YEAR of the COCK

YEAR
of the COCK

The Remarkable True Account
of a Married Man Who Left His Wife
and Paid the Price

Alan Wieder

GRAND CENTRAL
PUBLISHING

NEW YORK • BOSTON

Grand Central Publishing

Hachette Book Group

237 Park Avenue

New York, NY 10017

Visit our Web site at www.HachetteBookGroup.com.

Printed in the United States of America

First Edition: July 2009

10 9 8 7 6 5 4 3 2 1

Grand Central Publishing is a division of Hachette Book Group, Inc. The Grand Central Publishing name and logo is a trademark of Hachette Book Group, Inc.

Library of Congress Cataloging-in-Publication Data

Wieder, Alan.

Year of the cock : the remarkable true account of a married man who left his wife and paid the price / Alan Wieder. — 1st ed.

p. cm.

ISBN 978-0-446-58216-2

1. Adultery—United States. 2. Wieder, Alan. 3. Husbands—Sexual behavior—United States. 4. Husbands—United States—Biography. 5. Man-woman relationships—United States. 6. Penis—Size. 7. Penis—Enlargement. I. Title.

HQ806.W44 2009

306.73'6092—dc22

[B]

2008026064

A man, I tell my wife: all day I climb myself
Bowlegged up those damned poles rooster-heeled in all
Kinds of weather and what is there when I get
Home?

—James Dickey
"Power and Light"

Dear Reader

I have changed the names or otherwise protected the identities of many people involved in my story. Also, I completely fabricated some shit in order to make these 87 percent true events a little more entertaining. If you really wanna know what's true and what isn't, feel free to e-mail me at anneeducoq@hotmail.com, and I'll be more than happy to shoot straight.

Acknowledgments

Now that *Year of the Cock* is actually being published and I'm beset with anxiety over whether it's any good, I kinda wish I'd shown early drafts of it to a whole host of brilliant friends and colleagues whom I could now thank for their invaluable book-improving input.

Oh well.

At least the four people who've read prepublication drafts have been extremely helpful and kind. They are Kim Witherspoon and Pilar Queen, my agents at Inkwell, who immediately saw the potential of my proposal, landed me an unthinkable deal, and guided me every step of the way; Ben Greenberg at Grand Central, my tremendously talented editor, who encouraged me to kill my darlings without forcing me to, coaxed details out of me that I wouldn't have otherwise exposed, and made the whole thing a lot better; and of course my homeboy Steve Sobel, who gave me innumerable story ideas, joke punchups, and other creative suggestions at every stage of the process.

Steve also allowed me the space to write the book while we had a lot of other equally critical film and TV deadlines to meet as a team. I'm sorry, *boychik*, if at times I was a moody and over-tired (and often hungover) mess. Love you, buddy.

I thank anyone who allowed me to use his or her real names (you know who you are), and Steve and his wife Marita especially for allowing me to write so candidly about their relationship and about Steve's Reluctant Groom Syndrome. Steve and Marita are still very happily married and have since given birth to my goddaughter, Lulu.

Samantha: despite everything that has come between us, and despite everything I revealed about your life and our circumstances, you were an unflagging supporter of this project, and I am eternally grateful to you. I am sorry that you became an unwilling character in this messy story, and please trust that the only person I hoped to embarrass with this book was myself.

My psychotherapist of three years, Dr. Edward Newman, gave me the means to think straight, write honestly without shame, and be a man.

Liner-note style, I'd like to holler at my personal heroes, all of whom in one way or another kept me inspired or productively distracted during my writing: the rappers Cam'ron (Dipset for life!) and Jadakiss; the singer/songwriter Scott Reynolds; Richard Pryor and Mitch Hedberg (R.I.P.); W. H. Auden, Samuel Beckett, Jim Thompson, Philip Roth, George Plimpton, and Joan Didion; and my Grandpa Bernie.

And finally, a shout-out to my baby boy Roman Jude Wieder, a.k.a. "Chicken Nugget," for keeping me alive, happy, and hungry. I intend to hide this book from you for as long as possible.

a.h.w.

YEAR *of the* COCK

Oct. 14, 2005, 1:45 a.m.

I<small>T'S</small> D<small>AY</small> F<small>IVE</small> *and I don't want to be here or anywhere else.*

Being back here is doing me no good at all. I am not the man she once loved, nor even the one who walked out the door. I am not a man at all. I've made yet another wrong turn in this ruinous year and I should leave tonight, while she sleeps, write a pretty note and split forever.

For once I should give her what she deserves and just go the fuck away.

All my things are still boxed up in the closet where she stashed them, out of view: my books, the few clothes I'd left hanging, the canvases I painted for her a few years ago that turned out surprisingly good enough to hang on the dining room wall. I can't shake the thought of it—yet another imagining I can't dislodge: of my poor wife rampaging around the house, pulling my things out of drawers, off walls and shelves, disappearing any sign of the life we shared and are now, somehow, supposed to resume.

She's still so angry and if she only knew the half of it, what I'm thinking and doing when she turns the other way.

I am hurting and so so sad. I've fallen fast over the last days, gone a million steps backward and—shit that I am—taken her with me. I've returned full-bore to my rituals. Dr. Goodson ordered me to stop—"The thoughts are only reinforced by the behaviors," he said—but I can't—CAN'T—and, at this rate, may never. Late at nights I run a scalding-hot tub and strip off my clothes in front of the long mirror that hangs on the wall above the low cupboards in our second bathroom, the one furthest from the bedroom where Sam's fast asleep, with no idea that hours ago I left the bed and am now standing naked in front of that pitiless glass—again!— looking, palpating, pulling, stretching, inspecting, measuring.

My cock, my hair, my hands. My hair, my hands, my cock.

If she only knew.

When I first enter the tub I want the hot water to melt me to nothing, so that I can speed down the drain and be gone from Sam's life and my own. But then . . . then the water cools slightly, becomes livable, and I sip my whiskey, and for a moment it feels okay to still be alive, and as I begin to stretch my warm, wet cock I feel a flicker of hope.

Tug straight out for thirty seconds, out and to the left, out and to the right, outward rotary. Up, up and to the right, up and to the left, upward rotary. Down, down and to the left, right, downward rotary. Back between the legs, hold, right, hold, switch hands, left, hold.

Repeat.

Afterward I can see my flaccid penis twitching and pulsating in the mirror, veiny and chafed and flushed with blood: Fuller, stronger . . . bigger?

No, no, no.

My penis is too small, too small, too small. Dr. Goodson says—everything I've read says—that writing down the thought is supposed to give me some power over it, but no matter how many times I try, see the idea's raging illogic on the page for what it is, it does not surrender or fade.

You are a writer, *the doctor says smugly.* So write. Put it in words you can control. Tell a story. Find the funny.

Okay, Doc, if you say so.

My penis is too small. There's less hair on my head than before, no, more, no, less. These hands are stubby and weak and not mine.

How am I supposed to write anything with these hands if they're not even fucking MINE?

1.0

IN EARLY FEBRUARY 2005, the Year of the Rooster, I moved out on Samantha, my wife of two and a half years. I announced my decision to her on a Thursday evening, explaining very little, saying very little, with the same curt efficiency I'd use to update my production staff of a location change. "I just need a few weeks on my own to figure things out," I think I put it; but neither she nor I believed I had any intention of coming back. And by Friday afternoon I'd gathered up a few necessities (Hefty bags stuffed with clothes and toiletries, my Xbox console and copies of *Grand Theft Auto: Vice City* and *Medal of Honor*, a cigar box full of family photographs, a stovetop espresso pot, my mp3 player, a Tizio desk lamp, a *Moby-Dick* paperback), loaded them into my producing partner's pickup truck, and—to Sam's mute amazement—split.

Steve Sobel, my partner and best friend of twenty-five years, and I had just finished producing two high-profile network reality TV series (*My Big Fat Obnoxious Fiancé* and *My Big Fat Obnoxious Boss*) that had gobbled up the last eighteen months of our lives. Eighteen consecutive months of eighteen-hour days, lengthy location shoots, and marathon editing sessions had left my marriage in shambles and me too enervated to save it. After ten mostly happy years with Sam, I believed somehow, callous as it may come across, that I was done with her. Steve urged me to get into couples counseling and try to work things out. My mom and dad couldn't make sense of it: Sam and I had always been so perfect together. My friends were equally taken aback—aggrieved, even: "You were, like, my go-to example of how young marriage can work," one recently engaged friend said when I told him my wife and I were splitting up. "Jesus, Alan, I *proposed* because of you. What the fuck am I supposed to do *now*?!" And Sam, who had come to severely resent my absence while I was in production, had remained hopeful that our life would return to normal as soon as I was on hiatus. But now, at the first opportunity I had to rejoin my marriage, I was immovably convinced that my only option was to leave. I was just so *tired*: tired of her constant angry outbursts, of having to explain to her why I worked so much and so hard, of having to work so hard at the office *and* at home—too damn tired to repair the massive toll my profession had taken on us, only to watch the marriage go to shit again when the next series came along. My lifestyle and Sam's were simply incompatible, grown apart, our relationship beyond fixing, our futures irreparably unmarried. I'd essentially been living the life of a career-obsessed single man, and now I wanted, for the sake of expediency, simplicity—I'm still not sure what—to be single.

So began my journey into bachelorhood. After ten years in a committed relationship—my whole adult life—I suddenly found myself a single guy. My new life, I must say, got off to a very favorable start. Those first few days of freedom—*oh, those first few days!*—were exhilarating: I was giddy with my newfound unattached-ness and all the possibilities for self-gratifying behavior it would enable. Just about every married guy I knew openly and quite pitifully fantasized about how kick-ass his life would be if he could only figure out how to give Wifey the heave-ho. Now here I was actually going through with it! An indefinite future of suffocating sameness vaporized in an instant, giving way to an electrifying rush of unexpected wants and altered appetites: A few days after I moved out, I exited my agent's office in Beverly Hills and decided, on a whim, to purchase a stainless Rolex Perpetual Datejust, even though I'd always hated wearing wristwatches. I experienced a sudden strong craving for guacamole, which had previously made me gag. After a lifetime of finding hip-hop vacuous and repetitive, I became obsessed with the genre and started spending hours searching the Web for obscure Diplomats and D-Block mixtapes. I felt like a *different person,* at the cellular level, as if my brain and blood and hormones had conspired to neurochemically underwrite my new lease on life.

In my heedless and slaphappy first days as a bachelor, my marriage took on a grotesquely ugly aspect. My years with Sam seemed in close retrospect a soul-destroying gulag from which, after years of voluntary thralldom, I'd finally mustered the courage to escape. Being single, I was certain, was going to FUCKING RULE. Los Angeles is of course a town acrawl with sexy young women, even the least desperate of whom I felt confident I could lure home to my tastefully decorated future bachelor pad. After all, I was a six-five, decent-looking thirty-one-year-old with a bank account that—even cut in half—would be impressive enough. I *loved* to hang out in bars and drink vast amounts of alcohol, an activity which I got to do far too little as a married man. My career as a producer was burgeoning and my professional future far brighter than most dudes my age struggling to make it in Hollywood. And moreover, if all else failed, I still possessed my really enchanting collection of cereal-box toys—featuring a complete set, still in wrappers, of the Cap'n Crunch magic kit—which I'd successfully busted out, ten years earlier, to charm the pants off the then-twenty Sam.

The only thing working against me was my copious back and shoulder hair. As it happens, I suffer from a rare and lamentable genetic condition (inherited from Dad) called *senex scapulae,* which translates as "old man shoulders." It's characterized by swirling formations of pubiclike hair along the upper arms, shoulders, and neckline that link my luxuriant carpet of chest hair to the also-quite-shaggy coat on my back, creating one unbroken, and quite unsightly, poncho of hair. Fortunately, however, with the help of a skilled waxer—not terribly hard to come by in L.A.—this is a remediable affliction, and one that if regularly groomed would likely pose no major obstacle to my philandering. Profuse body-hairiness hardly kept Alec Baldwin in check, I thought, with not enough sense at that moment to realize how preposterous it was for me to compare myself to the suavest, sexiest, studliest man in history, whose fling with Ally Sheedy I'd so envied as a lad.

And with no wife or potential kids to worry about, I could do with my disposable income what I felt I should have been doing for the past decade: disposing of it! Gone forever were the days of scouring the aisles of Whole Foods for elusive discounts on Ezekiel 4:9 sprouted-grain bread, raw fruit snack bars, and organic seitan steaks with my health-and-money-conscious wife. Now I'd toss *whatever the fuck I felt like eating* into my cart, no matter what it cost. Gone were the days of having to sock away $300 a month for our future child's overpriced private high school and assumedly Ivy League education. Put another round of Patrón shots on my tab for the hot chicks in the window booth! Gone—at last!—were the days of giving a shit about anything other than work and play, making money and spending every last red cent of it on the advancement of *me*.

Fuck savings! Fuck my health! Fuck every grain of security and comfort my marriage afforded but also *required* of me. It was time, well past it, to be on my own. Steve—who, at the time of all this, was himself headed to the altar with his longtime girl-friend—had a long-running joke about the "fantasy" bachelor pad that he "fantasy"-lived in as a "fantasy" single guy. This imaginary den of iniquity overlooked a "fantasy" private beach and was complete with "fantasy" cool chrome kitchen appliances, a sweet "fantasy" hi-fi media room, and a "fantasy" '67 Stingray parked in the "fantasy" driveway out front. Well . . . *fuck* fantasy. Now I could rent an *actual* bachelor pad on an *actual* beach in Malibu or Topanga Canyon or wherever else I *actually* wanted to live, which was anywhere other than in my apartment with my wife. Fuck spending my Friday nights at home in my paja-mas and socks, eating a healthful home-cooked meal, drinking a glass or two of Coppola cabernet, and falling asleep on the sofa to a Claude Chabrol movie Sam had thoughtfully picked out on Net-flix. Now I was going to go out Friday night—and every other night of the week I felt up to it, for that matter—and get pie-eyed drunk in pursuit of the innumerable trivial sexual encounters I wished I'd racked up in my early twenties. And when I didn't feel like doing that I'd go home to my future bachelor pad, strip down to my underpants, eat a Wahoo's fish taco combo platter on my comfy Ligne Roset "Togo" sofa in front of my 55-inch flat-panel TV, jerk off to Brazilian porn, and pass the fuck out in my big, delectably empty California king-size bed.

I embarked at once on a mission to do and buy and experience *every single thing* that as a married man I'd been either forbidden or discouraged or disinclined to pursue. My imagined bachelor existence was a place of illimitable extravagance and opportunity, unfettered by the realities of what I could sensibly afford or even pull off within this space-time continuum. I would buy a vintage Lotus Elite and a brand-new Gibson Black Beauty Les Paul. I'd triple my already unmanageable collection of punk-rock vinyl. I'd start a band, even though the last one I'd started, in college, kinda sucked because I wasn't a very good bass player—but hey, now I'd have all the time in the world to practice! I'd pick up and go on a beer tour of Ireland. Accompanied by one of the three women I was juggling I'd finally take that road trip to Groom Lake, a.k.a. Area 51, and camp out under the stars, scanning the night skies for black-budget aircraft between sessions of open-air lovemaking. I'd adopt a quirky pet—like a pig, a badger, or a wallaroo. I'd take up surfing and dirt biking and Ji Do Kwan Tae Kwon Do. *I'd finally get to finish my novel*—oh, to be able to spend my Saturday and Sunday afternoons sitting *alone* at my future antique writing desk, sipping Cuban coffee, smoking cigarettes, and pecking away at the novel that, with a wife in the picture, I could never justify tending to in the meager time I had off!

And most important of all, I'd be free to *work*. To work, all day and all night and every weekend of the year if I so chose, free of the responsibilities of being a husband and the shitheap of guilt Sam would make me feel when the demands of production forced me to dodge those duties. Truth was, despite the unforgiving schedules on which most television is made—and especially reality television, that tawdry, tightfisted, bastard breed of entertainment that I helped propagate—I loved what I did for a living. I loved everything about it: the creative challenges and budgetary quagmires of preproduction; the breathless, unstoppable sprint of production; the exquisitely protracted torture of editing, a.k.a. "post." I loved sitting in an editing room more than just about anything in the world: more than driving around in my car listening to really loud death metal, more than drinking tequila gimlets, more than reading a good Charles Willeford novel on the beach, all of which I fucking *loved* to do. During postproduction on my most recent reality series, I would arrive punctually at ten in the morning, cheerfully join my unsociable but masterly editor in his tenebrous bay, and cut footage for fifteen, sixteen hours on end, powering through lunch and dinner, drinking black coffee till my eyelids twitched, stopping only to smoke a cigarette, take a crap, and—with ever-decreasing frequency—call my lonely and pissed-off wife. Then, when my editor clocked out around one a.m., and even my extremely assiduous partner had the good sense to call it a night, I'd *stay there*—crashing on the couch for a jerky hour or two before a surge of adrenaline woke me, somehow fully reinvigorated. Then I'd review the day's cuts from the top, again and again and again—looking for shots to improve, music cues to swap, running time to lose—and then scan the next day's material until I was too addled to make sense of it and I was finally forced to head home and, after a numbing bolt of whiskey, take my place in bed beside my wife, who, with ever-*increasing* frequency, I'd find crying herself to sleep.

Naturally, it never occurred to me how, even as a wifeless man, I would manage to keep working at this ungodly pace and *also* make time for the litany of whimsical new bachelor hobbies and activities enumerated a few paragraphs ago, let alone maintain a nurturing environment for a wallaroo—which apparently must be hand-raised, require two to three hours of vigorous exercise daily, and can become quite irascible and combative unless provided with a near-constant supply of Bermuda grass. But more on that later.

I must clarify something. Heady and impulsive as it all sounds, my decision to leave my wife was in fact a fairly rational attempt to lift myself out of a deep and prolonged funk. You see, in the year leading up to my separation, I had become disaffected not merely with being in my particular troubled marriage, but with being *married,* period. Yes, certainly, Samantha and I did have real problems as a couple—a whole bevy of tangible and plaguing relationship issues, in fact, many of them rooted in my exasperating work schedule and others that I'll get into later. Whenever I spoke to Steve about what was going on at home—how that poor patient bastard listened to me *krecht* and *geshrei!*—I could readily cite a rash of recent incidents to substantiate my domestic discord: *So check this out: I finally take her on this romantic getaway to Vancouver Island, which is all she was saying she wanted for six months, and she spent the whole weekend angry at me about the fact that I might—**might!**—have to work over our anniversary weekend—which is THREE MONTHS FROM NOW! God forbid we should make the most of the time we DO have together—God forbid we should actually ENJOY this four-hundred-dollar-a-night hotel with its deep soaker tub that looks out onto a panoramic view of the rocky headlands of the Pacific Rim in the peak of storm season and for which I wasted an* *extra hundred twenty-five a night, apparently, because she seemed to have no interest in having sex with me in it . . .* And so on. But truth be told, my relationship woes, in and of themselves, were not uncommon for a couple of our profile—one in the industry, the other not—and probably very survivable with the assistance of a decent marriage counselor. And despite all her animosity, Sam was and is a loving, smart, clever, beautiful, ambitious, and all-around exceptional woman (and a first-rate chef, to boot), who, it must be said, had stuck by me during a very challenging professional period that would have driven a less-devoted wife into the arms of another dude, or into the office of a divorce attorney hell-bent on bankrupting my workaholic ass.

No: my marital collapse, I now realize, did not really stem from our *circumstances*—the misunderstandings and misalignments that had accumulated between us as a result of a work-life balance out of whack. What propelled me to leave my wife was more penetrating and—*oy*—existential than all that. And it had begun long before—indeed likely catalyzed—the precipitous decline of my marriage.

Allow me now, if you would, to take you back two or so years, where my story properly begins. It's a crisp, bright Saturday morning in October '03, the Year of the Sheep. I wake up beside my sleeping wife—who looks beautiful and breathtakingly serene in her Hanro nightgown. The night before I took a Dead Sea salt bath, and I feel all clean and fresh and relaxed. I'm naked and semierect beneath the down comforter and am just snuggly as all shit. I think, *I'm going to have sex with my wife. Afterward I'll have an espresso and a raisin scone and read the paper for a while.* For a minute or two that sounds just perfect: *I'm going to have sex with my wife. Afterward I'll have an espresso and a raisin scone and read the paper for a while.* But then, all of a sudden, I start chewing on the reality—really *thinking* about it—and it doesn't seem so hot anymore: *Sex with my wife? Since when has that been interesting? Coffee and a pastry and Thomas L. Friedman? BOOOOOO-RRRRRRING!*

Why my hitherto happy marriage suddenly seems so terribly lame-o, and why today of all days, I have no clue: It just *does*. A blanketing self-pity comes over me, as I direct at myself the kind of smug sympathy I usually feel for men whose lives are vapid and stuck. *I'm going to have sex with my wife. Afterward I'll have an espresso and a raisin scone and read the paper for a while.* Repeating the phrase again and again, I try in vain to recapture its formerly comforting resonance, smother my burgeoning chagrin beneath a heap of counted blessings.

A question seizes my brain, as racking and intrusive as it is painfully clichéd: *Of all the places in the world I could be right now, of all the things I could be doing, does this—spending the morning in Los Angeles with my wife—even make my hypothetical top ten? Fuck, my top fifty?* Instantly, my mind is ablaze with alternate existences and life scenarios, even the most fantastical and asinine of which seem, in that moment, perfectly attainable, and none of which involve Sam—or, for that matter, *any* wife. I picture myself sitting in a café in Budapest, drinking a *Tokaji* with a Russian girl I met only days before in Istanbul. Taking a jog at sunup with my Airedale through the Bois de Boulogne, as my Sorbonne grad student girlfriend cooks me breakfast at her airy single across from Les Invalides. Driving up to Vegas to visit "Ocean," an intriguing Australian stripper at the Spearmint Rhino who once gave me a lap dance, and whom I'm now casually dating. . . .

I lie there for a good half hour in a cold sweat, my heart in a sprint, my imagination viciously determined to show me how small and nugatory my *actual* life is—what *little* I'm doing with my precious time on Earth. My boner wilts to the size of an eraser head. Just twelve hours before I went to sleep a contented married guy who was ready to begin the part of his life in which he would hopefully become a rich and successful TV producer, have a few kids, go on some exotic family vacations, maybe write a book or two in his spare time. And now, in the light of day, I am terrified that I'm *settling* for that very same low-hanging fruit of a future: sliding ineluctably, unless I do something radical, toward a destiny already in place, in which I'm a homeowner with two-to-three children and a wife I met just after college, when I was flat broke and renting cars for a living and she was the most valuable thing—shit, the *only* valuable thing—I had going.

I get up and go to the bathroom, wash my face, stand naked in front of the mirror, and give myself a good tongue-lashing: *Schmuck, wake up! How the fuck did this happen? What have you been doing for the last eight years, aside from working and hurrying home for dinner and folding laundry and paying bills and watching HBO and eating low-fat frozen yogurt and going home for Christmas and grocery shopping and yelling at your wife and getting yelled at? You're almost thirty fucking years old! Forty's around the corner! There's a whole world out there—a world of strange experiences and strange pussy in strange and distant parts of the globe—and you've utterly failed to avail yourself of any of it! Why? BECAUSE YOU'VE BEEN TOO BUSY BEING MARRIED, YOU COMPLACENT PIECE OF SHIT!*

After excoriating myself for ten straight minutes, I finally manage to calm down enough to crawl back into bed. I want to sleep for another hour but I find my wife wide awake and, it so happens, unexpectedly amorous. "I love you, Alan," she whispers as she wraps her warm body around mine, puts her hand down my pajama bottoms and—not to be crass—takes my penis into her tender palm. My mind instantly issues a reactive garble of negative thoughts that aim to stem any urge I have to carry off the thing that now fills me with morbid disgust: *Sex with my wife! The horror!* But then, after very little coaxing, my wang shoots up in irrefutable assent, and I am obliged to follow its lead. I proceed to have sex with my wife; I lift up the skirt of Sam's nightgown and caress her smooth belly and give it to her with gusto, finishing together in that gentle side position she really seems to get a kick out of. And—to my great relief—it's *absolutely fine*. Fantastic, actually: Afterward we softly kiss and lie in each other's arms with the same loving languor as when she came over in the middle of the night to the apartment I was house-sitting above Washington Square in the summer of '95, to have wild groping sex on the kitchen floor, on the sofa by the mantle lined with photos of a cool-looking family I wished intensely was mine, the building rooftop, and every other spot worth defiling at 25 Fifth Avenue. And when we're done, I walk to Starbucks in my pajama bottoms, buy a triple macchiato and a slice of pumpkin bread, and proudly embrace my fate: *If the next thirty to sixty years are just like this,* I think, *what is so bad about that?* I have a wonderful wife whom I love and a piece of cake that one can unobjectionably eat before ten in the morning. I'm good. I'm great. Now if you'll excuse me, I have some pedestrian op-ed pieces to read. . . .

But I am not good, not good at all. I am good for an hour or two at most before my anxiety returns full force, and an ill-founded notion blossoms into an unshakable *belief:* That for a guy like me, with my prospects and ambitions and bust-ass lifestyle, marriage was a nice idea but more or less untenable. That marriage was for marketing execs and guys named Bill who work in accounts receivable and play golf and live in Pasadena. That even the most contented of married men were in truth a mirthless, castrated lot whose lives were effectively terminated; and that those dudes who had the balls to be single—despite their claims to want to settle down, despite their complaints of chronic loneliness and purposelessness and their professed fears of dying alone—were, as a rule, hyperproductive, vivacious, insouciant, and strong. Guys who got shit done, got laid, and got to do whatever they wanted in between. Guys, it seemed, who had the right idea.

And in my particular line of work, littered as it is with failed relationships, I didn't have to look far to find living proof of this thesis: My sad-sack married production coordinator would arrive at work every day and relate a fresh story of a horrific row he and his wife of ten years had had that morning, in one instance of which the woman had actually tried to run him over with their Ford Excursion and wound up plowing into the garage door he'd spent two fucking weekends installing at her insistence. My line producer, two years married, was convinced that his wife loathed him, a theory that propelled him into cycles of torrid infidelity that he barely managed to keep secret, followed by bouts of consuming guilt that would prompt him to dump whatever chick he was banging and take his wife on an extravagant getaway that he couldn't really afford, but that did manage briefly to quell what he perceived as her seething contempt for him until it would resurface, unavoidably, and he would again have *no choice* but to seek solace in the arms of some new and unfortunate other woman, professing his love to her and breaking her heart in the space of ten days, only then to pass the next week of sleepless nights shopping for vacation packages to Cape Town or Cuixmala on expedia.com.

Meanwhile, conversely, one recently *divorced* editor with whom I worked closely was having the time of his life—throwing beach BBQs at his new Venice bachelor pad, riding around in convertibles with twenty-two-year-old hotties (I nearly dropped my iced cappuccino one morning as, at the intersection of La Cienega and Santa Monica Boulevard, I saw him wave to me from the passenger seat of a BMW M3 being driven by a delightful lass in a triangle bikini top), staying up till three and strolling into work at noon, Bay Cities Italian sub in hand, to fire up his Avid and launch into unsparing descriptions of the rowdy and, it would seem, empirically verifiable sex he was having nightly with different impressionable young women. And my thirty-eight-year-old boss, Chris Cowan, a dogged bachelor, had just dumped his girlfriend and was busy hosting booze-drenched poker nights and dating a sweet and smokin' hot ex-reality-TV temptress.

In the face of all this unarguable evidence—after being bombarded with it daily—I grew, in a matter of months, deeply fatalistic about my own relationship's prospects and openly cynical about marriage, wives, fiancées, long-term girlfriends, and, for that matter, steadies of any sort. All of a sudden I became that guy, The Bitter Married Guy At The Office, who upon hearing even the most mundane or innocuous gripes of his married male colleagues launches into inordinately angry invectives: *Oh man, you've had to spend your last three weekends at Home Depot because she won't stop nagging you about all the work you promised to do around the house? Dude, your wife sounds like she needs a fuckin' beat-down! What? She doesn't want your recently divorced fraternity brother staying in your living room for the next five weeks? Duuuude! Your fraternity brother! You gonna tolerate that shit? Where does the skank come off?! What's that? You found a Tenth Anniversary Trans Am in mint condition and can finally*

afford it but she won't let you buy it because it's not safe enough for
your baby? Christ, bro, when are you gonna grow some stones and
leave that stupid cunt already!

No one was spared this aspersion—employees, friends, my
hopelessly monogamous assistant—and especially not Steve,
whom I felt a special responsibility to shield from all the misery
he would doubtless bring upon himself if he were actually stupid enough to go through with his impending marriage. When
he was ten months from his wedding day and experiencing what
any married man would call normal pangs of suffocating panic,
I offered the following consoling bit of wisdom:

"Don't worry, partner. Just remember, marriage is merely a
gateway to divorce."

"Excuse me?" he said.

"Think about it," I said. "I mean, at this point, you can't really get out of the relationship *without* marrying Marita. I mean,
you've been together for seven-plus years, she's gonna be thirty-
three . . . It's only fair that you marry her. But *once* you marry
her, you can always divorce her, right? I mean, not right away,
but like in a year or two . . ."

"Ahhhh, I see," Steve said, carried along for a moment by the
alluring cogency of the idea. "'Cause my intentions were noble,
and I gave it my best effort, but in the end our marriage just
didn't work out . . ."

"Most marriages don't. Just check the stats."

"Thanks, man," he said. "I feel a little better . . . I think."

"Hey, anytime."

And so, as this distorted logic took hold, I found myself falling away, every day, from a woman I had adored without question for so many years. Moreover, I was reluctant to do anything
to reverse this downward spiral—no, if anything, I welcomed

it. As my work schedule dragged on, and our fights grew more frequent and explosive, I came on some level to *savor* the feeling that my marriage was speeding toward some fatal boundary past which it would be beyond salvaging, and past which, therefore, I could defensibly succumb to the irresistible prospect of swingin' bachelorhood. With mounting desperation, Sam proposed gestalt couples therapy, Tantric sex, cute things we could do together—like cheese-tasting seminars and meditation retreats—holding out hope, till the very end, that I still cared enough to "work on us." But I repeatedly sidestepped, postponed, and, when she issued ultimatums, adamantly refused. I just knew—with impossible clarity I knew—that I *had* to leave her, that any constructive effort to deny it would unnecessarily perpetuate our agony and waste money we'd both sorely need when it was all said and done. The question I faced was not *whether* to move out but *when,* and how to ensure that when Sam and I finally parted ways, she too would be convinced that it was our only recourse. I wanted to do that much for her.

So I deployed the bury-myself-in-my-career-till-she-snaps approach—a trusted and effective, if not exactly honorable, method of marital sabotage. In hindsight, it was perhaps a cruel and chickenshit thing to do, but it was also the most practical. Because I was already obliged to put in a fourteen- to sixteen-hour workday, it was easy to up the ante to eighteen, pushing Sam past her already extended threshold. Instead of coming home at one or two in the morning, sleeping till eight, and spending a few hours with her before heading back to work, I would purposely loiter at the office—usually drinking hard liquor, smoking weed, and playing *Madden Football* with our night editor, Tyler—for an extra few hours, return home past four absolutely cashed, pass out till ten thirty, wake up, and rush out the door again before she and I could exchange a word. I reduced our daily phone calls from five to two tops, kept them painfully short at that, and canceled our once-sacred lunch and dinner dates. "Sweetheart, I'm sorry, but Chris just gave us a shitload of notes on this cut. I'm gonna be up all night. Can we do dinner tomorrow?" I'd ask, knowing full well that she already had plans tomorrow and I'd be off the hook. "Babe, I'm sorry, but I got three producers sitting in my office. Can we talk later on?" when there was no one in my office, and I knew that it was already past her bedtime and there would be no "later on."

My hope was that after six or eight months of this passive-aggressive torture, my marriage would de facto cease to exist, and Sam would simply be compelled to move on. Being that she was a highly desirable woman, it seemed that any minute she'd commence an affair with some dude with a more normal lifestyle and a much sunnier attitude and an actual interest in spending time with her—a scenario I began, after a point, to desperately wish for; or she'd pack up her shit and move in with one of her many sympathetic friends who thought I was a total prick; or pack up *my* shit and finally kick my ass out. Returning home from an editing session in the wee, wee hours, reeking of coffee and cigarettes and, all too often, Knob Creek bourbon, I'd tiptoe into our bedroom and, before quietly turning on the light, wish upon a star to find our bed empty save for a letter, in her magnificent prose, telling me to fuck off and have a nice life.

Were it only that easy. Instead I found my wife, always my wife, sleeping fitfully beside a cluster of balled-up Kleenex. Sam didn't leave, no matter how painfully obvious I made it that I wanted her to. Day after day, night after night, the sweet woman waited for me, and she'd wait as long as it took. She tried to do her thing in the meanwhile: While I was at work she kept herself busy—meeting friends for dinner, watching TV, reading, writing, painting, taking a nighttime cooking class, often working late into the night herself. But then, when enough was enough and it was time to see her husband, to look into his eyes and see whether there was any love left there, she would call me on the phone and beg me to come home—just for a quick bite, just for an hour or two to watch a movie or walk around the neighborhood—and when I said no she'd shout, and cry, and call me all sorts of horrible names I wished she really meant.

But she never left. She'd never leave, because she'd promised me on our wedding day that she never would, in health or in sickness. So, I felt, I had to.

Those of you who are still reading this may be wondering how and why my wife tolerated, for so long, such raging assholishness from a man, even from one who, granted, had treated her very attentively and lovingly for eight solid years before everything went south. Did she not have a sliver of self-respect? I will explain everything, but the fact is, the primary reason for her steadfastness was that she loved me. She loved me to no end, more than enough for us both, which I would only realize a few months later when I was alone in a perfect little bachelor pad in Hollywood, lying in a big empty California king-size bed, staring down at my flaccid penis with disgust, wishing I was dead.

2.0

WHEN I MOVED OUT, I didn't have much of a plan, but I'd planned it that way. The day before I left my wife I'd asked my good friend and former boss, Chris, who lived alone in a huge house in the Los Feliz hills, whether I could rent his guest apartment for a few weeks until I found a place to live. Partly because he's a generous dude by nature, and partly out of guilt, I suspect, over having been the overseer of my marriage-wrecking work schedule, Chris kindly offered to let me stay in the apartment for as long as I wanted, even months if it became necessary, for *free*. This was a huge relief to me, as I already planned to continue covering the pricey rent at my old apartment so that Sam wouldn't have to move, and I gratefully took him up on the offer. All Chris asked me to do in exchange was keep an eye on Ching Ching, his lovably decrepit thirteen-year-old Shar-Pei who slept nineteen hours a day and whom I expected to demand little, if any, of my attention.

As I mentioned, Chris had just ended his relationship with his live-in girlfriend of five years, and was presently in full-on bachelor mode—playing softball several times a week, dating with decided nonchalance, and throwing out-of-hand house parties that raged till sunup. Steve theorized that Chris offered me the free apartment primarily out of self-interest—that his main motivation was that he wanted a roommate, a live-in frat buddy with whom he could get regularly drunk and who could keep the creator of *Temptation Island,* in his weaker moments, from reuniting with his ex. I have to admit that I was a bit thrown by Chris's largesse. But there seemed to be no potential downside to forging a closer friendship with a highly successful executive producer whom I happened to be very fond of, who had a kick-ass party pad, and who also seemed to enjoy boozing even more than I did. Any way you cut it, this was one sweet fuckin' deal.

Steve pulled up to Chris's house, a turreted, 7,500-square-foot Spanish-style hillside fortress that looked like something Pablo Escobar might find a little overstated. My ex-boss and now quasi landlord came into the driveway, tasty-lookin' Harp Lager in hand. He was wearing a fitted Cleveland Indians cap turned backward, a threadbare Argentina soccer jersey, side-pocketed Bermudas, and Oakley sport sandals, looking very much the jock he was. He greeted me warmly.

"Wieder! I have your apartment all cleaned for ya," he said. "But are you sure you don't want to stay *in* the house with me? You're more than welcome . . . Up to you, bro, but check this out."

We went up in an elevator to the fourth floor of his home, where Chris showed me a huge furnished guest suite whose high

French doors gave out onto a sprawling private balcony with the most spectacular view of L.A. I'd ever seen. I pictured going out there after work to drink a whiskey and write or play my guitar, or to share a dinner I'd prepared in Chris's chef's kitchen with a woman I'd met two days before in yoga class, and the idea struck me as deeply sad—given that any effort to make myself at home presupposed a certain degree of self-delusion that this ridiculous mansion was mine—but also terribly inviting.

"Why don't you just stay here till we can furnish the apartment?" he suggested, for some reason bringing upon himself the additional responsibility of outfitting the apartment he was already giving me for nothing. "I think Ching Ching would really enjoy having you in the house."

At that moment the wizened pooch was fast asleep in her down bed in the hallway, looking as if she had long outgrown her interest in man's friendship. Steve grinned at me privately as if to confirm his theory that it was not the dog who would truly relish my presence.

I agreed to live in the guest room for a few days, and Chris, a man whose suggestions are meant to be followed rather than merely appreciated, seemed very pleased. He then ushered me down the imposing marble staircase that wound around the exterior of the house, until we reached a small terrace at the mezzanine level. There, through a private entrance, we entered the efficiency apartment that would be mine as soon as I could get it up and running.

It was a terrific little pad, an entirely remodeled unit with untouched hardwood floors, spic-and-span appliances, a marble bath—a charming studio that would easily have fetched $1,700 a month in that neighborhood, on the posh outskirts of Hollywood and a stone's throw from Griffith Park. As we moved in my things, Chris began pitching past the sell, as we TV-mongers say, enumerating the apartment's many obvious perks long after I clearly needed no more convincing: "It's got central air, mini Sub-Zero fridge, dishwasher . . . and hey, Wieder, check out this showerhead . . ." Steve, for his part, began sauntering around the apartment making various lewd humping motions, in the corner beneath the skylight, in the walk-in glass shower, in the area where it'd be a natural place for a sofa or love seat—acting out, for my benefit, all the crazy sex I'd soon be having, in infinite creative configurations, in every nook and cranny of the single room.

"Very mature, Steve," I said reproachfully, then joined right in, humping the shit out of an imaginary female who lay, legs splayed, on the granite kitchen countertop. This sent my friend into a fit of hyenic laughter, as I knew it would.

"You boys have fun," Chris said, smiling but obviously less amused by the puerile antics of the two men whom he'd spent three years mentoring. "I gotta run to practice."

Chris tossed me a set of keys not only to the apartment but to the main house as well, telling me to feel free to come and go as I pleased, use the pool, Jacuzzi, media room, liquor cabinet. I thanked him and, casting aside a lifetime of devout agnosticism, the Lord for his munificence.

I made my few belongings as homey as possible in the barren apartment. I placed my stovetop espresso pot on the range, my clothes in the closet, the few books I'd brought on a built-in shelf, my Tizio lamp and Boston Acoustics alarm radio on a bright orange Kartell nesting table I'd orphaned from its two larger counterparts, still sitting at my bedside in my former home. I put a few provisions away, the proud spoils of my First Grocery Run As A Single Man: bottles of Bushmills and Grey Goose; a tin of Bustelo coffee; a six of Wittekerke white beer; a half-gallon of milk; dried pasta; a sourdough ficelle and a hunk of Iberico cheese; a bag of peanut-butter-filled pretzels; canned sardines; and assorted jarred spreads, dips, sauces, and condiments that would pep up the many probably crummy and insipid meals I would be consuming in the absence of my wife's fine cooking. And I put a few toiletries in the bathroom, among which was an unfamiliar and highly titillating box of LifeStyles spermicidal condoms—the same type I'd fumblingly applied in college, now a beacon heralding all the new vaginas into which my intrepid penis would soon be venturing (and uteruses I wouldn't be impregnating).

I decided I wouldn't need much in the way of furnishings to make the studio comfortable, that I would live spartanly until I figured out where to settle long-term. I needed a firm bed, some respectable-threadcount sheets, a two-seater sofa, a coffee table, dishware for two, and, to shore up this austere living arrangement, a decent flat-panel TV. I needed a desk and chair and a doormat and perhaps an area rug to complement the small Persian I'd swiped from my former second bedroom. Later on, when I moved into my *real* bachelor pad, I'd add the high-def surround-sound system and wireless kitchen appliances and Gregory Crewdson photographs on the dining room wall, but for now I needed to impart only enough livability to avoid embarrassing myself in front of whatever chicks I brought home—beyond, of course, the obvious indignity that as a fairly reputable thirty-one-year-old television producer, I was temporarily residing in—to call a spade a spade—my boss's maid's quarters.

That February we were in the middle of a spell of torrential late winter rains, an anomaly in sunny L.A., and that afternoon it was falling hard. It was Friday, my first real day off in nearly six months and my first without Samantha in over a decade, and after I put my stuff away and Steve went home to his fiancée, I had, to my delight, no fucking idea what to do with myself. I poured a stiff neat Bushmills and walked up to the pool deck, taking a seat in one of the chaises beneath a large patio umbrella, and watched the city guzzle the seemingly inexhaustible rain.

I dialed my mother and father to tell them the big news. I owed them a call. Both of them got on the line. I sipped my drink.

"I did it, guys," I said, probably a little too exultantly. "I moved out."

I'd kept my folks pretty well apprised, over the previous six months, of my deepening marital crisis, and had even warned them earlier that week that I was moving out any day now. So there was no real reason for either of them to get too worked up. But despite all the clear warning signs, my mother—a nervous little French lady who'd worried about me incessantly until I met Sam, a woman she adored and had depended on to take care of me—went out of her fuckin' *tête*.

"Oh mais non . . . oh mon fils," she exhaled, with thick French *désespoir*. "I can't believe it. Are you okay? How's Samantha? Poor girl! You think it will be easy to find another woman like that? Where are you living? At your boss's house? You can't stay there long. Nothing comes free, *Alain*. It will get awkward. You'll need an apartment. You'll have to keep paying for Samantha in the meantime. You can't put her out in the street! It will get very expensive. What are you going to do? Have you ever heard of anything so crazy? I can't believe it—"

"Catherine," my dad cut in, *"Tais-toi. Ça suffit*. He's going to be fine. He's a big boy, okay? *Arrête*."

My father, an American, often addressed my mother *en bro-*

ken *français,* especially when issuing commands that would sound too harsh in English. He'd developed the habit when my sister and I were uncomprehending youngsters and kept it up even after she and I became far more French-fluent than he.

"You act like this is nothing, Dav*eed,*" my mother said. "It's not nothing. I'm sorry—"

"I do *not* act like this is nothing. But our son was unhappy—"

"But you work it out if you are unhappy! You don't leave a marriage! Did I leave you every time I was unhappy? Which was a lot. *Believe* me."

"You should have left," my dad said. "You think you did me a big favor? A good riddance, it would have been!"

"Fuck you, *Daveed!*"

"No: Fuck *you!!!*"

My stomach convulsed at the sound of it, their immemorial pattern of senseless bickering into which Sam and I, too, had fallen. I gagged up a little whiskey.

"Are you okay, son?" my dad asked, looking to prove a point.

"I'm fine, guys. Better than I've been in a long time," I said.

"Good," my old man said. "We're both concerned about you, is all. Your mother and I both. We're here for you for anything, son, you know that."

Then, after a beat of strained silence, he said tentatively: "Umm . . . are you okay . . . *financially?* Do you need any money? Things are a little squeezed right now—I'm not pulling in what I used to, you know . . . I don't have too many good cases coming in these days, just some hourly stuff to put food on the table—the legal scene's gotten very competitive here—but I can probably figure *something* out if you're in a jam . . ."

Money offers from Dad typically came encased in this guilt-inducing spiel. Once a top-notch Miami litigator who'd saved up a nice fortune and was preparing to retire at sixty and travel the world, Pops had taken a major hit in the 2000 stock-market crash and was now back to work full-time—and not thrilled about it. Since losing all that dough he was complaining of chronic hypertension and heart palpitations. Terrible as it sounds, I didn't really feel too sorry for the guy. He still had plenty of cash and a nice waterfront house he could always sell if things got tight—a lot more than most men his age. But the last thing I needed was his myocardium infarcting over *my* finances.

"Thanks, Dad, that's good of you. Really. But it's all right. I have some big expenses coming up, but I got plenty of money. I made two hundred twenty grand last year—"

"Wow. *Two hundred and twenty Gs?* No kidding . . . That's more than *I* made," my dad said, more piqued than comforted. Then, only half-kidding: "On second thought, since you're such a Hollywood big shot, think *you* can send *me* some money? Keep your old mom and dad out of the poorhouse, heh heh heh."

A single subdued "heh" was all I could volley back.

"Maybe you want to come home for a while, live with us?" my mother put out there.

No fuckin' way.

"Yeah . . . maybe," I said. "Maybe, Ma. But I'm fine—really, for now I'm happy and well. Don't worry. Look, I'm about to duck into a business dinner. Let's talk in a couple days. Okay?"

"Okay," they said, and I hung up. *A tout à l'heure.*

I finished my drink and headed into the kitchen for a re-fill. Chris was there, back from softball practice, meticulously unloading a cornucopia from a Greenblatt's Deli bag: smoked turkey, corned beef, a pound of delicately shaved Swiss, pickled cucumber salad, spicy mustard, a sturdy sliced marble rye. Though a real goy from a Cleveland suburb, who by his own admission had never met a Heeb till his freshman year at Ohio University, Chris had a penchant for Jewish deli food and often made a dinner of it, not simply because he didn't know how to turn on his stove but also because Greenblatt's—a legendary Sunset Boulevard establishment that serves a cinderblock-size kugel so good you keep eating it after your stomach ruptures— had properly exposed him to how fantastically delicious our people's cuisine can be. He also had a penchant for Jewish girls, not simply because they came with a built-in excuse not to marry them.

"Wieder: dig in," he commanded.

We took several minutes in deliberate silence to construct towering triple-decker sandwiches. I could not help but notice that Chris, perhaps out of deference to me, defied expectation and forwent slathering his with a ruinous gob of mayo. We then retired to his comfy media room with a bunch of Grolsch Ambers and a fresh bag of salt-and-vinegar kettle chips. We ate, threw around some new reality show ideas, and watched some really silly shit on the TV, stuff I never found the space to watch at home: *Chappelle's Show, Family Guy, South Park, Aqua Teen Hunger Force, Wonder Showzen*, a TiVoed *Jimmy Kimmel Live*. So here's how I'm going to be spending my time, I thought, extrapolating this sublime aimlessness into the indefinite future. *This is fuckin' great.*

"So, how's your wife?" Chris said.

Jesus, talk about ruining a moment. "I have no clue," I said, using a finger to scoop out the intensely tangy potato chip dust from the bottom of the bag I'd absolutely demolished. I hadn't spoken to Sam for a full day at that point, having ignored her half-dozen phone calls. Nor had I thought about her much, to be quite honest. "Terrible, I would imagine."

Chris said nothing but nodded in a way that seemed to suggest, *You might want to check in on her tomorrow, bro.*

Then he said: "Hey, I got a sofa in the garage from my old house that I'm not using. Check it out. If you want it, I'll help you move it in. I may have an extra TV down there, too. Maybe we can run a splitter, get you some cable . . ."

"Thanks, Cowan. I'll owe you a coupla porterhouses at Morton's when this is done."

"Nah," he said. "We're good."

Via remote he turned on his PS2 console, and on came the launch screen of *Tiger Woods PGA Tour 2005*. He tossed me a wireless controller.

I detest golf, virtual and otherwise, but holy fuck that's a good video game.

Around one, after Chris had gone to bed in his room, I wandered up three flights of stairs to mine. The room had its own gas fireplace, and I switched it on, sending a cradle of bluish flames around an ashen porcelain log. In my old life Sam and I had agreed that gas fireplaces were vaguely depressing, but now it and everything else about my new living situation seemed just aces: *Whoa, check this out, a gas fireplace! I love this. Oooh, goodness. It's so toasty . . .* I put on my favorite corduroy sportcoat and went out onto the balcony and lit an American Spirit oh-so-meaningfully—Sam always hated it when I smoked—and it was the best damn cigarette I ever puffed on.

I felt amped about the coming months. The TV series that had hijacked my life for the last year and a half was now completely wrapped, and Steve and I were about to commence a lucrative development deal at FremantleMedia, the deep-pocketed production company behind *American Idol*. It was a cozy contractual arrangement that granted us posh offices in Santa Monica, the freedom to come and go as we pleased, the creative latitude to work on our own projects, and, most critical of all, the budgetary resources to hire a hot young assistant: all told, a television producer's dream. After five years of grinding work as hands-on writer/producers-for-hire, we were eager to take a break from production to develop our own slate and do our own thing—a professional autonomy that dovetailed perfectly with my liberation from the shackles of marriage.

The rain had slowed to a mist and, in the lamplight down on Los Feliz Boulevard, I could see so many puddles eddying confusedly, not knowing where to drift or drain along a hillscape drenched beyond capacity. The perpetual rainfall was already ravaging thoroughfares, causing lethal rock slides on the Pacific Coast Highway, toppling homes in Laurel Canyon, sending cars careening off Mulholland Drive. Los Angeles was seemingly on the brink of some aqueous apocalypse, but it was so lovely to watch that I hoped it would never end.

When I awoke the next morning, the rain had stopped, and the skies looked as if they'd be clear till after lunchtime. I'd had my first solid night's sleep in easily a year, what with the seven drinks and the gas fire and the absence of an inconsolable spouse in my bed. I brushed my teeth and threw on my running clothes, grabbed my mp3 player and headphones, and jogged down the hill to the base of Griffith Park. Then I headed back uphill on the bike path beneath the overhang of oak and walnut trees. The air was bracingly cool, and as I picked up the pace I felt keyed up, euphorically *alive*. On my player was the record *S.D.E.* (for *Sports, Drugs, and Entertainment*), by Harlem-based gangsta rapper Cam'ron—not his best work (nowhere near as good as the more recent *Purple Haze* or *Killa Season*) but a sturdy album with a few absolutely sterling tracks that really got me pumped.

It's worth reiterating that just three months before, I'd never even *heard* of Cam'ron or his talented crew, the Diplomats, a.k.a. "Dipset," and had absolutely zero appreciation for hip-hop. I'd had a lifelong and some friends would say totally monomaniacal obsession with punk rock (and most postpunk subgenres) and heavy metal, and every other form of music could go suck a dick. But then one evening, my night editor, Tyler—a lily-white, twenty-three-year-old kid from the L.A. suburbs who wore XXXL-size clothing and hip-hop Starter caps turned sideways and chain-smoked Newport menthols—introduced me to this fellow Cam'ron, and in the space of a week, I don't know, I was completely fucking hooked.

As I entered a muddy cove and began the final leg of my uphill climb, I felt a jolting wind under my hoodie and, as one song faded down, a powerful surge of anticipation for the ensuing track, "Do It Again." It's a melodic banger in which "Killa Cam" looks back at his life thus far and decides that despite having killed and nearly been killed and seen so many loved ones shot or turned snitch or shipped off to the hooskow, he wouldn't change a muthafuckin' frame. At the first ragtime piano beats I began pumping my fists and jumping up and down like a ninnyhammer, weirding out a group of shirtless, brawny middle-aged Russian men making their way down the hill. My favorite part's the intro:

Man, I fucked a lotta bitches, man . . .
("True," echoes Dipset capo Jim Jones.)
Made a lotta money . . . ("True.")

Made a lotta enemies . . . ("True.")

But would I do this shit all over again? Hmm. I don't
  know . . .

That's a good question. ("You right about that," Jones says,
  as if he'd dare contradict the boss.)

Would you do your life over again?

I know I fuck fat-ass Tasha one more time if I didn't have
  nothin' else to do. I fuck that bitch one more time, that ass
  was fat . . .

Cam'ron's breezy recap of his badass personal history got me
all fired up about where my life could possibly lead. But steeped
in self-evaluation as I was, the song also—a bit unexpectedly—
prompted me to beat myself up about where I'd *been*. Indulging
an invidious comparison, I wondered: *Have **I** fucked a lot of
bitches?* Definitely not: all told—I counted and recounted—I was
barely in the double digits. True, I met Sam when I was twenty
and never once cheated on her, meaning I realistically had only
about four good years in the game, but whose fault was that?
Okay then. Have I made a lot of money? Well . . . I was doing
all right, I guess . . . I was currently in the low six figures, with
the potential to reach the mid-six by age thirty-five—nothing to
sneeze at, certainly, but far from fuck-you chips, and definitely
small small change by Cam's standards. *Well—what about
enemies then? Have I at least made a few enemies? One enemy?
Have I ever done anything so unforgivably heinous that someone
out there wants me dead and may in fact be plotting my untimely
demise this very second? Hmm . . . enemies . . . let's see . . . does*
my wife count?

Back at the house Ching Ching met me on the front steps. I
would come to learn that every morning around this time, before

breakfast, the old dog would dodder down the exterior staircase to the mezzanine landing, gaze out near-blindly at the cityscape, and bark for ten minutes at nothing in particular—putting all of Los Angeles on notice that this house, now my house, was officially under watch. She was howling then, feebly but intently, as I passed up the stairs without interference. I then hopped in the shower, careful not to wake Chris—who'd warned me that he slept till two on weekends—and, by way of making a truly fresh start, immediately went to town with a brand-new bar of Zest Citrus Sport.

One smaller bone of contention I'd had with Sam was that she'd never allowed me to indulge my predilection for mass-market bath bars—soaps like Coast Blue, Lever 2000, Irish Spring Icy Blast, and the like—an almost fetishistic craving borne of those early-80s commercials featuring ordinary, morning-showering men and women joyously and unabashedly lathering up for all of America to see. No, my wife would permit us to bathe only with "nontoxic" body cleansers like Dr. Bronner's organic hemp peppermint soap or Alba Botanica Midnight Tuberose bath gel. To be honest, I'd never really objected to Sam's natural-soap-only policy and even found her products quite serviceable, if understimulating. But now that I had my druthers, and a DayGlo-yellow, hyperfragrant bar of Zest in my clutches, I must say I was all the more enthused to lather and scour and scrub every last bit of me, covering my entire body in a rich, tangelo froth that only a complex interfusion of inorganic and doubtless highly toxic ingredients can generate.

These saccharine bath soaps have always had a highly aphrodisiac effect on me, for some odd reason, and after I got all good and sudsy, I felt a strong desire to pull on my pecker. Like many men, I almost always feel a strong desire to free a few hostages while in the shower, admittedly, but this time the urge was dizzyingly heightened and rousing. I was not so enraptured, however, that I was not fully cognizant of my strange new surroundings and of the radically altered symbolics of this First Morning Beatoff As A Single Man. Yes, of course, I was caressing my erect wang in my boss's guest shower, as he lay snoring like an axle-back exhaust on the other side of the wall, but that wasn't really the issue. I'd lived with other dudes before and had always managed to get my morning-shower business done without a trace of self-consciousness or anxiety, wholly undistracted by the bumps and footfalls of my roommates as they scrambled eggs, put on loafers, shuffled work files, lifted barbells, or what have you in the next room. Rather, what I realized, as I feverishly glossed my gland, was that this form of release was now divorced from the safety and surety of *pure fantasy*. No longer was masturbation a temporary departure from my marriage into a thrilling and restorative unknown—a realm of unencumbered sexual possibility in which I could thoughtlessly fuck some sexy assistant art director I worked with, or porn starlet Ashley Blue, or Hilary Duff in the late Lizzie years, or any other gal who popped up in my dirty imagination. No longer was it a tonic upon which I partly relied, without guilt or repercussion, to maintain the psychosexual stability of my marriage. Now jerking off was merely a *minor prelude* to an *actual* and far headier pursuit, a preparatory exercise for a totally achievable goal that, simply by virtue of being tangible, would *surpass* anything I could concoct in my wildest fantasy. It wasn't, in other words, anything to get too excited about.

'Bout two, two and a half minutes in, right on schedule, I spooged down the shower drain and watched the first of what I hoped would be gallons of feckless bachelor's semen swirl away into oblivion.

Around eleven Steve arrived at the house to pick me up. His fiancée was working all day, and he'd dutifully agreed to schlep my ass around and help me get my new life equipped. We had a whole day mapped out, and I was pretty excited about it: to start off, brunch at Ned's on Magnolia, a venerable North Hollywood diner; then off to buy some basics—a bed, towels, sheets and pillows, dishware, pots and pans, maybe a desk and chair; then an afternoon espresso at the Coffee Bean & Tea Leaf on Ventura and Laurel Canyon—a favorite spot of ours that we'd dubbed the "Hottie Bean" because, in one of those fortuitous human nexuses known to crop up at some strip malls in and around L.A., it shared an outdoor seating plaza with a low-carb frozen yogurt place overrun with under-twenty-five hot chicks; and finally, toward evening, he was gonna tag along as I went to see a man about a Porsche.

As I said, at the time I left my wife, it so happens that Steve had just entered the back half of his engagement to Marita, his lovely girlfriend of seven-plus years, and was hurtling meteorically toward his Wedding Day. And unlike my own engagement and marriage two years prior—the whole process of which I had *embraced* with eagerness and joy and the best of intentions, despite how it all turned out—Steve's was proving a much tougher pill to swallow. Eighteen months earlier, my friend's engagement had begun on a note of heart-stirring romance when Marita, fed up with Steve's heel-draggin', literally *forced* him to propose by e-mailing him a link to an engagement ring on WorldJewels.com, with a subject line that said: "Or else." He caved, of course, and now he was coming to grips with the reality that in about nine months, any notion that he would one day leave Marita and become a free man again would be annihilated once and finally.

Thus far, Steve's engagement had been a slow-boiling soup of despair and denial. He was alternately haunted by the blood-curdling prospect of actually *walking down the aisle in front of all those people* to face an event tantamount to, in his estimation, a public gelding or execution; and hopeful that a miracle would intercede, like some eleventh-hour gubernatorial pardon, to knock the marriage off course before then. During every step of the planning, he'd fussed and fought and flailed, hoping that he could eventually break Marita's will and compel her to see as clearly as he did that a court document and an overblown party in a Loews Hotel conference room was no big value-add to their union. To no avail: Marita had brushed aside his tantrums, most of the plans were now in place and paid for, family on both sides had booked hotels and plane tickets—and Steve knew damn well that at this point, he was gonna marry the broad whether he liked it or not.

And if he needed any more convincing, his fiancée's family, an intimidating clan of first-generation Filipinos, was not above reminding him just how irreversible the event was. At his recent engagement party, one close cousin, an imposing Hong Kong Mafioso type rockin' Chow Yun-Fat's trenchcoat-and-Ray-Bans look from *A Better Tomorrow,* had taken Steve aside and whispered to him with a lethal smile: "I love Marita like my own daughter, so treat her good . . . or else I'll have you killed. Okay? Ha ha! Only kidding"—with a strong chop to the spine to let Steve know that actually he was dead fuckin' serious.

Now, a word about my lifelong comrade and business partner, Steve Sobel, whom I have been blessed to know since we were seven-year-old *mamzers* shooting his brother's BB gun at lizards after Hebrew school in his backyard on North Bay Road in Miami Beach. I did everything first with Steve: I watched my first hardcore porno with Steve (admittedly a little young at age ten), a crummy Betamax dub of *Swedish Erotica Superstars* featuring Bridgette Monet and the ball-achingly hot Seka that we'd found—*score!*—among a pile of absolutely filthy XXX magazines under his oldest brother Jay's waterbed. I drank my first beer with Steve when we were twelve, one of my dad's Heinekens that I thought he'd never miss because I only ever saw him drink Johnnie Walker Red on the rocks. (I underestimated Dad. The next day he promptly noticed the beer was missing and chased me around the house in a rage, brandishing a thick leather belt that he'd doubled over into a makeshift blackjack. He never really struck me but did frequently threaten me with that shitstain-inducing belt.) I smoked my first joint with Steve when we were fourteen, a considerate gift from his Deadhead middle brother, Paul, and at sixteen I lost my virginity on a golf course to a girl named Andrea Weiss while attending a Jewish youth group event in Orlando, not very long after Steve had lost his in a similar fashion—

What I am trying to say here is that Steve and I are tight bros from way back when, and no one is more qualified than I to say what I'm about to say. *Steve wanted to marry Marita, more than anything in the world, and be with her forever and ever. He just didn't know it yet.* Despite all his hand-wringing and professed cynicism about getting hitched—for all his lusting after every attractive female (especially those of Asian descent) he laid eyes on—he was, at his core, faithful, loving, and consummately monogamous. And all of his *tsuris* over the prospect of having sex with one woman for the rest of his days was simply about him getting okay with being the affectionate and devoted sap he knew he was.

Naturally, my own marital troubles notwithstanding, I was happy for my best friend that he was in love and getting wed. Actually, no, I wasn't, not at all. In truth I *resented* the idea that he was moving on to a new chapter of his life that was entirely incompatible with *my* new chapter. For, much as I liked Marita, I liked the idea of my longtime homeboy chucking his fiancée and joining me in bachelorhood much, much more. I'd spent the last five years with Steve in the television trenches, during which we'd seen far more of each other than we had of our women. And now, somehow, the idea of tearing up the Hollywood singles scene without him seemed unpurposed and insubstantial. Though I'd never had any major trouble chatting up girls, I felt I *needed* Steve to be my wingman. Not my *married* wingman, who would halfheartedly nurse a Michelob Ultra before heading home to the wife round nine thirty, but one who was in it to win it like me, as off-the-leash and totally committed as I was to getting sloppy laid—no matter how late we had to stay out, no matter how many fatuous conversations with bimbos we had to sustain, no matter how many liquid cocaine or chocolate cake shots we had to buy 'em to close the deal.

I had other single male friends to hang with, sure—some of them bona fide hounds, even—but none as glib and quick as my writing partner, and I knew how potent our combined mack would be. I'd repeatedly witnessed the out-and-out ass-kicking he and I could pull off in a network meeting—with Steve typically taking the lead as the off-the-cuff-comedian idea guy and me playing the part of the wry, cerebral producer you could trust to deliver finished episodes: We are a goddamn powerhouse in the room. So, obviously, I could not help but imagine the damage we could do among the drunken horde of belly-shirted aspiring actresses at Barney's Beanery and the cheesedick frat boys daft enough to think they could go toe-to-toe with Wieder & Sobel!

Of course—of course—I never considered actually trying to break Steve and Marita up, or anything of that sinister sort. It did, however, stand to reason that if my new life became as totally fucking awesome as it surely would, Steve, fiercely competitive chap that he is, would gradually find his own circumstance insupportable by comparison, his engagement would implode in the nick of time, and he'd be left with no option other than to get shitfaced and chase birds with me—that is, of course, until Chow Yun-Fat hunted him down and took him out execution style, and possibly me for good measure, with double-fisted Beretta 92Fs.

"So, bachelor . . . how was your first night?" Steve asked as I hopped into his beat-up 1997 Ford Ranger pickup, a commodious vehicle I'd made good use of lately but one I also hoped not to be spotted in later outside the Hottie Bean.

"Dude, it was awesome," I said. "Hung out, ate some Greenblatt's, drank a bunch of beers with Cowan, played PlayStation till one in the morning, pulled one off, and went to bed—*alone.*"

He took this in with a measured nod, not giving me much. Clearly—I could decipher his every tiny tic and mannerism by this point—he was very relieved to hear that I had not already received a blow job from a woman I didn't know very well. But he also looked a tad stung, probably because *he'd* spent the night eating grilled salmon and finalizing his wedding invites with his fiancée. What he was saying to himself right then, only half-convincingly, was: *Okay, that* does *sound pretty awesome and I do wish I got to do shit like that more often, but the bachelor routine's gonna get real old in about a week. Just watch: in a month he'll grow tired of being alone and get a girlfriend who'll prob-*

ably be young and hot but kinda stupid and irritating, and—just wait—he's gonna end up marrying her . . .

But, supportive friend that he was and never the killjoy, what Steve said out loud was, "Lucky fucker."

Dum-ditty-dum-ditty-dum-ditty-dum: I suddenly heard the opening drum solo of the Youth Brigade song "I Hate My Life" playing on my cell phone. It was Sam's ring: I'd assigned it to our home phone number one night six months before, when it was 3 a.m. and I was trying to finish a cut and the woman wouldn't stop calling and, well, I hated my life.

I forwarded my wife's call to voice mail, as I had so many others, and lit a cigarette. She didn't leave a message.

"So we put a deposit down on the venue in Malibu," Steve said.

"Oh yeah? The Beach Club? I like that spot," I said.

"We're sitting down with the rabbi on Tuesday. Tasting cakes on Thursday."

I tried again to be supportive, though I wasn't sure what weight the encouragement carried, if any, coming from me. My broken marriage aside, I'd never had to go through the whole demoralizing rigmarole of planning a wedding, because Sam and I had eloped and married in a Las Vegas courthouse, much to the envy of my male friends. Sam was cool like that.

"Sounds fun," I said. It did not. At all.

"Yeah," he said. "It actually *has* been kinda fun, surprisingly enough. I've actually enjoyed a lot of it. Some of it, anyway. More than I thought I would, actually. I really like this rabbi, I think—he's the interfaith guy I was telling you about. He's a little too quippy, but he's pretty funny, actually. Surprisingly funny—I mean, you know, he ain't Patton Oswalt. The ceremony's gonna be right on the beach. A private beach. Great view. Of the ocean. You should see this view. Marita's thrilled, so I guess I'm happy."

"Atta boy. See? You're getting there. Come the day, you'll be good to go."

"Totally," he replied feebly. "Totally."

We pulled up to Ned's and went into our beloved diner, a cramped single room with cement floors, ten wobbly tables, and mismatched dishware, where they served a slam-bang bagel breakfast sandwich with a side of buttery zucchini patties, the thought of which is making me drool like a bullmastiff as I write this. We were immediately welcomed by the sexy Armenian—maybe Turkish hostess whom, it occurred to me, I was now free to get to know better sometime, perhaps over an *ibrik* of Aladdin coffee; and free, too, to nosedive afterward into her plump and snuggly bosom in her room in the apartment she probably shared with her elderly non-English-speaking parents somewhere in Glendale.

We grabbed a table and ordered our food in one fell swoop without even eyeballing the menu—smooth Ned's regulars that we were—and sat in pleasant silence for a minute or two. But then my dear, disconsolate friend could contain his anguish no longer. He shifted forward in his seat and let out an odd snort, and his face appeared wan. I braced myself for the onslaught that was coming whether I was prepared to listen to it or not.

"Digame, hombre," I said.

"This is really gonna happen, Al," he exploded. "I mean it's *really, really* gonna happen. And . . . it's not that I don't *want* it to happen. It's not that I don't *want* to be with Marita for the remainder of my life. But I just don't know what to do . . . I mean, the only alternative is ending the relationship, which I *definitely* don't want. But walking down that aisle in front of my whole family—*her* whole family—holy fuckin' shit, *walking down that aisle,* promising that I'm *always* gonna be there for her . . . It really feels like a—like a hanging. That's what it is, a hanging. Might as well be a noose waiting for me at the altar!"

"Oh, come on," I said.

"I'm serious, Al! But you know what? I let it get this far. I did. I've got no one to blame here but myself. Who can I blame? Can't blame *her.* Marita's got a right to be married after seven-some years. And I know, in my heart, that I'm the right guy to marry her. And yet here I am with the clock ticking, picking flowers and place cards and sitting down with a man of the fucking Torah, and I'm only like forty-two percent in favor of actually going through with the thing! Forty-two percent!"

I thought for a sec. "Yeah, but . . . what percentage were you at when you gave her the ring?"

"Um . . . zero percent."

"Forty-two's a solid uptick from zero, bro."

"Yeah, I know. You're right. I've come a long way; I know I have. But the question remains: am I gonna reach one hundred percent by my wedding day? I mean, the chips are on the table here, dude. I only have nine months to go. *Nine months.* What happens—what do I do if I'm only at eighty-two percent on the day? Is that how most guys feel when they're getting married? Eighty-two percent sure?! Would you and I send an edit or a script to the network that we thought was *eighty-two percent* there? Fuck no! I mean, this is the biggest decision of my life, and *eighteen percent*—a solid and very insistent eighteen percent of me's gonna be like, *Do you take this woman as your wife? Who, me? This chick? NO FUCKING WAY!*"

I let out a booming laugh of which Steve took special note.

"That's kinda funny, huh?" he said. "Think there's a bit there, in the percentages thing?"

Perhaps not surprisingly, before starting a production company with me, Steve'd spent some years in Hollywood as a working comic actor and standup. He still hit the comedy clubs now and again just for kicks.

"Definitely worth exploring," I said.

The food arrived, allowing Steve a moment to cool off, lower his voice, and ask for some Tabasco. But then he went on—oh, man, did he go on. I just kept listening attentively but not saying much, glad to have a chance to repay him for the countless hours he'd listened to me hem and haw about whether I should leave Sam. No longer having a wife myself had so replenished my reserve of magnanimity and patience and overall good spirits that I felt I could sit there and listen to him for days. Either that or it was just amusing to watch him suffer, knowing that I was finally done with all this marital meshugas, I'm not sure.

"You know what's weird?" he said.

Right then, as I forced down a tennis-ball-size mouthful of bagel, egg, cheese, and jalapeño sausage, I thought gleefully, *If Sam were here, I woulda **never** ordered this.* "I got a few opinions. Pass the pepper, will ya?"

"What's weird is that *you* didn't seem to have any doubts about it when you proposed. You asked your parents for the family diamond, took Sam on that romantic weekend to Napa, proposed, married—*boom*—and you seemed totally fine with it all. I never heard you worry or complain, not once. But then again, look what we're doing today. I mean, no offense, buddy, but seriously."

"It's cool," I said. It was true that on the weekend I proposed to Sam I was unequivocal, one hundred percent onboard.

We stayed four nights in the couples suite at the Hotel Healdsburg in Sonoma, ate at the Dry Creek Kitchen every night, rode bikes through Russian River Valley, vineyard-hopped, antique-shopped, drank Chardonnay in a hot air balloon—the whole deal.

"You say marriage is a 'gateway to divorce,'" he said. "I don't know, man. If that's the case, why bother at all? I mean, I have to say, I'd really feel like a *failure* if I got divorced—again, bro, no offense. But then again, I don't want to merely *succeed* at marriage; I want to feel *good* about it. I want to be happy and excited about it. Is that too much to ask?"

"..."

"I just can't for the life of me understand these dudes who are like, '*I can't wait to find a woman I love to spend the rest of my life with, to have a big family and grow old with.*' What's their secret? I mean, I think I'm a pretty romantic guy, but come *on*. These schmucks plan their proposals for months and find the perfect ring and the exact setting that was the one she pointed out in the window of Harry Winston two years ago when they spent a winter weekend in New York and he actually remembered, and they take their girlfriends to the top of some windy ocean bluff in Kauai and get down on one knee. '*Will you marry me?*' They wear their stupid little wedding rings, announcing to the whole world, '*I'm married, look at me, I love my wife so much that I married her.*' It's just all so *gaaay* . . . And yet, on the other hand, I *do* love my fiancée, possibly as much as those homos love theirs, or maybe even more. I mean, my life royally sucked before Marita and I got together—I mean, you remember."

I pictured the apartment he was living in before he and Marita got involved, a nasty-carpeted bachelor in a sad butterscotch complex in Valley Village, right across the street from a Wiener-schnitzel. He was twenty-five at the time but still living like a college freshman, with his unfolded clothes stuffed in plastic milk crates and a fridge full of half-empty cans of refried beans and other burrito fixin's. The one good thing about his building was its abundance of postcollege cuties in tank tops and stretch-fleece short shorts going to and from the laundry room—all of them broke and desperate enough to be living there. *Hmm,* I thought, *I wonder if they have any vacancies . . .*

"Check this out," he went on. "The other day Marita wakes me up at the crack of dawn to go to our food tasting. We have to drive all the way to Long Beach for a *food tasting* for my *wedding.* We're actually gonna sit down with our wedding planner and taste shrimp mole and sirloin tips and say, 'Oh yes, mmm, this is just delightful. And what type of sauce is served with this? Ooooh, really? Wonderful.' And I'm just *DYING* inside, Alan! I'm like, *How the fuck did I get myself into this?!*"

"Beats me, dude," I said.

"So we get there, and we meet our wedding planner, Dana, who's just this officious little princess, and Marita's of course happy as a clam. And then these three nosy Waspy catering company ladies come out and greet us, all enthused. They've got this whole spread meticulously laid out for us on this linen table-cloth, and I'm like, I gotta *perform* here, ya know? I can really fuckin' blow this right now; I can break Marita's heart. These three falconesses are standing over me and I've got this pasted-on smile, and I know they can see right through my bullshit. These broads've met enough grooms to know that I don't wanna be there. I just *know* they're judging me; I can *feel* them thinking, what is my poor fiancée doing wasting her life marrying *this* turd? So they bring out these dishes—we're doing a Chino-

Latino theme, so it's all stuff like paella and minty rice, mu shu pork empanadas—"

"Sounds delicious. Good combo."

"It is. The food's gonna rock . . . But—but anyway, I'm standing there in front of this elaborate culinary array, and I can hardly get a bite down. I'm sweating like a pig, I'm scanning the room for an emergency exit and thinkin' of making a dash for it—maybe leaving the country altogether. And the one chick brings out a plate of rice and says to me, 'Do you like it? Is there too much saffron? We can take down the saffron. *You* tell *us*. Remember, this is *your* day. You have to ask yourself'—she literally says this—'you have to ask yourself, Is this the rice I want to be served on my wedding day?' And I'm thinking to myself, *Huh?* ***What*** *wedding day!? This food is all fine and well, and it was very kind of you to make me this paella, lady. But at this point in time there's a fifty-three percent chance there's not gonna* ***be*** *a fucking wedding day! But while you're on your feet, throw a few more currants in there, bitch!!!*"

I laughed hard again, lovin' it. "And the worst part of all this," I said knowingly, "is that you can't share any of it with Marita."

He sopped up the rest of his ketchup with a tiny sliver of zucchini strip unfit for the load, and as he brought the overburdened patty-fragment to his lips it collapsed, plopping right into his lap.

"Fuckin' hell," he said.

Part of me wanted to put him at ease—to offer, as a friend who'd now seen some of married life's ups and downs, a bit of gentle and sagacious counsel that might correct his grim picture of what lay ahead. But I guess I was a bit irked by his implication that I was a failure at marriage and that consequently my current situation was a mess. So I took a tougher tack.

"Bro, listen to me," I said. "Fuck the 'gateway,' fuck the whole notion. It's just a stupid thing I say. And anyway, you're not me. Here's the deal. Don't even think about the rest of your life right now. You do and you're fucked. In fact, don't even think about your life at all. Your life means shit. Think of your life right now as this elaborate and wonderfully benevolent favor you're doing for someone else. No man *really* wants to get married, any more than he wants to take out the garbage, or grow old and die. But what *you* want doesn't even figure at this point. Fuck what you want. Marita's spent the last seven years of her life with you. Important years. She's been loyal and sweet and for some unfathomable reason still loves your ass. And you've stuck around; you've had plenty of opportunities to stray—I can think of one in particular, on production day twenty-eight on a beach in Costa Rica—but you chose not to. Now you *owe* it to the woman to marry her and give it a shot. Give it a shot, and if it's gonna work out, which you and I both know it is, it's gonna work out. And if it doesn't, you're gonna come out okay, too. I promise. But hey, I sucked at being married—right?—so what do I know."

He smiled at my reference to the time when, during our two-month stint in Costa Rica's Tambor valley as segment producers on *Temptation Island,* he and an extremely lecherous gaffer wound up (through a complicated set of events for which Steve was only *partly* responsible) partying and salsa-dancing on the beach of Bahia Ballena with two local *mami chulas* from San Jose. Things got so heated that Steve was compelled at the last minute to confess to his chick, Alejandra, that he had a girlfriend back home and couldn't fool around with her, much as he *quiere*'d to. (The lighting guy didn't get any *culo,* either, by the way, but only because he was kind of a creep.)

"Dude," he said, "if you start givin' it to all these girls now my head's gonna explode."

"So I just won't tell you about any of it, then."

"About any of *what*, exactly . . . ?" he asked, feigning ignorance—and intentionally provoking the very response he most dreaded.

"Why, any of the anonymous, multihole hardcore fucking and sucking I'm going to be doing," I said in perfect stride. This was our twenty-year private comedy routine, our well-honed pattern of pointless provocation and even more inane rejoinder, which only we found amusing. "Oops. Sorry, man. My bad."

"Ahhhhhhhh!!!" he screeched, and we laughed. Then he said: "The tough thing is, Al, I *want* to know about it all. I want to hear every unholy detail of the fucking and sucking. And I'll enjoy the hell out of it, too. As a friend. I *had* five years as a single dude-out-of-college before I met Marita; you didn't. Now it's your turn to have fun. God bless. I'm behind ya, bro. And yet . . . I've also got a very delicate balance going here. If you start banging chicks left and right it could really foul it up. It could potentially cause . . . just estimating here . . . a twenty percent displacement in my marriage-willingness ratio. If I take a twenty-point hit before my wedding day, I'm *screwed!*"

"Well . . . wish I could help ya, pal," I said to my friend, who'd had sex, it is true, with triple the women I'd had. *But not for long,* I thought. "Honestly I do. But the women of Los Angeles need my penis. They wish they didn't need it so very badly, but they can't help themselves. Starting with this one right here . . ."

I motioned over to my future Armenian lady friend for the check and smiled not my usual smile. She took note of it and smiled back. What the fuck, I figured, and wrote *What is your phone number?* on the bill, which I handed back to her along with my American Express Platinum Card. Cheesedick move, to be sure, but when she retreated behind the register and opened the check holder, I could see that she was surprised and charmed by it. And lo and behold, when the charge slip returned, her name, *Tati,* and her number were written on the customer copy in a bubbly cursive ("i" dotted with a little heart and all) that I found highly suggestive and erotic.

"Score. Wow, it's that easy," I said, taunting Steve with my first digits in a long while.

Steve then proceeded to open an imaginary drawer below the table, pull out an imaginary shotgun, put it in his mouth, and blow his brains out all over the unsuspecting family seated behind him.

After breakfast, my friend's mood brightened, and my first weekend afternoon as a single man—like the evening, night, and morning preceding it—was just ducky. First on our list was taking care of the apartment necessities, a pressing but potentially dreary chore that I believed would be much more agreeable under the sweet spell of Schlitz Malt Liquor. I decided I just *had* to have the amber, almost lager-y Red Bull variety (not to be confused with the energy beverage) that I'd so enjoyed as a teen, and I insisted that Steve drive to several convenience stores in search of it before I settled for a forty-ounce of Bull Ice, the ironically ghetto-ass nature of which tickled me greatly until I actually took the first few ghastly mentholated gulps—grabbing the bull by the horns indeed. Nevertheless, I managed to suck the whole forty down, and by the time we reached Bed Bath & Beyond I was pretty fucked up; and what little desire I'd had to comparison-shop featherbeds and step-on waste bins had fizzled altogether.

Soooo . . . I asked my chauffeur to take a little detour to Ahead Stereo, where I decided to purchase a full complement of fabulous new hi-fi components instead: Musical Fidelity integrated amp, Rotel CD player, Definitive speakers, Rega turntable—a lustrous audiophile rack whose $6,500 price tag I boozily rationalized by telling myself that if Sam was ultimately gonna get half my dough anyway, I might as well recklessly squander our joint cash assets on a bunch of esoteric equipment she probably wouldn't bother to seize during the divorce. (Brilliant, I know.) Afterward, Steve and I cruised to the Hottie Bean, where we shamelessly gawped and ogled eighteen- to twenty-four-year-old female yogurt store patrons (often accompanied by their MILF-y moms, who seemed to dig us far more than their daughters did) for two solid hours as we made our usual plans to conquer the world, one reality TV humiliation-fest at a time. And finally, right on time at five thirty, we arrived for our appointment at a tidy bungalow in West Hollywood, where a buff and shirtless middle-aged man named Ray was chamois-ing the immaculate silver 1986 Porsche 951 that I'd seen an online ad for and just had to check out.

"Sobel," I said, still slightly Bull-whipped, as we pulled into the driveway, "I think I'm gonna buy that car."

"Easy, White Dawg," Steve said, referencing the underground Caucasian crunk rapper from our home state of Florida, whose tight song "Sittin' on 22's" I'd been annoyingly humming all week. "Remember the plan," which was to absolutely refrain from buying anything I could imagine being forced to sell when the time came, and it would come very soon, to cough up my ex-wife's guaranteed year of alimony.

"You used to be fun," I said.

The Porsche 951, a.k.a. the 944 Turbo: with its 2.5L, 220 bhp

straight-four; intimidating flip-up headlights; grille-less nose
and strapping, dual-spoilered rear, the Land Shark, unlike any
other Porsche before or after it, struck just the right balance
between head-turning glamor and down-and-dirty, asphalt-
munchin' machismo. Ever since I was a young kid, long before
I finally passed my driver's exam after two failed attempts, I'd
been creamin' my jeans for this car. My neighborhood sleepover
pal Stewart's college-aged older brother Perry drove the first 951
I ever saw—a sweet one in metallic blue, in which he brought
home a seemingly endless stream of (in his words) filthy whores,
much to our prepubescent awe. (I can still hear the giggles and
gasps of pleasure that came from behind Perry's bedroom door
as Stewart and I, our teeny-weeny boners protruding beneath
our Underoos, eavesdropped in the hallway.) Ever since then, I'd
told myself that someday—someday, when *I* called the shots—I
would drive one just like it.

Hello, someday.

I introduced myself and Steve to Ray, shaking his big, gnarled
paw, which engulfed my bony hand like a lion swallowing a
baby gazelle. I noticed that Ray was without a wedding band,
which I assumed meant that he was either a really butch older
gay dude (likely, given the neighborhood) or a grizzled hetero
bachelor who'd racked up God only knows how much tail in this
vehicle. I preferred to assume the latter.

"Lemme ask you: why the 944 Turbo?" Ray asked after I'd
rounded the car admiringly. He was clearly testing me a little.
He wasn't gonna sell the car to just any young punk who came
along.

"He just left his wife," Steve interjected. "—Not for me," he
then clarified, producing a tepid chuckle from Ray.

I shot Steve a put-a-sock-in-it look, fearful that my loudmouth friend would fuck up the good 951 seller-buyer karma that I knew would be critical to striking a deal.

"Honestly, Ray," I said. "I just love this car. I've loved it forever. For some people it's the GTO, or the Mercedes 450 SL—but for me, it's always been the 951. And my wife, my soon-to-be-*ex*-wife, never wanted me to get one. Wasn't safe enough, no ABS, no airbags, in the shop every other week, a fortune to fix, blah blah blah. I was fine with it. She's a great woman, and I loved her a lot, so I drove a Saab 900, and right now I'm in a nice Lexus SportCross—both good cars; I haven't exactly been suffering. There's bigger problems to have. But now I'm a free man, free to be a selfish bastard, and I'd like to be one in this car."

More than anything else I said, my use of "951," the little-known factory designation for the 944 Turbo, signaled to Ray that I was a genuine enthusiast who would probably take proper care of his pride and joy.

"You guys wanna whip around the block?" Ray said, in that moment looking very much the overgrown teenager I hoped to still be when I reached his age.

We all hopped in: Ray, still sans shirt, riding shotgun; Steve (the shortest of the three of us) squeezed into the Lilliputian back "seat"; and I—for the first time since young Stewart and I horsed around in Perry's cockpit that smelled richly of pine air freshener and Drakkar Noir cologne, pretending we knew how to drive stick—actually behind the wheel of the grand tourer of my dreams, the 944 Turbo. As we took off through West Hollywood towards Beverly Hills, Ray kept insisting, "Punch it, Alan, punch it, don't be shy," and I gladly obliged, pressing through neighborhood turns, grumbling down Rodeo Drive, tearing ass along empty Burton Way. This was one dope-ass ride.

Ray was ten times the 951 nutjob I was and had spent five

years and clearly many thousands on some pretty bodacious up-
grades and mods, all of which he described in carfreaky detail
as we zipped along: He'd replaced the stock turbo with a Hunt-
ley Racing something-or-other, which was capable of deliver-
ing over 300 hp to the rear wheels and felt fuckin' *dangerous*.
He'd added a cluster of crazy Formula 1-lookin' pressure gauges
to the dash, along with a glass-pack muffler whose obnoxious
growl, much to my delight, drew the indignant stares of nearly
every passerby. And the stereo he'd installed was just *ree-*
diculous: a humongous Precision Power system that took up half
the hatch and with its blinking digital voltage readouts and ca-
pacitor LEDs looked like a time bomb fixin' to blow; and pushed
a three-way, ten-speaker setup that, thundering over the muffler, nearly powdered my eardrums. Awesome!

"So?" Ray said when we were standing on his lawn again,
back on planet Earth. "Check or cash?"

"God damn," I said.

Truth was, much as I was enamored with the idea of driving
the car away without a second thought, I was on the fence. Rad
as they were, all of Ray's aftermarket bells and whistles were
actually a little much for me, and had driven the asking into the
$24,000 range—a lot of gouda for an '86 car with 94,000 miles
on it. Also, as Steve duly reminded me, in order to buy the car
I'd have to maneuver a highly conspicuous chunk of Sam's and
my savings out of our joint account—which would have been a
big fiscal fuck-you to my wife, especially given that I'd already
blown seven grand on the hi-fi stereo, immediately after which
I'd bought a flashy new smartphone, a slimtop computer, and
$400 worth of DVDs and Xbox games, figuring hey, what's an-
other four grand. An $11,000, obviously, that I could have used
to pay down the bachelor pad I had not yet secured, or Sam's

interim living costs, or my forthcoming legal fees, or the zillion other transitional expenses I'd soon be on the hook for.

Once I got good and stewing, the whole thing started to seem like a shitty idea. I broke into a chilly *shvitz* along my spine—a trusted neurophysiological indication that I was on the cusp of doing something stupid. But then I got a grip: *Relaaaaax, Wieder,* I thought. *Truly now: What's the worst thing that can come of buying this car? I have a good job. I'm not rich, but I have enough dough. My best earning years are ahead of me, way ahead. It's not like you're buying a fuckin' Bugatti here! What happened to "fuck savings," tough guy? Take out a loan. Live off peanut butter for six months. God, you're a pussy! You want the car. You've wanted it for twenty years. Quit whining about how your wife never let you do anything fun, and figure it the fuck out!!!*

Yo yo, Alan, Alan, it's like this: are you a hustla or ain't ya?

"Can I put five thousand down tonight to hold it and give you the rest later in the week?" I asked Ray.

And just like that, before I could say Zuffenhausen, the day's damage was done: $35,000 on a truckload full of high-tech gadgets and a low-tech car, and still I didn't have a mattress to sleep on, or sheets to put on it, or a pot to piss (or cook mac and cheese) in.

On the drive home, I began to agonize over the prospect of having to drop at least another $2,500 on items I actually needed. But then a stroke of good luck befell me: Steve recalled that he still had, tucked away somewhere in his garage, most of his belongings from his days in the nasty-carpeted bachelor apartment in the sad butterscotch complex in Valley Village!

"It's probably all pretty rank by now, but you're welcome to it," he said.

Whattaguy. We drove to his house—a quaint North Hollywood cottage Marita's father had helped them purchase just after their engagement—and rummaged through the garage. And lo and behold, in a damp corner where a small leak had sprung, we found three large moving boxes containing a trove of workable bachelor-pad booty: a set of cast-iron pots and pans; a four-slice pop toaster; a Ziploc freezer bag full of random knives, forks, and scattered soup and dessert spoons; a cutting board, a waiter's pulltap corkscrew, and an electric can opener; a cool circa-1980 Kitchenaid blender that I recognized from Steve's old house in Miami Beach; and many other utile bits and bobs.

And most critically, towering along the back wall, there stood what else but a very promising-looking California king-size mattress!

"It's a good one. *Tempur-Pedic. Swedish. Not bad—eh?*" Steve said in his funny alta-cocka voice. New, these things ran like $1,500, so I was psyched. "It was Mom's. She gave it to me after college when she upgraded to a Craftmatic."

As it turned out, the mattress was *not* so promising when we dragged it out. Because of the leak the recent rains had gotten to it, and my heart sank as I discovered that an entire edge of it was soaked through and starting to mildew. That's to say nothing of the assorted other stains—coffee, spaghetti sauce, sex juice—that had accumulated on both sides over five years of young bachelor use. It was not quite what you'd see laid out on a city sidewalk for the sanitation department to haul off, but close. It also smelled . . . bad.

The foam mattress flopped and floundered as we carried it to the driveway for a more thorough inspection. It was getting on evening, so it was tough to make out exactly how grody it was in the fading light. Steve, for his part, was more concerned with the leak and went back into the garage to see what was up.

An aproned Marita came out of the house to see what mischief we boys were up to. I kissed her hello. She eyed the mattress.

"You're gonna sleep on that?" she asked me. "You're gonna let the girls you bring home sleep on that?"

"Considering it," I said.

"Honey," Steve said from within the garage, suddenly sounding very much the mature home-owning hubby. He was shining a flashlight along a drippy ceiling beam, beaming himself at having located the source of the seepage. "Looks like we got our first leak here."

"Really?" Marita went into the garage to confirm. "Awww," she said. *"Our first leak."*

They got all huggy and smoochy and boo-boo-ba-ba, and for a moment I missed Sam like something terrible. For a moment.

"Alan," Marita said, her arms wrapped around Steve's neck. "You staying for dinner?"

"Thanks, sweetie, but I think I've monopolized enough of your husband's day," I said.

"Bah," Steve said. "Hang out. It'll be fun. I'm grillin' *pork chops . . . on the new grill.*" He'd just bought one of those mondo suburban gas grills with the stainless steel hoods and thermoset work surfaces, tool and beverage holders—the works—and was eager to share it with me. Or, knowing Steve, show it off.

The day had been full, and the idea of throwing down a pork chop, drinking a glass or three of wine, and nodding off on a comfy Pottery Barn sectional sofa beside my best friend and his fiancée sounded all right. It did. But it also bored me to tears.

"Maybe tomorrow night, guys," I said. "Think I'm gonna go out to eat."

Steve told Marita he was gonna drive me back to Chris's, help me carry my stuff up to my apartment, and be back home in an hour. She was anxious to get dinner up, but she was okay with it. It seemed to me that the saintly woman was always okay with everything.

"So what's the call?" Steve said re the mattress. "You takin' this piece of shit? If not, help me drag it over to the sidewalk, 'cuz I'm tossin' it."

I figured I'd schlep the mattress home and if it was still absolutely frightful in the morning light, I'd give it to a transient.

"Let's load 'er in," I said.

We put the mattress in the pickup bed, laying it on top of my stockpile of boxed electronics and household hand-me-downs, and secured it with truck rope. It was a fortuitous setup, because on the way back to Chris's house it started to rain again, so at the very least the mattress—already sodden anyway—would serve as a great makeshift tarp.

"Man . . . I gave it to so many girls on that mattress," Steve reminisced, as we sped along the 101 South back to Hollywood. "Every which way."

"That's nice, Steve," I said.

The multi-CD player had finished with Nas's *It Was Written* and moved on to 2Pac's *Better Dayz*. Steve had been a hip-hop fan since high school—long before I ever got into rap—but, unlike me, he'd never made a whole big to-do of it. We rapped along in unison, like the Miami Beach Jewboy dorks we were, to an oft-recited line from "Still Ballin": "I love my females strapped/no fuckin' from the back/I got my currency in stacks/California's where I'm at—right?"

We reached my temporary hillside alcazar and carried the day's acquisitions up to the guest apartment—including Steve's stinky, condiment-and-cum-spattered mattress. It saddened me to bring something so tainted and foul into my new life, but for some reason I was determined to salvage it. I stood the mattress on its side beside a heating vent, thinking maybe it would dry by morning. I hoped to God the foam slab was not harboring some horrific infestation of mites, earwigs, silverfish, and who knew what other garage creepy-crawlies—like some Trojan horse destined to carry ruin into my new home before I could even settle in.

I gave Steve a big ol' hug that I hoped was fair compensation for putting up with days and months of my personal crap, and bid him good night. He seemed more than a trace sad to go.

"Sobel," I said, as he was about to drive off.

"Sir."

"You've got a good woman," I said.

"Yeah," he said. Then: "Hey, what's on the docket this evening, bachelor?"

"No clue," I said. "Think I'm gonna take it easy tonight," which was code for, *I'm gonna get right fucked up, probably at my regular hangout, the Coach & Horses on Sunset, and see where the night leads.*

"Oh Alan," he said, knowing my code too well. "Ya old drunk. Do me a favor. Take a cab. My future kinda hinges on you not winding up in jail, or dead."

"You'd get by without me. Barely."

"You're a real dick, Alan Wieder."

"I know," I said, as he drove away.

Chris's X5 was not in the driveway, which by this hour meant that he was probably out for the night, probably wining and dining his reality TV hottie. So I made myself right at home. I went up to the main house and poured a generous double of Johnnie Walker Blue—Chris didn't fuck around when it came to liquor—and caught the tail end of *Heat,* one of my all-time faves, on his massive flat-screen. Ching Ching soon tottered in and galumphed onto the leather sofa beside me, perhaps with her dwindling faculties mistaking me for the man whose usual seat I presumptuously occupied, and for whose life I felt more than a little envy.

In a few hours I felt hungry and took a ride to Whatever The Fuck Restaurant I Felt Like Eating At. With Sam it had always been such an ordeal, such a *conversation*, just to decide what to do for dinner on a Saturday night—a stultifying discourse in which I would invariably fall into the role of reluctant restaurant pitchman, and she the nearly impossible sell.

Feel like sushi? I'd say. *We can order Hirozen and watch a movie . . .*

No, she'd say, *I shouldn't do fish—the mercury.*

Okay, I'd say. *How about Dominick's?*

Hmm, she'd say. *Italian . . . I do love the courtyard . . . great stuffed mushrooms . . . but it's kinda heavy, no? Not tonight.*

All right, what about the Malaysian place at the Farmers Market? You liked that tofu-sprout stew, remember? Or how 'bout a bunch of salads from Skaf's Lebanese?

Umm . . . she'd say. *Is that what **you** want?*

For her it was fun, I suppose, a cute guessing game in which I got to pin down her fickle wants; but for me, it was a cruel and senseless torture. And the knowledge that *this was just what married couples did*—that our dysfunction was all too common and kind of funny in a certain light, the clichéd stuff of married-guy observational comedy—only prompted thoughts of murder-suicide all the more.

Fuck it all to hell, I thought, as I entered Cheebo, a bright-orange-awninged bistro on Sunset, not far from my old apartment. Though we'd never eaten there, Sam always used to make light fun of it as an obvious first-date kinda joint—which it *was*—a trendy, eclectic-menu'ed restaurant where diners crayon on butcher-paper-covered tables as they wait for eighteen-dollar mac and cheese. "Let's go to *Cheebo*," she'd say sarcastically, preying on its admittedly goofy name. And to be honest, the one time I'd eaten there alone some months before, on a night when Sam and I were in a bad fight, the "steak frittes" was just okay—and spelled wrong. But the votive candlelit place was nothing if not cozy, its waitresses cute and offbeat and pleasantly chatty, its selection of bottled beers competent—and the fact that it was a stone's throw from the Coach & Horses bar was, on such a night, a sufficient selling point.

The lovely hostess/waitress sat me at a great table in back and brought me a Cheebo-tini, a sweet-potato-vodka martini that seemed worth a taste. I took a sip—not bad—and brought out a four-hundred-page tattered manuscript that I had not even glanced at in many months.

This was *Polak,* my would-be Great American Novel. I'd been tinkering with it between TV productions for five years. It was roughly the story of an emotionally stunted Polish-born New York street sweeper who's driven to brutally murder his infertile wife and the baby she compelled him to kidnap. But I ain't bitter. The premise needed work and the book was in coarse, disconnected pieces, but I was relieved to find that I still felt good about the project and confident that, sans time-sapping wife, I'd soon whip it into shape.

As I read through the draft, I Cheeboed on a mix of high and low cuisine: veal carpaccio with shaved truffles, and a mesquite pulled-pork sandwich. Both were middle of the road. Then I needed something real to drink and headed down the block.

At the time, the Coach & Horses was one of my favorite

spots in Hollywood, a glowy-red, pleasingly musty railroad-car of a bar whose jukebox is the only one I've encountered that contains the Descendents, Misfits, Bad Religion, Minor Threat, *and* the Circle Jerks. (I *know*. Can you believe it!?) This was the doing of the managing bartender, Liza, a mercurial, curly-haired brunette with a mesmerizing countenance, impeccable taste in music (obviously), and a big, juicy butt that one got to glimpse every ten seconds when perched at the bar. Though I'd introduced myself to her on four or five occasions (and masturbated to her many more than that), she didn't know me from the lonely-looking dude sippin' on a twenty-four ounce can of Pabst Blue Ribbon who was now begging, fruitlessly, for her phone number.

I heard her politely fend the poor guy off: "Sorry, Mike . . . No . . . I can't. Sorry . . . No . . . That's sweet of you, you're very sweet, but no . . . You can give it to me, but I won't call you . . . I don't date customers . . ."

Oh, but she will, I thought, *she will.*

I dropped five bucks (fifteen songs' worth) into the jukebox, took a seat by the video poker machine, and drank. And drank. A couple starter shots of Booker's True Barrel 126-proof whiskey that lit my brain afire, three Bushmills on the rocks to lay the buzz sideways, and Newcastle beer after beer. Liza was flirty but unyieldingly professional and on point, and I watched, rapt, as she beat back the Saturday night swell—pouring her fine martinis, flinging killed bottles into the trash from halfway across the bar, pausing every now and then to bounce along to Fugazi's "Waiting Room" or some other bar favorite. By the time my first track came on, the Descendents' "Hope"—one of the theme songs of my lovelorn late-teen years—I was good and shitty and full of adolescent longing for her. I thumped my fingers on the bar and tried my best to keep key with Milo Aukerman's inimitable scratchy-sweet voice.

So now you wait for his cock, you know it'll turn you on.
He's gonna make you feel the way you wanna feel.
But when he starts to lie, when he makes you cry,
You know I'll be there: My day will come.
I know someday I'll be the only one.

The song's story of a boy's sidelined affections transported me into an elaborate rescue fantasy involving me and my quirky drink-slingin' future girlfriend behind the bar. In a flash I saw myself luring Liza away from some douchebag boyfriend she probably had who, in my imagining, played in a sucky garage band and did piles of coke and treated her like shit and didn't love her like I could . . .

Then a phone call on my fancy new cell phone buzzed me out of my reverie: Samantha for sure, I thought—yet another of her distraught attempts to plead with me to come home, demand some explanation for why I was treating her so abominably.

I checked the phone: The call was actually from a Tampa number I didn't recognize. I sent it to voice mail just to be safe. But then came a follow-up text from the same number:

Hello oldman. *Now* can we go to Souplantation? ;)

Well, would you look at that, I thought. It was Ms. K, an adorable twenty-three-year-old story assistant (and recently relocated fellow Floridian) with whom I'd carried on a months-long innocent flirtation at our production offices. Clearly word of my separation had spread like a Malibu wildfire: a good sign, I supposed. "Oldman" referred to my AIM moniker "oldmanwieder"—"old man" was my college tennis team nickname because I had the agility of an octogenarian—and the cute *asterisks* meant *now* that I was single, was I free to take her to an all-you-can-eat soup-and-salad bar on La Cienega about which she and I had once had a charming conversation in the office kitchen?

Fuck yeah I was free to take Ms. K to Souplantation. But I played it cool:

> Wow. I see girls move pretty quick these days.

Then within seconds:

> U r a hot commodity. Someone's gotta take u off the market. :)

A hot commodity, eh? All cocky, I punched back:

> Whatcha doin Friday night?

Then her:

> A date. Mark Benson the editor. I was set up.

Mark was a fine reality editor and a nice enough chap, but come on. This is *me* we're talking about. So I went for it:

> Poor guy's gonna be heartbroken.

Her, confused:

> ???

Me:

> When you tell him to buzz off and hang with me instead.

Her:

> :O You're funny.

And boom, just like that, Mark's rendezvous with Ms. K went bye-bye—sorry, buddy—because she was salad-bar-bound with yours truly instead.

Bad Religion's "I Want to Conquer the World" gave way to the Misfits' "Hatebreeders"—*whoa oh oh whoa!*—to the Circle Jerks' "I Just Want Some Skank." Finally noticing my fervid chanting and finger tapping—and that I'd turned my attention away from her to my cell phone screen—Liza came over.

"These are your songs, aren't they?" she said.

"Mayyyybe," I said, guilty as charged. "Did I do okay?"

"I like 'Sour Grapes,'" she said, naming a catchy Descendents tune from their most overlooked album, *Enjoy!* "For future reference . . . Alan, right?"

"Duly noted," I said, popping a slight boner at the totally unexpected name recall.

She reached behind the bar and brought up a murky russet cocktail.

"Hey, I just made this seven and seven by mistake. Do you want it?" she asked.

Life was just getting sweeter and sweeter.

I swerved and weaved Lilo-style back to Chris's house around two thirty, the first of many DUIs I flirted with over the next months. As I stumbled into the dining room, I discovered fifteen or so rowdy white gentlemen sitting around a felt-covered table heaped with half-empty bottles of expensive alcohol, cigar-stubbed ashtrays, and chips of both the potato and gambling variety.

Poker night. Shit. I'd forgotten all about it.

"Hey! It's Wieder!!!" Chris shouted at the top of his lungs, one drunken fool greeting another. "He finally made it!"

"WIEDERRRRR!!!" came a collective greeting that would've made Norm Peterson proud, from Chris's peanut gallery of softball buddies—three-quarters of whom had never seen me in their lives.

"We're just starting a new round. A hundred bucks to get in," Chris said.

The huddle of liquored-up jocks made room for me at the

table. I poured myself another generous Johnnie Walker Blue—wasted on me, wasted as I was—and took a seat.

Stacking my chips in neat rows, I said to everyone, "You fuckers ready to lose some money?"

Not the greatest line, but enough to produce roaring laughter from this jolly group.

I don't remember any of what happened next, but apparently, 'round sunup and three hundred lost dollars later, I went out to the balcony for a smoke and blacked out.

3.0

THE THING IS, my family and friends weren't wrong: We *were* so perfect together, Samantha and I, from the moment that—after two hours of ogling her from across the bar, trying in vain to catch her eye—I finally mustered the liquid courage to approach her and buy her a Red Stripe.

We met in the snowy winter of 1995, the Year of the Pig, the weekend before Valentine's Day. I suppose the approaching holiday boosted the chances that Sam and I would find romance, but even more propitious (to me, anyway) was the specific *location* of our first encounter: my first favorite place in the world to be drunk, the Night Café at 106th & Amsterdam in New York City, in the heart of a drug-and-rodent-infested section of Spanish Harlem that real estate marketers euphemistically called Manhattan Valley. At that sublimely scuzzy bar, pretty much every

Friday and Saturday night for my latter half of college, I and my circle of friends would gather to piss the night away drinking beer, listening to Urge Overkill on the jukebox, and playing the hiply retro Galaga machine till our missile fingers went numb. I'd never seen Sam there before and was instantly sucked in by the sight of this very pretty and put-together woman at my beloved craphole bar, in her preppy peacoat standing out from the pack of riot-grrrly female regulars I usually tried to lure back to my dorm room.

Spotting Samantha hit me hard not merely because she was exceptionally beautiful and sophisticated looking, but also because at the time I was growing deeply disaffected with my college clique and hungry for some way out. From the outset everything about Sam seemed *different*—her style, her demeanor, her sense of self. She seemed to have arrived from some thrilling period and place totally apart from the one I was presently mired in. At Columbia, the crew I ran with—death-metal-head cultural studies major Matt, Seattle-born indie-rock snob Jeremiah, pomade-doused wannabe greaser Greg, edgy NYC rocker Abigail, lost Lunachick member Moira, and assorted hangers-on—were all very cool kids, and for most of college I'd felt lucky and honored to have been embraced by the hippest crowd—I'd venture to say the *only* hip crowd—on our relatively small campus. But we were also an exclusionary group of punker-than-thou pissants who judged others solely on how many indie bands' CDs and poststructuralist texts they had on their bookshelves, by whether they'd heard the Melvins or read Maurice Blanchot. The truth is, we really weren't all that kind to *each other,* either. And now that I was an almost-twenty-one-year-old senior who was starting to wig out about what I was gonna do with my life once my student ID expired, our too-cool-for-school proclivities had begun to seem shallow and troublingly inapplicable to the terrifying future awaiting me in the real world below 114th Street.

I'd also grown disenchanted, by extension, with the punky Barnard Sylvia Plath types I'd made a habit of dating. Arty and off-key chicks of all stripes were drawn to our circle in droves, and somehow I had a knack for homing in on the most insane ones in the bunch. By my senior year I'd developed a rep among my friends—most of whom had long-term steadies—as a guy who ran through girlfriends, but the reality was that all the women I fell for turned out to be so unstable that, often despite my best efforts at monogamy, my relationships would implode as quickly as they began. At the time, of course, these women all seemed sooooo *fascinating,* each in their own unique way; I accepted their volatilities as part and parcel of their mystique, and even relished my role as the port in their stormy emotional lives. But now I look back and wonder what the fuck I was thinking. My freshman year there was Jamie, my first three-week girlfriend, a Sisters of Mercy-worshipin' goth chick who painted disturbing self-portraits and always had strange wounds on her legs that really freaked me out. Then there was Elana, a mercurial sculptor who once a week would come down with a paralyzing "migraine" and lock herself in her dorm room for forty-eight hours, doing I never figured out what, while I fetched her soup and finished her French homework like a schmucko. Then Andrea, the depressive bulimic ballerina, whom I pined for—oh man, did I pine—when a nervous episode forced her to drop out of school (and drop me). And Carmen, the hot, heroin-addicted agoraphobe . . . Noelle, who had great taste in music but cried in my arms incessantly and was just clearly mental from the beginning . . . Paola, a tortured graphic artist I saw over breaks in Florida, who lived with her verbally abusive mother . . . Alexis, a totally daft young woman who, when I broke up with her, threatened to attack the next girl I dated with a lead pipe . . . and, most recent, Sarah, the aspiring photographer and raging alcoholic whose hair I once held while she puked in a bathroom stall in Wallach Hall . . .

Was there something seriously wrong with me? Every guy falls for a troubled gal every now and then, but with me it was an obsessive pattern. And even worse, I wasn't really getting laid much outta the deal. How is it that this Nice Jewish Boy From Miami Beach had yet to date one—*one!*—girl who wasn't a complete freak whom I felt compelled to fix, protect, or rescue?

What was it with me and wounded women?

When I laid eyes on Samantha—this girl to whom I would now turn to save *me* from my mean-spirited friends, from my own worst instincts—I was twenty minutes into a game of Smoking Chicken with Greg, a tall, stick-skinny, red-headed, Pittsburgh-born lush who was my closest comrade in the group. Smoking Chicken, part of a repertoire of games my friends and I played while drinking, basically consisted of two people taking turns exhaling as much cigarette smoke as possible into the other person's face, at extremely close range, till one person cried uncle and quit.

"Your move," Greg said without a trace of levity, as if we were Kasparov and Karpov sitting across a checkered table in Tchaikovsky Concert Hall. His words carried along the last wisps of a positively nuclear blast of unfiltered Lucky Strike smoke he'd just blown into the general vicinity of my face. Greg was our group's reigning champion at Smoking Chicken, not really because of any special technique but because he had the profoundest disregard for his own physical well-being and therefore for the obvious hazards of this very cruel and idiotic game.

Tears of agony welled beneath my trembling lids, my nasal passages felt like they were on fire, and I was about to toss my Shiner Bock all over the KISS-themed pinball machine behind me. I wanted to quit. I was so done with this shit. I didn't want to play Smoking Chicken anymore, that night or ever again.

But I stood my ground: I pulled a massive drag of my Pall Mall 100, bringing into my lungs and mouth almost a fourth of that extra-long cigarette's throughput, and waited a pregnant beat, trying to psyche Greg out. I then released the smoke in a precise swirling formation across his entire face, moving deliberately across his eye sockets, beneath his nostrils, hoping that my meticulously distributed cancer-spritz would finally get him to bow down.

Not a chance: Greg just stood there, taking it all in, grinning perversely through the bank of smoke, even *inhaling* some of my exhalation and—no joke—volleying it back to me in a perfect smoke ring: the game's ultimate fuck you.

"Chicken," I sighed, stubbing out my cigarette and, in the game's official gesture of surrender, snapping the butt in half.

"What a duffer," he laughed. "You always quit."

"I guess I continually underestimate your masochism," I said.

He smiled, pulled another Lucky Strike from the pack Fonzer-ellied in the sleeve of his black T-shirt, and said: "Galaga?"

I totally didn't want to watch Greg blast alien insects for at least the next forty-five minutes till he lost his first man—because, come to think of it, he was annoyingly good at that game, too. I glanced over at the bar at Samantha for the thousandth time. I could see now that another fellow was chatting her up—Mike, a guy who piped up a little too often in my Contemporary American Lit section. My stomach clenched a bit in a spurt of premature jealousy.

Man, I was blowing my moment big-time. It seemed impossible that this girl would ever be back at the Night Café—or that, as I would be graduating in eight weeks, I'd ever have a chance to talk to her again. But, hungry as I was for his approval, I had a really hard time saying no to Greg, to any of those guys, about anything.

"Sure," I said. "Light it up."

When Greg was through his third flawlessly executed bonus round and had already accumulated like six extra men, Matt, the super-cocky de facto leader of our pack, came over and made a gesture that little did he know would change my life forever: he offered us heroin.

"Let's roll, nerds," he said. "Party at Abby's. Satan awaits."

"Satan" was the street term for the crop of inexpensive dope one could then easily buy on every corner on Amsterdam from 106th to 109th Street. It's a little shocking to say now, but at that time smack was the recreational drug du jour at Columbia. Pretty much everyone I knew, including me, was snorting it every weekend like it was no big thing.

Greg had already abandoned his game and slipped on his leather jacket. For him, not even beating my ass at Galaga took precedence over dope. He looked back at the screen ruefully as his now-unmanned and defenseless twin fighters were blown to smithereens by a swarm of those nasty orange-and-blue dragonfly things that appear at the higher levels of the game.

"All right," he said. "Let's dust."

The idea of spending the rest of my Saturday night the same way I'd spent the last thirty or so—doped up in some dorm room full of Foucault texts, listening to Nation of Ulysses's *Plays Pretty for Baby* or watching some dumb Russ Meyer movie for the two hundredth time—now made my skin creep and crawl. I also recalled that the last time I'd done smack I'd been peer-pressured into doing a line too many and wound up passing out in the bathtub in a puddle of thrown-up falafel balls. I started to drag my feet.

"Wieder, what's your deal? You coming?" Matt said, leaving off the *ya big fag?* that was always implicit in Matt's tone whenever he asked anyone to come do drugs—or, really, do anything he wanted to do.

"Nah," I uttered reflexively, surprising myself and my friends especially. "Pass."

Feeling good, I stepped out onto the street to smoke an unfiltered Pall Mall in some fresh air. Snow had been dumping down for at least the last two hours, because there were eight powdery inches on the ground, enough to engulf the hole-ridden low-top Vans that I rocked, freezing feet be damned, through the thick of winter. Then I ducked back into the Night Café and sat alone at the bar for another hour, drinking and watching Mike mack on Samantha.

The bloke seemed to be doing all right—he obviously moved faster than *I* did—but I could tell that he was being a bit of a nudnik. I could tell especially when, as he rambled on at one point, Samantha looked across the bar at me, smiled, and slightly rolled her eyes, as if to say: *If you got the legs, boy, come on, let's walk.*

On Mike's next bathroom break I steeled my nerve, bought a Red Stripe—the beer she'd been drinking—and sidled over, wondering what to lead off with. Then it came to me in a stroke of genius, or perhaps of destiny.

Putting the beer down in front of her, I said: "What are you messin' with small change for?"

It was the exact line my grandfather, Bernie Wieder, used when he met my grandmother at the dog track one summer Sunday in 1936—when she was on a date with another man. Grandpa happened to be a broke-ass salesman at the time, blowing his last few nickels on an afternoon trifecta, while Grandma's beau was an executive at the Bank of New York. But somehow, the line totally worked for Bernie, and from the way Samantha lit up, more amused than outraged by the absurd ballsiness of it, I could tell straight off that it would work for me, too.

"Is that like some Marlon Brando line I should know?" she said.

"Come on, I'm not that cheesy. It's an old family pickup line."

"It's a pretty good one, actually," she said. "But with all due respect to your family lineage, I believe Small Change was messin' with *me*."

She smirked cutely. I was so in.

"You cut your hair," I observed.

I'd seen her a few times around campus as a shoulder-length golden blonde, but presently her hair was close-cropped and dyed dark brown. I preferred the old look, to be honest, but the new one was all right, too. Of course, revealing that I'd noticed the hair change at all was probably a bad move, but I was feeling adventurous.

"Yeah," she said. "Kinda going through a Jean Seberg thing right now."

Uh-oh, I thought. *Red flag.* I'd seen Jean Seberg in *Bonjour Tristesse* and *Breathless* in a French film survey, and while I found her totally intoxicating, I also knew of her self-inflicted demise in a Paris suburb. On the other hand, the idea of playing down-on-his-luck Michel to her enigmatic Patricia did greatly intrigue me. *Shit,* I thought, *another wack-job. Here we go again . . .*

"It's working for ya," I said.

"Nice of you to say."

We stared at each other wordlessly for a moment. Up close for the first time, I finally got an honest look at her, and lemme tell ya, beer goggles or no, this was one hot chick. She had sea-green eyes, high pronounced Slavic cheekbones that sloped down onto bountiful lips you just had to kiss, and exasperatingly smooth skin, like one of those girls in a Clearasil commercial who have no business shilling the product because they've clearly never had a zit in their lives. She wore no makeup at all and didn't need any.

"My hair, by contrast," I said, "is not at its best tonight. It kinda looks like a space helmet right now."

She laughed. "You also reek of cigarettes."

Slightly embarrassed, I started to explain: "Um, my friends and I kinda play this stupid game, Smoking Chicken—"

"I saw," she said, saying *say no more.* "Is that a game you and your friends play frequently?"

"No . . . usually we play this other one called Blood of Collie, where we challenge each other to drink shots of Jack Daniels mixed with Folgers instant coffee."

She smiled through her very visible disgust. "I also enjoy tennis," I added.

Laugh number two, a solid one. "I'm Samantha Silver," she

said, first name and last—I loved that—and offered her pretty, unpainted hand.

"Alan Wieder." I took her hand and said faux-pretentiously: *"Enchanté."* Then I bought it back with a piece of information that no female undergraduate could resist—especially one, I predicted, who'd recently adopted the hairstyle of a notorious Francophile: "Hey, I'm allowed. My mom's French."

"Really? You're half French?" she said.

Works every time.

Just then Mike returned from the loo to find me in the middle of my now-impregnable cockblock.

"Wuddup dude," I said.

"Hey," he said, his peeved gaze panning from me to her.

In the impasse, Samantha gave us nothing. She swigged the Red Stripe I'd bought, stood up, and said, "Boys, play nice. I gotta catch some Zs."

"I'll walk you back," Mike and I both said.

"Okay," she said.

The three of us trudged through the thick snow and arrived at her impressive off-campus prewar doorman building on Cathedral Parkway. Then at the door she hugged both of us with equal warmth and summarily headed in, leaving her two escorts standing there in a foot of snow, quite literally with their cocks in their hands.

"Not cool of you, bro," Mike said.

"I know," I said.

Three days later—after I'd managed to track down Samantha's number and was hemming and hawing about whether to call—I ran into her again at the Tamarind Seed, a great mom 'n' pop health-food store that was then on 112th & Broadway. She was at the raw bar, adding steamed greens to a heaping salad;

and when I saw her there I put away the soy ice cream sandwiches that were going to be my lunch and opted for a salad, too.

I grabbed a recycled cardboard plate ever so nonchalantly, waiting for her to notice me and be pleasantly surprised to discover that the charming if stinky drunkard from the other night at the Night Café happened to share her penchant for natural foods. (Which wasn't exactly true: I was just one of those half-assed college vegetarians who subsisted on healthyish junk like carrot chips and cane juice-sweetened cocoa puffs.)

"Hello there," she said, eyeballing the sad concoction I'd tossed together without really thinking, because I was thinking about her.

"Hi," I said. "I'm losing faith in this salad fast."

She slyly dumped my plate in the trash and started me over, talking me through the myriad bins of sprouts, seeds, and strange slaws. Then we took a table in the seating area and, over the first nutritious meal I'd had in four years, talked till dinner.

We had some things in common, other than the Tamarind Seed: We both had roots in the Tri-State Area; older siblings we wished we were closer to; and a love of Richard Pryor, the Staten Island Ferry, Whoppers malt balls, and this one little-known tragicomic Belgian movie called *Toto le Héros*. We were both very chubby as kids and had studied the world's dorkiest instrument, the clarinet. She was Jewish, too, the first Jewish chick I'd ever pursued: Though she had the naturally blonde hair and fair complexion of a shiksa, she was a straight-up Yid, with parents in Jersey and a grandma and two great-aunts in Florida and everything.

But more important, we had so many of the right things *not* in common: Though we'd met at a bar, she didn't really like to drink much or do drugs. She knew a ton about high fashion and loved to spend afternoons walking around Barneys and Henri Bendel, looking at things she hoped one day to afford. And she disliked—fair to say *hated*—punk rock. In fact, when I told her that my popular-on-campus noise-rock trio, Swipe, had recently decided to call it quits, the conversation went like this:

"I saw your band once."

"Yeah?" I perked up. "Whadja think?"

"I liked your cute Snoopy and Woodstock ski hat and your bass guitar, but that's about it."

Well, her music taste was for shit, obviously, but at least the woman could appreciate vintage Peanuts apparel and my stunning FireGlo Rickenbacker.

As I would learn over the next weeks, Sam was not one to pull punches. But I relished—craved—her blunt perspective, because it gave me a much-needed kick in the ass. It drew me, every day, out of my present stasis and got me to entertain new possibilities and pursuits for my Life After Butler Library. My disaffection toward my friends was, I began to realize, symptomatic of a much larger, and largely unconscious, frustration that I'd spent so much of my college years steeped in underground culture and obscure, Marxist-leaning critical studies that I lacked any practicable framework for adapting to a larger society that didn't give a shit about any of that useless crap. It was a textbook case of Benjamin Braddockian ennui coupled with a paralyzing superiority complex: I just considered myself *too cool*—too strange and interesting to go to law school, to work for any kind of institution or corporation, to *be* anything. I loved music but despised all the labels that had the resources to pay me a livable wage. I figured I'd become a novelist, but I wasn't willing to put my name on anything that anyone without a taste for abstruse metafiction would want to read. So presently my grand plan was to accept a full-time managerial position at a rent-a-wreck on 96th Street, where I'd been working part-time since my sophomore year, and apply to Ph.D. programs in Comparative Lit for the following fall—the idea of both of which made me want to step in front of the M4 bus.

On our fourth date, over Dynasty Chinese, I was trying a little too hard to convince her—and myself—that a literature professor's life was one I'd find fulfilling.

"I figure I can probably finish my course work in four years, start teaching, write my dissertation in another two . . . It'll be tight, 'cause my dad said he's cutting me off, but I'll get funding . . . I *think* I'll get funding. I'd get at least eighteen grand a year. I can live on that. And I'll only be, like, twenty-eight, tops, *maaayyyybe* twenty-nine, by the time I hit the job market—which is still young. Pretty young. Right?"

It was a line of reasoning I'd gone over in my head a billion times, never very persuasively. "Plus I'd get a lot of time to write, summers off, and I *love* to teach—I mean, I've never really taught anything, but—"

She stopped me. "Alan. Are you sure you want to spend your thirties living in Bloomington, Indiana, or some other bumfuck college town? 'Cause my brother says if you want a tenure-track job you have to be willing to move anywhere."

"Who, me? No way," I said. "I'll totally get a position at like Harvard, or at least NYU or something. I mean, I think Columbia would hire me in a second."

But I knew Sam was right. I'd seen the stats, and the chances of me securing a professorship in any metropolitan area were very poor, despite my undeniable genius.

She changed tacks. "How about getting a job in publishing? Mandy says you're an amazing editor." She was referring to a very attractive friend we had in common, whose countless papers I'd revised in an ultimately futile effort to one day see her vagina.

"Nah," I said. "Being around other people's published writing all day would just depress me."

"And being around a bunch of sad-sack professors who can't get published won't?"

The woman did have a point there.

In my last weeks of school Sam took me all over New York City, like in some sappy romantic-comedy montage, showing me enchanted points and places I didn't even know existed: The Met roof garden. Siberia Bar in the Fiftieth Street subway station. Balto the Wonder Dog. The Cloisters. She was raised in the city and knew so much about so many things, far beyond her years: contemporary art; French lounge singers; cool little movie houses and breakfast joints below Houston Street; even East African cuisine, because after her freshman year she'd taken a semester off to backpack across Kenya. And she also knew about the things that made people tick, or worry, or silently hurt. She had an almost extrasensory insight into the human state, on which I came to depend to help quell my unquiet psyche.

But in as many ways, Sam was just a little girl, too—silly, deferential, naïve, affectionate, tender as can be. She collected Mrs. Grossman's stickers, loved to have her hair brushed, and made up little love songs of which I'll spare you the cutesey-wootsy details. She had guilty pleasures and charming habits: She had an encyclopedic knowledge of the works of Danielle Steele; and kept by her bedside, in a little journal on the cover of which she'd written her initials, *SRS*, with one of those sparkly gold-paint markers, a running list of things she liked: "the sound of rain stopping when you go under an underpass"; "the smell of Crayola crayons"; "lilacs." It was just all so *enamoring*. And she could *cook*, too—holy shit, this twenty-year-old woman already cooked better than my fuckin' French mother.

Not two months into the relationship, I had to wonder: *Was this it?* Had I met just the woman for me, at just the right time: a strong, witty, sophisticated, and totally captivating Jewish girl who knew how to make a killer *clafoutis* and didn't seem put off by the fact that I had more body hair than George "The Animal" Steele; had an uncommon capacity for shaking up my self-indulgent malaise; and, on top of everything else, looked like a Finnish model?

By graduation Sam and I were spending every night together. During my commencement ceremonies, my parents met her, took me aside, and—mindful of the sketchy chicks I'd usually dated—implored me not to screw this one up. Within a year she and I had both graduated and were living together in her cozy prewar on 110th Street. She was beginning her career as an interior designer, and I had landed my first publishing job at Seven Stories Press. We were a very happy young New York couple, deeply in love, spending our evenings having great dinners and great sex, and our nights fantasizing about all the places we wanted to take our hypothetical children . . .

But that was ages ago. So much had come between us, so much shit between then and now.

It started when her father died. One August morning in the second year of our relationship, Sam's dad suffered a fatal heart attack in the back office of his manufacturing company in Hackensack. He was only fifty-five, and she—and I—barely twenty-three and just getting on our feet. But the suddenness of the man's death, while awful, was not totally unanticipated; he'd chain-smoked and eaten terribly, and Sam had worried about him dropping dead for as long as I'd known her. The far bigger shock, to everyone in the family, was the financial mess they faced afterward. It came to light almost immediately, in a barrage of pitiless phone calls from insurance agents, lawyers, accountants—an onslaught of bad news that robbed the family of any chance to mourn. First, there was the catastrophic revelation that Dad's $2 million life insurance policy had lapsed some months before, due to a filing error. Then came the news that his business, which was in the middle of a multimillion-dollar expansion, was deep in the red and would now be forced to close its doors. Long story short, by the time they liquidated their assets, unloaded the business, paid vendors and bills and back taxes, my girlfriend's once-well-to-do family would be left with almost nothing.

The immediate reality of sudden financial distress just waylaid Sam and her family. But far more tangled and ugly than their financial quagmire were the familial grievances and antipathies it deepened. Sam's was not the happiest family to begin with. Her relationship with her mom, especially, had always been rickety. But now with her father gone, and the money gone, there was no way for the Silvers to prop up even the illusion of stability. Sam's mother faced the unseemly prospect of having to *go back to work at retirement age,* after twenty-odd years of not doing much, and she deeply envied the fact that her daughter could more or less return to her life in upper Manhattan, with a (seemingly) good guy, and have a future. Sam's older brother was forced to assume primary financial responsibility for their mother and, with a new family of his own to support, wasn't thrilled about it. Sam, in turn, was hurt that neither her brother nor her mother were doing enough for *her* (the youngest, after all). Sam thought she should have been shielded from *all of this* because her father—whom she loved more than anyone else had, and in whose eyes she could do no wrong—would have wanted it that way.

Basically, the whole thing was one big holy mess, and some-how—*somehow*—I'd landed smack in the middle of it. And as I was helplessly drawn into the vortex of this psychodramatic family tragedy, which was causing my poor girlfriend so much sorrow and shame and distress, and was just about the most heartbreaking and unfair thing that could have happened to her, all I could think was, *FUCKIN' HELL! NOT AGAIN! WHY ME?!*

Almost overnight, it seemed, I'd managed—*somehow*—to go from dating a nice, stable, and self-contented Jewish girl to a distraught and disillusioned woman with a cascading failure of personal problems. *Shit! I'd been conned!* Before all this went down, I'd made a pretty significant investment in the idea that Sam's family was much like mine: an affluent, averagely dys-functional Jewish clan with whom it would be tolerable to have a routine phone conversation every Sunday, and spend Passover, Thanksgiving, and a few days over New Year's. Our respective families would stay largely out of our lives; occasionally toss a little extra dough our way to help us buy a new appliance or go on vacation; and eventually, if all went well, go halvsies on our wedding brunch. *Now* I was deeply involved—*Christ, hopelessly in love*—with a chick who had a dead father, a broke mother, and a shattered family picture that was shaping up to be a giant pain in my ass. *Fucking shit!!!*

I acknowledged that none of it was Sam's fault—of course

it wasn't her fault—but still! *Sam was supposed to be **different** from the other girls, the stable one, my way out! Did I really need this—did I really need to take on the burden of **being there** for yet another woman, to spend God knows how many evenings talking her through the shame, the worry, the anger, the disappointment, to effectively become—at only twenty-three years old, when I had so much of my own shit left to figure out—**her husband?***

But I didn't leave. *I should have,* I thought now, *I should have packed up my shit and left eight fucking years ago, at the first sign of trouble, at the first indication that this girl was going to end up as tragic and needy as the rest of 'em—no, she would become the most tragic and neediest yet. I should have left when I still had the chance to have a life, to drink and fuck and fuck off as much as possible, to go anywhere I pleased, wake up where I wanted, blow my money, be responsible to no one: a kid.* But I never left, never even so much as packed an overnight bag and stormed out in a huff. Far from it: instead, as the going got tougher, and Sam struggled to keep her head above water, I seized the opportunity to *support* her—a role at which, after all, I had a certain mastery. I became possibly the greatest boyfriend ever. Sam's monthly financial allowance from her father was gone, so I took on extra work as an English tutor so that we could afford to stay in our pricey apartment and Sam could keep her low-paying architecture position without having to work a second gig. Then, when she wanted to stop working altogether and pursue her grad degree—which Dad had promised to pay for—I got a better job and offered to pay her way. When she wasn't in the mood to cook, I fetched dinner; when she was too tired or sad to edit her term papers, I busted out my trusty red pen. I surprised her with gifts—*so many gifts!*—to let her know how much I truly loved her, when it seemed that no one else in her life did.

I spent months—*years!*—helping Sam navigate the shitstorm of complications unleashed by her father's untimely passing: her mother's ensuing depression and string of lost jobs; her brother's estrangement from their mother; Sam's own falling-out with her mother, her grandmother, her mother the second time, and eventually her brother—an endless concatenation of events that I feared would before long put me, too, below ground. And then, at twenty-eight, I married the woman.

Of course, I'm wildly overstating—hey, it's what I do. Sam's unfortunate circumstances did not reduce her to some lifeless piece of human wreckage whom I continuously had to buoy. Despite all the crap in her life, she studied hard, she finished grad school, she started her own interior design firm, she made money, she achieved everything she set out to do, she made me very proud; she still cracked wise and sang silly songs and added new things she liked to the list in her little journal; she threw fantastic dinner parties and bought me the most thoughtful birthday gifts imaginable; she was a good, loyal woman to me and, through it all, my best friend by miles. For the most part Sam and I remained a happy couple—loving, communicative, devoted, openly affectionate to the point of grossing out our friends. And she always backed my career. She coached me through a series of job changes in New York, and then, in 2001, supported my risky decision to leave the corporate world, move us to Los Angeles, and become a freelance TV producer—even if, toward the end, she could not tolerate the long hours that trade required of me.

She was Samantha, always my Sam: I never met any other woman I wanted more than the one I married, despite everything that had happened to her. But nevertheless, on the day her father died, something about us was lost; and in the eight-odd years that followed, we never really recaptured it. What began as a series of breathless encounters—first true love in the city, full of joy and danger—became a series of hardships we'd *survived* together, that had bonded us, before either of us were ready, through an on-slaught of adult pressures: money, family, life's impermanence and frailty. And the woman who had been so inspired and self-assured when we met had become—rightfully, perhaps—so fearful, and dependent, and sad by the time I walked out the door.

Look, I take accountability for staying with Sam, believe me, I do. I stuck by my wife's side because I loved her unconditionally, yes; and also because some part of me must have *needed* to help her—because, ultimately, I probably liked the idea of saving her more than of her saving me; the feeling that without me, the woman would fall into irretrievable despair and maybe even kill herself, that no one else in the world would or even had the capacity to help her survive her situation, to love her through it like I would, like I could. Being her provider and protector made me feel tough and grown-up, like a guy who knew a thing or two about real life and the crappy hands it can deal. But in ways I couldn't see until it was too late, it also had burned me out, made me calloused and cynical and so fucking *tired*; and I didn't want the job anymore.

So yes, I loved my wife deeply and probably still did when I left. And yes, she was beautiful and funny and complex and I should maybe have been thankful that I was able to find such a rare woman to marry, despite all her stuff. But I wasn't thankful, no. Right now I hated her fucking guts for all the years she'd shaved off, for everything she came to need from me when I was far too young a man.

3.1

It was the sixth day of my new life, and as my souped-up silver '86 Porsche 951 bellowed around the southbound bend of Los Feliz Boulevard onto Western Avenue, I felt like the biggest badass in the world. It was four-something on a Friday afternoon, and I'd just stumbled out of bed because I'd slept all day instead of going into work. Under my current development deal at Fremantle, my physical presence in the office was optional—an invaluable perk on that particular day, because the night before I'd closed down the Coach & Horses for the third time that week and driven home seeing triple.

On my offensively loud new stereo I was bumpin' one of my favorite raps of all time: "This Is What I Do," by Diplomats member Hell Rell, nicknamed Ruger Rell for the two-tone semi-automatic he totes and professes a great fondness for popping off. Rell, who was just released from prison at the time of this writing, is by far the most sadistic and graphically violent of the Dipset—which is saying *a lot*—and at that time, perhaps not surprisingly, I took much delight in the rapper's ruthlessness. I was hopelessly addicted to this one track especially, playing it back to back to back to back; and I sang along now to the spell-binding chorus:

> *I stack chips, this is what I do.*
> *Run through divas, give 'em to my crew.*
> *Send work outta town, this is what I do.*
> *Be with my niggaz, this is what I do . . .*

My windows on both sides were wide open, and I was drawing looks at every stoplight—from a Mexican family in a pickup truck, from a reprehending mom in a Prius, from these two black dudes in a white-on-white Denali, who started cracking up at the sight of me. But I was so pumped and happy that I could give a shit what anybody thought. I was a free man; in only a few hours I was taking a twenty-three-year-old hottie on a first date in my exclusive new whip; and as far as I was concerned, the world and everyone in it could fuck off because, well, *This is what I do.*

My phone buzzed, and seeing that it was not Sam—her unreturned calls had started to abate, thankfully—I picked up.

"Steven!" I said, all chipper.

"Yo," Steve said. "Tryin' some new shit out at the Comedy Store tonight. Think this is funny?"

"Shoot."

"So . . . I'm a guy who loves talking dirty. I'm not afraid to admit it. But talking dirty's not for amateurs. One flubbed line and you can definitely kill the mood. Like, this one time I was having sex with a chick and I was really getting into it, all like, *'Oooh baby, you're so hot. Look at you. You're so naked. You like that? Yeah, you do, don't you. Fuck my pussy—'* Uh . . . it's kinda hard to backtrack at that point . . ."

I laughed hard and naturally enough to convince Steve that he was in good territory.

"Yup," he said. "It's gonna slay. How ya feelin', boychik?"

"I need a redeye and have a serious case of the whiskey shits, but other than that I'm fantastic," I said.

"Didn't you get any of my messages? The format run-through for *Seriously* got rescheduled for today," he said. He was referring to a deliciously mean reality pilot we'd recently sold to MTV called *Seriously, Your Band Sucks!*

"Shitbombs . . . Really? What time did they move it to?"

"Um, like six hours ago, bro."

"Ruh-roh!" I said, doing my best Astro Jetson to defuse my obvious fuckup. "Sorry 'bout that."

"No biggie. I handled it. Lois wasn't there"—meaning that I'd dodged a serious bullet, because the president of the network (at the time, Lois Curren) would have been rightfully displeased to see that one of the show's exec producers hadn't had the courtesy to show at a critical production meeting.

"Where'd you tell 'em I was?"

"Blacked out in a gutter somewhere," Steve said.

"Way to cover, partna."

"It's nothin'," he said. *"Jesus,* is that your engine?"

"That's only at twenty-five hundred rpms. This car's a fuckin' loaded gun, dude. I just ate this old Fastback for lunch!"

"Cool," he said, but I could tell that the idea of me—a notoriously blunderous driver—street racing across Los Angeles gave him serious agita. "Yo, Marita's out tonight. Come over. We'll get Tony's Mexican, play some *San Andreas,* maybe hit the Foxfire Room."

"Can't tonight, bro. I have a date."

"You dirtbag . . . Ms. K?" he said.

"Ms. K."

"Wheeeee!" he said gleefully. It was a crass inside joke we'd been making about the joyous sound that Ms. K, an endlessly bouncy postcollegiate party girl, probably made in the sack.

"Wheeeee!!!" I even more gleefully echoed.

"Where you takin' her?"

"Souplantation," I said. And in the heavy silence that followed: "I should clarify: she *asked* me to take her to Souplantation."

"Ah," he said. "The classic 'I'm-low-maintenance' first-date move. Next time you'll drop two-fitty on her at Koi and still feel like you owe her something."

"Naw," I said. "No bitch gonna fuck wit my paper."

"Okay, G," he said. "If you say so."

"Hey"—I'd almost forgotten—"how'd the cake tasting go?"

"Not too bad, actually," he said. His tone suggested that he thought I'd be surprised to hear it, but I was not. "I mean, it started out *really* bad. I had a full-blown panic episode in the bakery bathroom and didn't come out for like twenty minutes. And when I did I was white as a ghost. But then we met the cake artist and started looking at all these color options, choosing tiers and fillings and frostings—dude, what this guy could do with marzipan was just *astounding*—and suddenly . . . I dunno, bro . . . I got kind of *into* it."

"So you liked it. You had fun at your cake tasting with your fiancée. That's good, no?"

"Well I wouldn't say I *liked* it," he said, trying to buy back his extremely gay-sounding enthusiasm for edible embroidery. "I mean, it was, like, when I was faced with all those options, and started seeing the whole cake-cutting ceremony as this big *event,* the *reality producer* in me came out. And I was, like, okay, let's figure out how to *shoot* this thing . . ."

Of all the things I'd heard him say to justify his enjoyment of some aspect of his wedding planning, this was by far the most absurd. But I let him have it.

"Totally," I said.

"Anyway," he said. "What do you care about my stupid wedding? In about, uh . . . eight hours . . . you'll be finding out what kinda panties Ms. K's been wearin' all this time."

"Mmmmmm . . . *pannnnties,*" I said. "*New* panties."

"Panties are great. I expect a full report on Monday—that is, if you bother to show up for work."

"Wheeee!!!" I exclaimed, and waited a few beats for Steve to respond to the call. Nuthin'.

"Whee?" I tried again.

"Yes, Alan. Whee," he said halfheartedly, and hung up.

I pulled into a Coffee Bean on Sunset feeling like I had the scythe of Cronos wedged between my brain hemispheres, but after a large, doppio-spiked black coffee and a couple carnitas tacos from Poquito Mas, I was back like cooked crack. I checked the Rolex: I had a good three hours to kill before I had to pick up Ms. K for our salad-bar date, so I decided to pass the time doing something I'd long fantasized about: *Being a single dude at Amoeba Records.*

Everybody on this coast knows Amoeba. It's the greatest record store I've ever been to, and as you might imagine, I've been to a fuckload. It's a massive rock-flier-lined warehouse space on Sunset that contains basically every record or CD worth having, ever—a sprawl of thickset aisles that a music hound like me needs *at least* six or seven hours at a stretch to pick through. The one time Sam and I had made the mistake of going there together, after about an hour and a half—when I was only through "F" in Used Rock—she started passive-aggressively shadowing me, clearly trying to get me to speed things up. I knew it was totally selfish and unfair of me to expect her to endure one of my marathon music-browsing sessions, but I still wanted to wring her neck.

But on that particular Friday evening, the store's sweeping inventory was not as big a draw as its tendency to attract loads of hot rock 'n' roll tail. Because my primary agenda was not to shop (though I did intend to pick up the Dipset's *Diplomatic Immunity Vol. 2* mixtape and a fairly rare record by the short-lived '90s postpunk band Vitapup that the manager was holding for me) but rather to carry out a critical pre-first-date objective: *Get some other chick's phone number.*

You see, when I was seventeen, Ben Cavanaugh, a college-aged coworker at the Vermont resort where I spent a formative summer working as a tennis instructor, gave me a piece of advice that I took very seriously. I took it seriously because Ben, though a mediocre and indolent tennis pro who relied too heavily on the ball machine, had managed to diddle both of the hot swim camp counselors, the aerobics instructor, and the cute undergrad who ran the snack bar; while I, though a very skilled and conscientious pro, had only made out with one girl all season, another tennis teacher who was just all right lookin' and drunk at the time. "Before you go on any first date," Ben advised me, you must go out and get some other chick's phone number, and keep that other chick's number in your pocket during your entire time with the first chick.

As a fairly practicable confidence booster, it made sense off the bat; and from that point on and throughout college, I followed the ritual religiously, keeping a growing list of other chicks' numbers in a pocket-size spiral notepad that I came to guard with my life and that did, as a matter of fact, allow me to win over not a few women through the palpable apathy it empowered me to affect.

I took a quick lap around the store. My number-hunting prospects were bright: In Used Hip-Hop, there was a sexy I-surmised-Thai gal flipping through Scarface recordings—a rapper about whom I knew enough to teach a college survey. In New Rock, I was briefly smitten with a pale brunette who, though far from hot, was holding up HORSE the Band's *R. Borlax*—an intriguing screamo record from '03 that *nobody* knows about. Finally, I spotted my prey: A tiny-waisted, blue-streaked blonde no older than twenty-two, sporting an AFI T-shirt—the consummate sign that she was, though well-meaning and probably educable, a punk-rock poser of the highest order; and therefore in desperate need of my vast musical wisdom and, in due time, my ding-a-ling.

I peered into her basket and was surprised to see, nestled among a bunch of shitty My Chemical Romance-type titles, one rarified release of considerable esteem: SNFU's mid-'80s-hardcore masterpiece . . . *And No One Else Wanted to Play*.

"Not to be nosy, but I love that record," I said. "'Loser at Life/Loser at Death' is one of the greatest songs ever."

"Yeah, my boyfriend loves them," she said.

Oomph. In my head I heard the lugubrious sound Pac-Man makes when he bites it: *Dew-dew-dew-dew-dew.* But I also thought back to the success I'd once had with Grandpa's legendary "what are you messin' with small change for?" line; and decided to play the odds.

"So does my *girlfriend,*" I said. And when she laughed: "Don't worry, I'm not hitting on ya. You just looked like you could use a little advice. Besides, you're way too young for me."

Now I had her; I could see it in her pretty hazel eyes, swimming suddenly in the vulnerability my diss had elicited.

"Like what kind of advice," she said.

"Like, if you *have* to buy a NOFX record, which I can't at all recommend, it really should be *White Trash, Two Heebs and a Bean.* Everything they did after that is ca-ca. But if you're open to a much better '90s power-pop band, check out Crimpshrine's *Duct Tape Soup.*"

God, I sounded like *such* a pathetic record store dork. But it was working!

"I never heard of Crimpshrine," she said.

"That's what I'm here for," I said.

"What are *you* buying?" she asked, looking into my basket. "Styles P? Is that, like, R & B?"

Oh sweetie, I thought, *the things I could teach you.* I took her on a quick tour of Used Rock, sharing just the tiniest fraction of what I knew, and before long she was spilling her whole life story. She'd just moved out of her parents' house and was living down in Hermosa Beach—where she shared a town home, to her parents' dismay, with a professional call girl. My mind went to the obvious places. She was waiting tables at a beachside bar/café but trying to become a photographer. *Aren't they all,* I thought. Her boyfriend, it turned out, was a tech for a really lame platinum-selling O.C. band I won't name and would be on the road for the next six months. He was supposed to have arranged for her to go on the tour to take photos of the band, but—surprise surprise—at the last minute it didn't work out. And now he hadn't called her in weeks or returned any of her texts . . . the *jerk!*

"Hey," she said, when we were finally on line. "Do you MySpace?"

"No," I said, feeling like a real old fart. "But I do have a very cool cell phone."

"Gimme your number and I'll text you mine," she said. I dug the cybersexual sound of that. She then texted me right there thus:

when can I get my next lesson professor? :) xoxox Jan

And unlike her boyfriend, I *totally* texted her back—also right there, as she stood watching, waiting.

Office hours tomorrow night, 8 p.m.–midnight. Star students only.

She received it and smiled brightly, dropping her melancholic mien: I was so in. Then, not ten seconds after I'd sent her away with a half-dozen of my music recommendations and put my phone—containing her number, in an updated version of Ben Cavanaugh's tradition that would no doubt have made him proud, wherever he is—in my pocket, I walked up to the cashier, a punked-out hottie with lotsa tattoos, and the most amazing thing happened:

"How *is* the Locust?" she asked, as she price-scanned that band's 2005 release, *Plague Soundscapes*. "I been hearing a lot about 'em."

"They're *insane*," I said. "Just saw 'em live. They dress up like extraterrestrial bugs and play these dope plexiglass guitars. And they were so loud and crazy I felt like puking afterward."

"Rad," she said.

"Of course, it mighta also been the four Irish Car Bombs . . ."

She chuckled. "Yum. They're just so *chocolatey* . . ." She started saying some stuff about Ugly Pretty, the group *she* sang in, but misogynistic as it sounds, rock bands with female singers annoy the crap out of me; and I kinda tuned her out. Then, as she popped my purchases out of their plastic security locks with an expert wrist flick that jangled the thick cuff of bracelets and bands on her wrist: "Wow, the Diplomats too, huh? Interesting mix," she said.

"I'm an interesting guy," I joked.

"Oh yeah?" she smiled, and turned around to swipe my Visa on the machine mounted to the wall behind her. With her delightfully bubbly rear facing me I spotted, on the back of her neck, an arresting tattoo of an X-ray image of a handbag containing a gun—and split seconds later, I felt a trickle of drool cross my lower lip: *Whooaa*. Then she swung back around and said: "And you're modest, too."

"It's a rare combination, I realize."

Then, as she handed me my bag, forcing a bold move, I steeled my nerve and laid this shit on her: "Hey, long as I'm doing my cocky routine . . . Sunday night at the Troubadour: I got two tickets to the Hot Snakes. Come along?"

"Wow, you got tickets?!" she said. It was a sold-out-for-weeks show that I'd already promised to take my friend Jeff to; it was downright perfidious of me to offer his spot to some chick I met two minutes ago, but I knew he'd understand.

She, whatever her name was, started to equivocate: "Um, I'd like to go. But I don't even know you . . ."

"Well I don't see how turning me down is gonna help that problem," I said. "Come on, it'll be so loud you won't even have to talk to me."

She said, "Can you pick me up, though? Because my car's kinda fucked right now."

Could I pick her up. *Could I pick her up.*

Fuckin' A! For many guys this may have been an everyday feat, but for me it was an unprecedented score: Not only the requisite other chick's phone number, but some *other*-other chick's number, and even better, dates with both of 'em lined up on the following consecutive evenings! I was on fire!

I tossed my shopping bag in the back of the Porsche—*Could I pick her up?* she'd asked—and drove my now tumescent ego back to my, I mean Chris's, house in the Los Feliz hills. Now I was in a bit of a haste to get back to Beverly Hills Adjacent in time to pick up Ms. K, and I still had to get freshened up and—in another essential first-date precautionary measure—rub one out.

Then, all of a sudden, something kinda weird happened.

In the shower my daily soap-and-stroke routine was taking way too long, and the last thing I wanted was to rub my dick raw on a night that might, if all went well, lead to a few hours of dry-humping. So I hopped out, quickly toweled off, and popped into my laptop a pornographic DVD from an absolutely filthy gonzo series that in a clutch I could always trust to induce an orgasm in a minute thirty or less: Anabolic Video's *World Sex Tour*.

Now, over the course of my life, I have consumed what I can confidently claim is a prodigious amount of pornography. In fact, I would defy any man who is not an all-out porn addict to prove that he has a more thorough and wide-ranging knowledge of porno series, sites, styles, or stars. I fucking *love* porn, I really do, and during my ten-year relationship I'd come to master the clandestine rigmarole that cohabitating males must go through to purchase, stash, and view it without getting busted. And apart from a few select online destinations, nothing in my porno purview could hold a candle to the global peregrinations of Anabolic's Erik Everhard, Jon Dough, and Lexington Steele—three culturally curious dudes who'd made a career, and a respectable fortune, traversing the seven continents to screw gorgeous exotic women every which way, on behalf of all those average guys who, like me, had somehow gotten stuck giving it to one girl one or two ways, one or two times a week.

But for some strange reason, on this occasion, hours before my first date on my first-ever break from my ten-year relationship, Anabolic's unwavering magic was somehow lost, oddly defamiliarized and depressed. Things were *different*—suddenly, distressingly different. For some reason I couldn't fathom, the habitually comforting sight of my three favorite wanderlusty porn studs triple-penetrating some poor Lithuanian woman, who I could only hope was taking home a nice chunk of litai for pretending to enjoy it for my benefit, left me sickened and stressed and semi—no, *totally*—soft, unable, after a series of increasingly flustered attempts to get things going—*unable, my God!*—to make it happen.

And the reason for this was that I could not, as I had unerringly in the past, focus on the *act,* the seeming rapture she found in its overt degradation, and the mindless fancy that *I* was there, too, joining in, experiencing, pulling out, finishing in her mouth, on her ass. For the first time ever I could not live in the simple stupid fantasy of it, the heightened mind-state that allowed these men's reality to be interchangeable with mine, however briefly.

Instead, I was now focused on the one thing that the average male porn viewer must learn to block out to some degree, or live with, or laugh at.

Penis.

Their penises, so big and punishing, supremely male, plunging like mangrove roots into sodden earth.

And my own penis, so small by comparison, not even drooping, barely filling my stubby wet hand, useless, pathetic, sad, disappearing before my eyes.

4.0

OH MY GOD, Stephen's being such a douche," Chloe said, sipping from a glass of $1.99-a-bottle-at-Trader Joe's Charles Shaw Syrah, a not-terrible-for-the-money California red affectionately known in L.A. as "Two-Buck Chuck."

Chloe was Ms. K's twenty-one-year-old roommate, and I was sitting beside her on a red IKEA futon that had seen better days, waiting for Ms. K to emerge, perfumed and primped, from her room. The girls' pad—a wall-to-wall-carpeted 2BR on the second floor of a shabby courtyard building on Weatherly Avenue, on the fringe of Beverly Hills—was a full-on First Apartment Out Of College: a mishmash of clearly-handed-down furniture and appliances; dorm-roomy Ansel Adams and Matisse posters on the wall; mountain bikes plopped in the middle of the living room—a far cry from the Danish Modern-eclectic home that Samantha had so impeccably appointed.

On the big-screen TV in front of us, four prettified high school seniors from MTV's *Laguna Beach*—Jessica, Dieter, Stephen, and Kristin—were conversing inanely around a dinner table. It was a reality genre-changing series that I'd been loosely following out of professional necessity; and as I watched now—as Kristin sent her nascent beau Stephen into a jealous rage by taking a call from another guy, Sam, right in the middle of their double date—*the bitch!*—my working knowledge of the show was standing me in good stead.

"Hey, cut the dude some slack," I said, forcing down a savorless sip of Amstel Light—the only beer these broads had in their fridge. "I'd be pretty pissed, too, if Kristin was playin' me like that."

My neurotically aborted masturbation session was behind me and, for the time being, out of my head—written off as a perfectly normal and natural pang of self-doubt for a newly single man who'd shown his penis to only one woman in ten-plus years. I was back on my game and, as was my wont, so focused on laying eyes and perhaps more on a new girl's bad places that there was little room for thoughts of dick—the Anabolic guys', mine, or any other dude's.

"Yeah, I guess it's sorta sweet of him," Chloe said. She stretched out on the sofa, and I was able to confirm that in addition to a bewitchingly freckled face and ringletted black hair—for which I've always had a thing—she definitely had a slammin' bod beneath her pink Juicy velour sweats. "I wish *my* boyfriend were more jealous sometimes. He doesn't give a rat's ass *who* I talk to."

Jesus, what is it with these girls and their stupid boyfriends? I made a power move:

"What does your boyfriend do?" I asked, fairly confident

that whatever the guy was up to wouldn't be as cool as what I was up to.

She paused uncomfortably. "Um, he's, like, PAing right now on different reality shows. But he hates reality television. He's going to direct features."

Oh, is he now? For all I knew the guy was the next Paul Thomas Anderson—I'd seen a few below-the-line grunts sell a spec script for high-six figures or land a studio directing gig, thus enabling them to leave my world of lowest-common-denominator schlock behind—but it always made me smile to hear the snooty ambitions of some greenhorn who didn't have the good sense to mask his disgust for the genre in which, reality was, he'd probably be stuck for a while.

"Well, if he ever needs *PA* work, I'm always looking for good people . . ."

She accepted the offer politely enough, but the idea of her man fetching coffee for Ms. K's potential man really made her fidget and twist. She changed subjects: "Where are you guys headed tonight?"

"We're going to Souplantation. Then I'm taking her—"

"Big spender over here." She smiled pertly. She needed a good hard spanking, this one.

"Hey now, be nice. It was *her* idea. I suggested Boa—"

"You can take *me* to Boa," she said. "Only kiddin'."

Hmm, now there's an idea. I wonder what she's doing Monday . . .

"She's been a nervous wreck all day," Chloe said.

"Really?" I said, trying not to seem as totally psyched as I was to have this piece of info.

"Yeah. She's never been out with a much older guy. Not that you're *old*-old."

"Well I *am* 'oldmanwieder.'"

"Yeah, Ms. K told me about that. That's a kinda creepy IM name, though, don't you think? Kinda like you're a pervy grandpa, or a pedophile, or somethin'."

Ms. K finally came out, and my oh my was this a fine young lady. She was what a dude would call a spinner: a superpetite dirty-wavy blonde with a teeny waist and flat tummy, but with ample-for-her-frame, spheroid breasts and an equally perfect li'l apple butt. She was wearing snug designer jeans, black casual dress shoes adorned with sewn flowers, and a black tank top beneath, in sea-green, one of those cleavage-enhancing half shirts knotted at the midriff that all the girls were wearing that year. Altogether, it was a supercute ensemble that looked like it was put together at various shopping mall boutiques that Samantha would never in a million, billion years go to.

Her belly-button ring protruded beneath her black tank, and as she reached over Chloe to grab her Sidekick from an end table, I spied in the bowing rear waistline of her jeans a tribal tattoo of some sort of winged insect on her lower back. *Whee*. Here I am, at long last, and not a moment too soon: *Whee!*

Now, despite my lecherous description, Ms. K was no slut or ditzy dirty girl. She was a recent graduate of the University of Michigan, with a double major in psych and media studies. She was holding down a very challenging job in postproduction on a fast-tracked FOX reality series (which shared edit bays with the show I'd just completed), at a company known for not suffering fools; and she had a rep among the senior post producers as a smart and diligent story assistant. But she did have an unremittingly upbeat and welcoming way about her that, in contrast to my wife's rising antipathy toward me, made her seem preternaturally bubbly, playful, and *fun*. That was it: She seemed really *fun* to me, and thus appealed to a whole set of appetites that had—over the two-year period when I was working like a dog and my marriage failed to offer me any respite—become fallow.

At one of our company's series-premiere parties, at which Ms. K and I had first met and chatted for a while, I found out that the girl could hold her liquor, which always scores points with me; that she, like me, hailed from Florida; and that she was a sharp girl with punchy comic timing who aspired to write for a sitcom and made me laugh enough to think she actually could. We connected right away. Afterward, we crossed paths at the office more and more frequently, stopping to banter wittily, dish on colleagues, flirt, and eventually discuss our mutual semi-ironic affection for the Souplantation chain, and how it would be so funny if we went to lunch there sometime but no we really shouldn't, because I was—crap on a cracker—*married* . . .

Truth was, Ms. K's affection for Souplantation was borne less of irony than of practicality, and also of nostalgia. She ate there several times weekly, because it was all-you-can-eat, relatively healthy, and dirt cheap (story assists make a pittance); and she really liked the not-half-bad chicken soup. But the real reason behind her attachment to the restaurant was that it had a location in Tampa where she and her friends back home had often gathered to gorge themselves after a day of smokin' and drinkin' at the beach, all seven or eight of them cheat-eating off three endlessly refillable plates piled high with dressing-drenched salad, overmarinaraed fusilli. This cookie-cutter establishment, drab and devoid of any sense of place though it was, made her feel more *at home* than anywhere else in Los Angeles, a strange solace that I, too—dislocated and suddenly so alone—now found within its anonymous walls.

The connection that my first date with Samantha was *also*

at a salad bar, albeit of a much different sort, had completely escaped me until a few seconds ago, but I don't feel like getting into that now.

As Ms. K and I took a corner booth beside a large fake split-leaf philodendron and unloaded our trays, she said, "Guess what I have in my purse?"

I looked down at my shredded-carrot-smothered salad, sprinkled some pepper into my tortilla soup.

"Take-out from Mandarette?" I said, referring to a Chinese joint I liked in West Hollywood.

"Nooooo, silly," she said, and waited, sweetly, for me to guess again.

"A homeless man who will stare at me with hatred as I devour this mac and cheese."

"You're weird," she laughed.

She cracked her large studded leather handbag and revealed a stash of minibottles of assorted liquors and wines, which she'd either smuggled off an airplane or bought specially for this occasion—either way, clearly an act of great foresight and ingenuity.

"Cocktails!" she beamed.

"Is it too soon to say I love you?" I said.

The booze really was excellent news. It would help dinner go down for sure, and as we now sat awkwardly across from each other in this sad, overlit restaurant (across the aisle from a threesome of nurse-accompanied eighty-somethings probably on furlough from the assisted-living community around the corner on Olympic Boulevard), confronting the no-longer-cute hypothetical idea of a first date at Souplantation, it probably wouldn't hurt the conversation flow, neither.

Fortunately, our booth was pretty well concealed by the lush leaves of the phony plant, so we'd be able to get tanked unnoticed. She splashed a minibottle of Stoli into her soda-fountain Cran-Grape, a beverage choice that had seemed questionable until then. I dumped the water from my iced water into the plant and poured two Jacks over the rocks. *Oh Kentucky whiskey, old friend.*

"Cheers," I said, and we clinked rims and—at her suggestion—bottoms, too. Of all my first sips, it was one of the tastiest and most needed.

"I haven't done this in so long," I said, and though no clarification was necessary: "Gone on a date, I mean."

"You seem pretty okay with it all," she said. "I mean, given that you just left your wife of ten years a week ago."

And how should I seem? I wondered—not knowing, for her sake or mine, how bummed out I should feel, or pretend to feel, about the fact that my relationship—shit, my whole life as I knew it—was over.

"I was only married for two and change," I corrected her.

"Well, same diff," she said. "It's okay, I'm not judging you—"

"I know," I said, not so sure.

"You never cheated on Sam, in all your time together?"

"Nope. Never. Never even smooched another girl." Which was true, and as it occurred to me that the twenty-three-year-old Ms. K was probably more experienced betwixt the sheets than I was, and that it would be tough for me to carry off my whole seductive man-of-mystery act with a girl who already knew so much about me and my, it would seem, nonexistent dating history: "Pizza square?"

I nudged in her direction a pile of heat-lamped pizza slices, the adipose taste of which strongly recalled the cheesy, oily-crusted cafeteria pie at North Beach Elementary, for which I'd traded not a few Mom-packed lunch bags as a pudgy grade schooler.

"Wow," Ms. K said, a bit ruefully. "*Ten* years together. That's like, really special."

Um. Must. Change. Subject.

"I mean, that at least you've experienced that. My longest relationship was six months. And I've *never* been in love."

Ruh-roh! It seemed that now that she'd pursued and hooked me, Ms. K was having a bit of homewrecker's remorse—judging not me but *herself.* Or maybe she was merely gauging how serious I was about leaving the woman I once and perhaps still loved. Either way, it was imperative that I nip her equivocation in the bud.

"Look, I'm not gonna bag on my wife," I said. "I obviously stayed with her for so long because I love—I *loved* her. I mean, I'm very angry at her, and I easily could go on and on about how miserable she made me. We had eight great years together. The last two were very unhappy—for *both* of us. And we're just . . . better off now."

It sounded to me like a clichéd load of shit—partly because it was a prepared response I'd rehearsed in the car on the way to pick Ms. K up. But it was, ultimately, honest, and it evinced enough sensitivity and thoughtfulness on my part to put a welcome kibosh on the whole marriage issue. For now.

Having by this point nervously downed my whiskey, three pizza squares, and, in a regrettable move, a buttermilk corn muffin, I switched to a, er, lighter topic.

"How's the soup?"

"What I like about the chicken soup," she said, as she used her fork to extract large chunks of white meat from the broth and lay them on a small plate she'd set aside for the purpose, "is that the pieces are big. It makes me trust it more than if it were just dried-out little chicken scraps, like it's fresher, ya know?"

"This tortilla soup has the little scraps, which is interesting," I said.

"Hmm, that *is* interesting. *Haaate* the scraps. Truth is, I don't really care for the soup part, or the noodles, really. The noodles aren't terrible, as soup noodles go. But I really only like the chicken pieces." Then, holding out her fork: "Here, try—"

I'm not a big fan of chicken, but I nibbled at the soup-saturated white meat, finding it indeed surprisingly tender and fresh.

"You did too much with your salad," she observed.

"Oh yeah?" I said, just listening, enjoying her.

"You put *everything* in the salad. Look at your plate: olives, carrots, cheddar cheese, three kinds of lettuce, two dressings— Alan, it's anarchy! You gotta limit the salad ingredients, especially here, where you're not payin' by the pound. My technique is, I usually decide what *kind* of salad I'm making before I even start. I pick a theme—Chinese Chicken, Southwestern, Greek, Pizza Parlor—and avoid any ingredients outside that theme."

Compared to my usual agglomerated mess, Ms. K's salad was a picture of simplicity and clear intent: romaine lettuce, diced tomatoes, hard-boiled egg, bacon bits, avocado, blue cheese crumbles—

"Cobb?" I said.

"Bingo. The fake bacon's a drag, but other than that, it's *purrrfect*."

She had an Elaine Benes-esque aura—quirky, droll, outspoken, peevish without being pessimistic—that was undeniably sexy, especially on a girl this fuckin' *cute*. She had an opinion or riff on *every single thing* we talked about, and we suffered no shortage of conversation pieces: the TV we were respectively making; who was fucking whom on her staff and mine; peanuts (me) vs. almonds (her, fiercely); why our home state of Florida produces and/or harbors so many serial killers; Golden Grahams (her) vs. Cinnamon Toast Crunch (me, fiercely); her latest favorite book, Wally Lamb's *I Know This Much Is True,* which she thought I was a snob for never deigning to read; my favorite comedy, *Midnight Run,* which I thought she was crazy for calling dated—but which, come to think of it, she'd watched a lot more recently than I. Not that I had many, or any, recent dates by which to judge this one, but I knew enough of fire and ice to tell that our chemistry was thermogenic, clearly *working*.

And did I mention that this chick could *drink?*

After Souplantation, we hit up El Carmen, a trendy tequila bar in Hollywood. As we knocked back tequila gimlets—a toothsome variation on Philip Marlowe's usual—our conversation got more serious, but not much: high school heartache, college dissipation, the places we wanted to travel, the stuff we wanted to own, the people we wanted to become. She'd spent a few years working as a bar and restaurant manager and knew enough of the tequilas on the extensive menu to keep the gimlets changing, and she could even explain the subtle differences that were totally lost on my palate as I got drunker.

At some point late in the evening I just had to do it—reach across the table and grab her bare forearm, and squeeze it slightly. My touch had not given a woman such goose bumps in many years, too many. I liked her, more than I should have liked any girl then, let alone my first one outta the gate.

She put her hand on mine and said, "This has been fun."

Fun.

On the drive home in the Porsche I played for her (at a volume more muted than I would have liked) the funny Cam'ron song/rant "Fuck You," in which my rap hero lays out a long list of haters, hoods, and hos he doesn't particularly care for and tells them all, one by one, to get royally dicked. I would never have dreamed of playing the track for my wife—not because she was a stick in the mud but because, well, I don't know, I just didn't think she'd get it. But Ms. K, on the other hand—blithe-spirited, tequilaed up, and at the stage of things where she was interested in whatever I was interested in—found a vein.

"Dude seems pretty pissed at a lot of people," she joked.

We double-parked in front of her building on Weatherly, a generic, dumpy box that anywhere else in the world would be low-income housing. To the west was the backside of the Four Seasons Hotel and the stretch of increasingly posher Bev-Hills territory beyond Doheny. We sat there for a long beat in that awkward pre-face-sucking impasse, my engine idling in grumbly neutral, urging me to make a move already.

"So what do you think of the new car?" I asked, fishing for the compliment for which I'd waited all night in vain (and that'd eluded my $4,000 Rolex, too, for that matter).

"Um . . . yeah, it's all right. It's nice. Loud . . ."

"All right?" *Not that we're toolin' around in a Silver Spur or anything, but come on, woman, show me some love.*

"I'm not really into sports cars," she said. "Besides, a guy as charming as you doesn't need a car like this. It kinda makes me sad, in a way, when I see guys in these cars—I dunno, it's like they're trying too hard."

"So my new Porsche makes you sad."

"Not *you*—*your* car doesn't make me sad—but you know what I mean . . ."

I heard the sound of twenty-five Gs being flushed down a porcelain bowl—*whooshhhh! chug chuggle chuggle*—and soon after that Cam'ron's line, loud and crystal clear on the sound system: "Fuck you if you floss."

"What I mean is, you're not like most of the guys I've dated," she said. "I usually go for cute party-boy/player types. Or I should say, they go for me. Like this one CAA agent I went out with, he had a car like this—a BMW M5—thought he was hot shit . . . but he was an asshole! And he couldn't even get it up. I'm over the whole Hollywood thing, and I guess . . ."

"You guess . . . ?"

"I guess I don't see you being one of those guys. You're sweet, Alan. And *nice!* I mean, if you met my mother, she'd grab you and be like, '*Please* marry my daughter!'"

Whoa. Shawty better not be gettin' any bright ideas.

"Nah. One marriage is enough for me, thanks," I said.

"Yeah, right. You'll be married again within a year," she said, and kissed me on the mouth, in a move that my lips, tongue— that every lubberly part of me was totally unprepared for.

What's this chick's angle? I thought.

And then I thought, as I found my bearings and kissed her back, remembering that I used to be pretty good at this: *Oh Alan. Who fuckin' cares?*

We slurped and pawed at each other for ten minutes across my, uh, protruding gearshift. Then Ms. K said: "Come in for a bit?"

"I dunno," I joked. "I should probably be getting home . . ."

When we got upstairs Chloe and Darren Aronofsky were cuddled on the living room sofa, watching *Saw* on the big TV. Some poor bastard on screen was trying to weave his way through a deathly maze of razor wire. Ms. K said "Wudduuup" as she purposefully led me by the hand down the hall to her room.

Till I walked through Ms. K's bedroom door I had forgotten the many wondrous pleasures of Being In A New Chick's Room. It had been so long—*soooo* fucking long!—since I'd entered that intoxicating place where an unfamiliar female slept and rose and (un)dressed and read and watched TV, since I'd sat on her bed, seen her *things*—her bottles of lotion and perfume on the dresser, her array of chunky, scented candles, her cute little white MacBook on the desk, her mess of tossed clothing on the wicker chair by the window.

She disappeared into the bathroom for a few minutes, and I lay down on her bed, high-fiving myself so many times in my mind.

When Ms. K came out, she had changed into a flimsy Madonna concert tee, clearly with no bra beneath, and some stretchy pajama pants that appeared perfectly suited for a few hours of dry-humping.

Till we were rolling around among her soft jersey sheets, kissing, exploring, grinding, stripping off shirts, pants, I'd forgotten that the many wondrous pleasures of Being In A New Chick's Room are far surpassed by those of Having A New Chick's Nipples In Your Mouth.

Steve's prediction proved true: around two in the morn Ms. K's panties were revealed to be a pink-striped thong with a turquoise lace waistband, and they were awesome.

This was awesome.

Whee.

4.1

Back at my place I awoke with a raging boner, an intensely tumescent stiffy more turgid and throbbing than any in recent memory—as if the possibility, no, the certain knowledge that I was on the cusp of givin' it to a new woman had, overnight, radically enhanced the vascular strength and capacity of my pisser.

I took a few moments to test and toy with my ferocious morning wood. Hands-free, I twitched, flexed, and flung my penis beneath the top sheet, watching with admiration and amusement as it proved staunch enough to wave—almost *pole*like—the white fabric back and forth like a flag of surrender. Then enough was enough. With my balls starting to ache from two consecutive days without release, I needed to clear the snorkel big-time.

Under normal circumstances, I would have just wanked it right then, sans visual aid. Given my level of arousal, it would've sufficed to tap the mental image bank, which last night's date (not to mention the pending two) would have more than replenished with new beat-off material. But because the previous evening's porn viewing had been such a debacle, so anomalous and unsettling, I now felt compelled—odd as it sounds—to *reverse the experience*: to replicate the circumstance in which my, er, little difficulty had occurred so that I could try again and *succeed* this time around—so that I could be absolutely certain that there was nothing wrong with me down below; that my equipment was truly ready to leave the safe confines of married life behind and take on the big dirty world. I'd had no penile worries or issues whatsoever during my snoggle session with Ms. K, but still, until I trumped my earlier mishap, I wouldn't be able to root out the incident's still-lingering sting of inadequacy, ugliness, and failure. Knowing me, I would wonder, and worry that it would happen again, and *dwell*.

So once again, I brought over the laptop, another *Anabolic World Sex Tour* DVD—this time, *Volume 20: England,* a worthy compilation of scenes shot on location in Great Britain—and, for good measure, a bottle of Cetaphil moisturizer, a pricey but smooth and nourishing lube. I was going to make an *event* of this, to gauge my focus, pleasure, and staying power through an extended and immersive jerk-off session that would yield an undeniable conclusion, one way or the other.

In the chapter menu I pressed play on a scene in which Bulgarian-born self-described man hater Eva (the only non-British chick on the tape) grudge-fucks three Anabolic studs—Mark, Omar and, yes, the omnipresent and monstrously endowed Lexington Steele—whilst unleashing a torrent of antimale vituperations like "Men are fucking disgusting pigs!" at her three costars as they indifferently beef-bomb her every available crevice, gap, and hole. This was some pretty fuckin' nasty shit. I watched the entire scene with great concentration, start-to-finish—a far longer process than my usual four-minute panty removal/blowie/vaginal/anal/DP/facial zip-through—all the while checking in with myself, making sure I was *okay,* that I was enjoying it as much as I thought I should and, for so long, so mindlessly had.

I watched the tape and looked down at my penis in my hand, and at the Anabolic guys' massive rods, and at mine again, and again, and again. And—to my unspeakable relief—my schlong, through this entire exercise in unfair comparison, remained unbendingly firm, strong, spirited, ready to go. It did not deflate, or dwindle, or disappear. It seemed normal, fine—better than fine, substantial even. Even held up against Lexington's twelve-inch cervix-slammer, so much bigger than even this either totally badass or profoundly tragic cock-devouring Bulgarian émigré could comfortably handle, my penis remained very hard and looked perfectly respectable.

I stood in the mirror proudly, taking stock of my erect dick from this angle and that; and, at long last, Spallanzanied my pent-up load into the toilet.

Oh thank God.

There was a loud rap on the door. Pajama bottoms still drooped around the ankles, I pulled back the blinds of the guest apartment's single small window: *Yikes! Chris!*

I grabbed my espresso maker off the stovetop and opened the door, trying to look like I was occupied with something other than pounding my pud on my boss's property first thing in the a.m.

"Wieder!" Chris chimed. Then noticing the coffee pot dangling curiously from my hand: "You all right?"

"Um, yeah, uh, I—"

He tossed an eyeball quickly around the room behind me like a warrantless policeman looking for just cause to search the place.

"Wieder: What are you doing?" Smiling: "You got a lady friend in there?"

In his professional life Chris was, like any reality television producer worth his salt, a Machiavellian architect of human suffering and perversion, but off the set he was a genteel and conscientious Midwestern-valued dude who expected honesty above all else. So:

"Um. I was kinda beating my meat, boss."

"Ah," he said, not shocked, but not exactly satisfied, either. "Well. I came by to tell ya: Lakers-Pistons at home tonight. ICM has a skybox. Sobel's in. You?"

"Fuck yeah. Can I bring a date?"

"Sure. Does she like basketball?"

"She does now."

I thought about Jan, this punky ingénue I'd met one day ago and knew nary a thing about, and I wondered whether it might not be such a good idea to bring her to an event at which Steve and I would be expected to schmooze with some of our talent agency's bigger wigs. But then I thought, *Oh fuck it.*

"Listen, bro," Chris said. "One other thing I wanted to mention . . ."

My heart clenched. Prefaces like this from Chris were invariably followed by some stern but well-meaning and mentorlike reprimand for something I'd fouled up: a piece of underwritten host copy, a botched camera plot, sloppy music edit, or in this case:

"Your wife came by the office today looking for you," he said. "I wasn't there, but she showed up at my desk and talked to Jon," his assistant—a shy pleaser whom I'd subjected to a half-dozen rants about my miserable marriage, and now this.

I felt a whole tangle of things: sadness, vindication, chagrin, embarrassment, pure indifference, fear of what the woman might pull next, of what I'd drive her to do if I continued to ignore her—but above the noise, an anger without pity: *How dare she try to shame me, make me look like a **bad man**, at my office, at my **work** of all places!*

"I know it's none of my business," Chris said. "And don't feel like because you're staying here you need to take my advice. But you still haven't called her? I mean, she didn't even know the show had wrapped."

Not only had I not yet called my wife, but I still hadn't even checked the last voice mail she'd left me three days earlier. But

I hadn't deleted it, either. It was just *sitting* there, a splinter of information I knew I'd have to contend with eventually, but not now; a voice wracked with grief, barely recognizable, that could no longer say anything I had any wish or will to hear.

"I'll call her today," I said, this time choosing expediency over honesty.

He nodded. "I rented a limo tonight, so we can all get shit-faced. It's swinging by here at seven sharp."

"Copy that," I said.

A few hours later, Jan—my Hermosa girl with the bad taste in music and even worse in boyfriends—pulled up to Casa del Chris in a '92 Explorer whose bashed-in bumper was attached with duct tape.

"Sweet! Is this your house?" she said, as she stepped out.

But what was so awesome about that house was that I didn't have to stunt like I owned the place. I imagined it was a bit like living in a *petit appartement* at Versailles: even the lowliest courtiers residing in one of the Château's added-on wings or outbuildings was accorded, simply by living within its gilt-iron gates, a certain measure of *obeisance*.

"Nah. My former boss's pad. I'm between places and staying here for a bit. Come on up. Let's have a drink before the car gets here."

I did not grab her hand, a gesture which court etiquette would have deemed in poor taste. Instead, as was proper, I put out my bent arm and allowed her to place her fingers lightly on top of it as we walked up to the pool deck, where Chris, in the baseball cap I rarely saw him remove, was bobbing in the Jacuzzi.

"Good afternoon," he said congenially. He checked out Jan and smirked at me in approval, like he would in the field when

Steve or I had wheedled a reality participant into doing or saying something really juicy on camera: *Good work, Wieder.*

"Hi. Thanks for inviting me, Chris. What a view! Wow," Jan
said, turning around to take in my boss's vista, every bit as overblown as the house itself and the shows that had built it.

"Yeah. We *love* it here, don't we, Chris?" I joked cornily. "We
looked *forever* before we found this place . . ."

Jan slapped my shoulder playfully, as if to say, *You're so silly.*
"So like, you produced *Temptation Island, Joe Millionaire,* AND
My Big Fat Obnoxious Fiancé?" she said to Chris. "Those were,
like, the three greatest reality shows *ever.*"

I'd never seen Chris blush like that: "Aw, shucks."

Then Ching Ching gimped up the stairs onto the deck, to
see what was cookin', and Jan hit the mainline to Chris's heart:
"*Awwwww.* Hey, old-timer! What's her name?"—checking the
collar —"Ching Ching! *Sooo* cute!"

I gotta hand it to her: she made some impression. First
off, it turned out Jan did like basketball—a lot. She liked all
sports, really, which I usually didn't care for in a woman; but
on a twenty-one-year-old alt-rock chick it was quite endearing.
She'd grown up outside Philly, and her dad and two broth-
ers were face-paintin' wacko Flyers/Sixers/Eagles/Phillies fans
with whom she'd been forced to spend many afternoons and
evenings in the Spectrum and/or Veterans cheap seats, watching them scream their heads off at their city's historically
mediocre teams. So, in the company of the aging fratboys-and-
jocks-turned-Hollywood-agents among whom she'd suddenly
found herself, watching the L.A. Lakers from a Wolfgang Puck-
catered Staples Center Luxury Suite, she could totally *hang.* My
wife so couldn't hang.

And the girl had cleaned up well, too: gone was the fauxpunky getup she'd been sporting the day before. Now she had on a low-key, shopgirl-chic ensemble of skinny jeans, a striped yellow camisole, and an aqua cardigan—a very specific and detailed description that, I do realize, must make me seem like a big fag. The blue streak, too, was buried deep within her hair, which was pulled straight back in a clear attempt to add a few years, to no avail. She was obviously very young, and cute as hell, and I couldn't believe my good fortune that she was with *me*.

"Just reminding you, it's a school night," Steve remarked, while Jan was at the buffet refilling the plate of spicy chicken wings we were sharing. Then noticing my glower at the low-carb beer he, speaking of fags, was nursing, he said: "I know, I know. I'm tryin' to drop ten el-bees before the wedding. I spent two grand on the tux; I wanna look good! I know I shouldn't care—the whole point of being married is that I'm now free to become a big ol' tub o' goo. But I do care. It's sad, but I do."

"Nah, it ain't sad," I said. "Married dudes get fat to purposely make themselves undesirable—to eliminate options. *That's* sad. You, on the other hand, are thinkin' ahead. And by the way, she's twenty-one."

I meant to correct his insinuation that I was on a date with a woman of high school age, but I ended up only reinforcing the disparity between me and Jan, my life and Steve's.

"Twenty-one!" he said. "Twenty-*one! Fuck me.* I don't think we can be friends anymore, Al. SMCC?" he guessed, meaning Santa Monica Community College.

"California Art College, actually. Studying photography. Waitressing at a pub in Hermosa Beach to put herself through school."

"*Love* that," Steve said. "I bet at work she wears Daisy Dukes with really high tube socks . . ."

"Yum-my," I said. "I'm goin' there Tuesday night for two-dollar pitchers. Wanna join?"

"Yeah, Marita would totally go for that," Steve sighed. Then he said: "Hey, lemme ask you something—"

He suddenly leaned in close to say something in my ear, as if what he was about to share was highly confidential and important.

"You gonna try to give her your ding-dong?" he whispered.

"That would be the basic objective, buddy."

Jan returned, expertly balancing in one hand a plate laden with wings, skewered meat, and BBQed shrimp; and in the other two popped bottles of Sierra Nevada, around which her slender, painted fingers snaked in the most graceful of grasps. I'd never dated a waitress before and couldn't help but consider the applicability of her vast, uh, bottle-handling experience in other areas.

"Does Alan's friend have something he'd like to share with the class?" she said.

It was an audacious move on her part, calling out her date's closest *consorte,* but I dug it. I chomped on a beef satay-stick, relishing Steve's squirmy discomfort. Then I bailed him out: "Steve here was just wondering if you shoot weddings. He's getting married in a few months and is on the hunt for a photographer—"

"Uh-huh," she said. "I'm sure."

"—and he was also wondering whether I was planning to try to hump you at some point."

"You dirty bird," she giggled, and again socked my arm affectionately. She was earnest and sweet, and so breakable. "Congrats on your wedding, Steve. You and your fiancée must be so excited!"

"Oh yeah, we're *both* very excited," he said. "Except for me."

"*Awwww*. Yeah, right. I can tell that you're excited. Maybe if homeboy here needs a date, I'll even get to meet the lucky girl . . ."

I pictured arriving at my best friend's wedding with Jan on my arm—the stir it would cause, the things people would say: *Alan, the best man, Steve's friend since they were little kids, left his wife and is here with this young girl! Can you imagine? My God, his poor wife! Men are all the same . . . !*

Then I imagined slipping away from the party to have sex with her in some dangerously indiscreet place, Sonny Corleone-style.

"Perhaps," I said.

The Staples Center crowd spilled out around ten, heads hanging from a bruising 90–111 home loss. Steve said his good nights and went home—he and the wife-to-be were romantic-day-tripping to Solvang early the following morning. But for the rest of us, a rowdy crew of twelve or so drunken thirty-something dudes and a few complaisant women stuffed into a limo designed for ten, the night was just getting started. Our destination: Barney's Beanery, a historic West Hollywood sports pub, where we immediately laid siege to a row of booths, ordered a slew of heady pitchers light and dark, and settled in for a night of hardcore liver clobbering.

"You having fun?" I asked Jan, as we stood in front of the bar's lame-ass jukebox.

"So much," she said, flipping CD covers. "I'm afraid to choose anything, because you'll make fun of me."

"Oh come on," I said. "I'm not *that* much of a snob."

She dropped her head and stared at me from the tops of her eyeballs: *Who are you kidding?*

"Do you like the Ataris?" she said.

"Um . . . sure."

"You *liar!* You *hate* the Ataris. Not punk rock enough for you, are they, Alan?"

"Well . . . *no,*" I said.

She chose a bunch of tracks, whether I liked them or not, and we took a pair of stools along the bar. Now that we finally had a chance to talk, I went at her with full guns blazin'. At her insistence, I regaled her with tales of life behind the scenes of reality TV, even exposing a few closely guarded producorial tricks of the trade (*for shame!*). I busted out every dependably charming personal detail: that I once played in a band; that I owned a vast collection of cereal-box toys; that, yes, my mom was a Frog. And I also *listened*—to her goals and plans for achieving them, her indecision over whether to take painting or 3D modeling as next semester's elective, or whether even to finish school at all. Ten years with a woman who'd had her fair share of personal woes had made me nothing if not adept at listening, or at least pretending to.

"So you were in a band, too," she said. "Gosh, what is it with me and guys in bands! I can't seem to get away from 'em. What did you play?"

"Sang and played bass, neither very well."

"You *sang?* Oh my God. Sing something, Alan! Oh, you *have* to sing."

Karaoke had begun on an ad-hoc stage beside the air-hockey tables, and a long line of people were swirling drunkenly around the K.J., putting in their requests for "Bohemian Rhapsody," "Sweet Child o' Mine," and other feats of vocal wizardry that normal people had no business attempting to replicate in a public setting.

"Please sing!" she said. "I'll totally kiss you if you sing."

"You first."

We went up to the stage together and flipped through the massive three-ring binder of songs. She quickly picked a Yeah Yeah Yeahs tune, but I started to fret. I had no issue with getting up there and belting out a song or two—I've been told my voice ain't terrible. But, in true form, I couldn't find anything *cool enough* to sing, that epitomized *me*.

"Wuddabout T-Rex? That's your generation, isn't it?" she said.

"Ha ha."

Ah! Then I found one: the Dead Milkmen's "Punk Rock Girl." It was either that or Slayer's "Angel of Death," a hardly bar-friendly metal classic that, no matter how admirably I matched Tom Araya's blistering vocals, would probably have caused a platter of supernachos to be hurled in my direction. And many more drinks later, when my name was finally called—after Jan had pulled off a respectable Karen O, and right after a duo of positively shitfaced fratboys mutilated "To All the Girls I've Loved Before"—my somewhat obscure nerdcore favorite turned out to be a quirky and pleasing diversion that had the whole place at least moderately intrigued:

Punk rock girl, you look so wild.
Punk rock girl, let's have a child.
We'll name her Minnie Pearl.
Just you and me, eat fudge banana swirl.
Just you and me, we'll travel round the world.
Just you and me, punk rock giiirrrrl . . .

I stepped off the stage into a highly amused—and, I believe, justly impressed—collection of new friends and one pretty young girl who, I could tell, was just lovin' my shit. I remembered how much fun it was to sing in a rowdy bar, to lose control, to *play*. I resolved to get my bass amp out of storage the next day—working out dissonant riffs at home had never gone over too well with Wifey, so I'd put it away. *I'll start writing songs again,* I thought, *get on craigslist and find a drummer* . . .

"I gotta wee-wee. Then let's get outta here," Jan said.

As I went to gather my coat and Jan's and make a quick exit, one of Chris's softball buddies suddenly cornered me, red-faced and off his gourd.

"Wieeedder," he said, putting a hand on my shoulder and applying much of his wobbly weight. "You lucky bastard. That chick is *smoookin'*. Good move on eighty-sixing the wife, bro."

"Thanks," I said, not knowing what else to.

"I mean . . . fuck! You just upped and *did* it. I *worship* you, man. Fuck! One day, decided you had it up to here, and buh-bye, bitch!"

"Well, I wouldn't—"

"I've been so miserable at home for, like, ever, bro. My wife *hates* me. Everything I do, *everything* sets the bitch off: I don't even know anymore why the woman married me. I almost wanna come home and just find her on the sofa suckin' some other dude's cock, ya know? 'Cause then it's like, decision made, I gotta *go*, ya know? But instead I work my ass off, pay all the bills, I try to make her happy . . . and . . . and we've got two little ones, ya know? Two sons. And I love 'em to death. Fuck if I'm gonna leave my boys on her account. My dad split when me and my sis were young. I *can't* leave—or maybe, I dunno, maybe they'd be better off not seeing their dad be such a fuckin' puss! You don't have kids, so bam!"—he clapped his hands together, loudly, strangely—"Clean break. But what the fuck am I supposed to *do,* bro?"

Despite how much he and I seemed to have in common—I'd unloaded an eerily similar harangue on more people than I could count—this Bitter Married Guy struck me, in that moment, as the smallest, most pathetic man I'd ever met. He was a fucking *cliché,* drunk or no, a weakling who deserved to be kicked rather than pitied. We had nothing in common, he and I, nothing to talk about, not anymore.

"You'll figure it out, man. Just hang in there," I said, as I put Jan's coat around her and moved toward the door. "Sorry, dude, but I kinda gotta split . . ."

Jan and I got a cab back to Chris's. I suggested we hop in the 951 and take a ride to the beach, but once we reached the *palais*—sure to be vacant for at least another few hours—she asked if we could fire up the Jacuzzi instead.

This struck me as an excellent notion.

It was pitch-black on the pool deck, and a cold drizzle was falling. I ducked inside the house to grab a bottle of wine and turn on the pool lights and jets.

When I came out Jan, already in bra and panties, was standing over the tub, dipping a toe in the steamy roiling water. Her gossamer panties exposed an almost assuredly hairless pussy; and in the chill air her li'l Jelly Belly nipples had come out to say hi.

Oh my.

"Come on, let's get in," she said. "I'm friggin' freezing!"

I stripped down to my boxers and came up behind her. Then I wrapped my arms around her, to warm her up, and started kissing the back of her neck. My erect cock came to rest in the crack of her ass.

"You dirty bird," she said.

Speaking of clichés: next thing I knew I was a Successful TV Producer Who'd Left His Wife and was now gettin' all sloppy with a twenty-one-year-old hot chick in a Hollywood Hills Jacuzzi.

But hey, some clichés are clichés for a reason, right?

4.2

A SHOT OF APPLETON RUM plunged to the bottom of a pint of Red Stripe, shoving a golden spume to the top of the glass; and as my date cheered me on, I downed the thing—a Jamaican variation on the Car Bomb, known as a McLester Bomb, that the bartender had insisted I try—in two seconds flat. I was five drinks in already, and there were still two opening bands to go.

"Bravo!" she shouted, clapping boisterously, having herself just put back her second double Stoli Gold rocks.

Tonight's date completed my weekend trifecta: Ms. K on Friday, Jan on Saturday, and now on Sunday—a night of the week that Sam and I would've spent eating grilled lamb chops and watching HBO in our pj's—this chick I'd picked up at a record store, whose name I couldn't remember till we met up at the bar at the Troubadour rock club in West Hollywood.

None of the women with whom I was making time were exactly sensible drinkers. But this one, Breanne, was a full-on fiend and *craaaazy*. I could tell from the outset that she was gonna get me into some serious trouble, and I fuckin' *loved* it.

The opening bands—or at least what we could hear of them

through the soundproofed walls—were sucky, so we hung out in the bar area and rapped a bit, with diminishing coherence. She was quite tall and even prettier than I remembered, with choppy black hair that looked a little too styled to have been self-cut with a straight razor—the look she was clearly going for—and skin more fair than pallid. Her eyes were deep cobalt one minute, sparkly green the next. She had a tiny little nose stud, a great raised birthmark on her upper lip—*loved* those—and a silky neckline I could not wait for an appropriate moment to touch.

As I mentioned, Breanne lead-sang and played guitar in this band, Ugly Pretty, a punky all-female four-piece that, from her description, sounded in the vein of Slant 6, a mid-'90s Dischord act that she was soooo excited I'd heard of. Music had always been my most expedient way in with girls, ever since my first day of college, when my Chemical People T-shirt sparked a conversation with a lovely hallmate who also dug the band and whose boobies, as a result, I got to dandle later that evening. Now, so many years later, I was pleasantly reminded of how quickly a shared knowledge of esoteric punk rock could build trust and attraction between a guy and a girl.

But Breanne had plenty of other things to talk about as well. She was one of those people who'd opted to see and experience the world rather than attend college and get some dumb corporate job like I had, and she had really *lived*—in Tokyo, South Africa, New York, Austin, Oaxaca, Buenos Aires, a neoshaman community in Arizona, and, I inferred from an oblique reference, a rehab in Minnesota.

I told her how much I liked the tattoo of the handbag-stashed 9mm Browning on her nape, and the strange flowering vine around her right forearm and wrist.

"It's a Queen of the Night," she said. "An old boyfriend who was a rancher took me to see one once at the Texas border. It's like this cactus that looks like a dead bush all year until, one night, but only for twelve hours, from sundown to sunup, it blossoms, lighting up the night with these huge gold and white flowers."

"It's also the name of an excellent Whitney Houston song," I said, which I knew because my wife was big into R & B divas.

She giggled, really tipsy now: "You should *totally* get a tattoo. It would look really sexy on you!"

"Ya think so? Of what, you think? And where?" I had actually once brought up the idea with Sam, but had just as quickly dropped it when she made the valid point that tattoos don't look so hot on dudes with as much body hair, and as little muscle definition, as I had.

"You should get one right here," she said, rubbing the soft and anomalously hairless inside of my forearm. Her touch was voltaic.

"I dunno," I said. "I'm so bloody *noncommittal*. I can't even decide on a bedside lamp."

But she was already running with the idea of seeing me actually *do* something punk rock, to back up all my academic posturing. "Let's do it tonight! My friend Javier runs an all-night tatt studio in Echo Park!" she said.

"Um . . ."

I remembered just then that I'd been in pretty much the same exact situation twelve years earlier, my sophomore year, when some chick I was hot for dared me to allow her to pierce my ear by hand in her dorm room with a piercing stud of questionable sharpness and sterility, and no anesthetic other than the forty of Ballantine Ale I was chugging. I couldn't say no: she *dared* me! And once and again, I went along with it like a dope:

"Okay, fuck it, I'm in!"

"Yay!"

The Hot Snakes barreled through two albums' worth of material in under an hour—a meteor shower of terse, pounding two-minute tracks. Breanne and I hopped around the packed house, and sang along, and loosely embraced; and when we emerged from the club we were sweaty, and coming off our buzzes, and saying "That was so awesome!" a lot in raspy voices.

We drove to the Short Stop, a down 'n' dirty bar in the Echo Park 'hood east of Hollywood, where we met up with a couple of her bandmates and their sketchy-lookin' rocker boyfriends. I bought everybody a round by way of making a good first impression, and it was a winning icebreaker with these broke-ass fools. We drank a fuckload and smoked some powerful weed in the alley behind the bar; and later on, when Breanne's guitar player offered me a bump, it seemed to me as good a moment as any to try coke—the drug I'd always most feared, because of a heart-valve issue I have—for the first time.

"What kind of tattoo should he get tonight?" Breanne put out for group discussion, conveniently at the very apex of our collective intoxication. "I'm takin' him to see Javier later."

"Awww, you're a virgin!" said one guy named Will, a spirited metal-head who himself had just gotten fresh ink—an arresting tableau of a man working furiously by car headlights to bury a woman in a desert ravine—on his inner bicep. "Javier's shit is fuckin' bad*ass!* You should totally go, like, BALLS OUT, and get like a crazy depiction of the Black Mass all up your arm and shit, with like people feasting on human flesh, and a frenzied blood orgy, and newborn babies being crucified alive . . ."

"Yeah, *totally*," Will's catatonically stoned sidekick said. "Go *crazy* . . ."

My blood ran wild; the room spiraled and flashed out of view. I was coked up and drunker than I'd ever been. It seemed that everybody at the table—in the whole bloody bar—was pointing at me, whispering, snickering, but I could give two shits about it.

By the time Breanne and I got to Javier's shingle, a brightly lit and thankfully very tidy tattoo parlor off Sunset, I'd made up my mind: I'd get my initials, **a** and **w,** one on the inside of each forearm, in a lowercase gothic font.

It was, of all things, Sam's idea: it was the tattoo she thought would look cool on me if—*if*—I were to get one, which, she'd made abundantly clear, she *really* preferred I didn't.

I don't know whether I got the tatt more out of love for my wife or out of spite. But when I awoke in Breanne's bed on Monday afternoon—completely naked, save for the cotton bandages taped to my arms, the permanent ink beneath—it sure felt like the latter.

A hammering white light came in through a collapsed shade. I was cold-sweaty and sick to the core. I pulled back the covers and looked at this chick I'd fucked, ran a finger between her breasts, down her long flat torso. She was dead, dead asleep.

On my cell on the nightstand there were *twenty-nine* missed calls and three new voice mails, all from you-know-who.

Oh for Christ's sake, I thought. I shambled out onto Breanne's balcony and played the messages, and the one or two or three others I'd been ignoring. And for the first time in many days I listened to my wife—listened to her scream, and lay blame, and imprecate, and sob so hard she could barely get my name out—*A-l-a-n!*—as she pleaded for forgiveness, understanding, one more go, her voice every bit as feeble and faraway as I'd expected, even worse; it never got any better with Samantha, always worse.

Then I called Steve and said, "Dude, I can't come in today," took a hot shower, and crawled back into this sleeping stranger's bed.

5.0

THERE WERE SO MANY WOMEN I hoped and planned to fuck. Aside from Ms. K, and Jan, and Breanne, there was this chick named Amber, a sweet-tempered, redheaded country girl from Alabama who, through some apparent happy genetic accident, had the physique of a hip-hop video ho. Steve and I had worked with her on a few productions and, in our predictably boorish fashion, referred to her by the nickname "the Pants," because man, this chick, front and back, looked *goooood* in pants.

And there was Jacquelin, a model-y half-Puerto Rican server at a restaurant where I'd often do working dinners, who would shamelessly flirt with me, never seeming to mind, no, seeming to *like* the fact that I was a married man; and who I felt confident would be equally receptive to the single me.

And there was Melanie, or Mel, a doll-faced casting assistant who'd worked for me on a recent ABC pilot, who laughed at *everything* I said; and Julie, a sassy associate producer who laughed enough.

There was—oh shit, was there ever Gabriela, a mid-thirties art director who was the hottest chick I'd ever passed up a clear opportunity to hook up with—*schmuck!*—late one sultry and seductive summer night on location in fuckin' *Tuscany,* for Christ's sake, during the taping of *Joe Millionaire 2,* when it seemed that everyone, crew far more than cast, was getting ass except for love-bound losers like me and Steve.

And Michelle, the sexy-smart editor with whom I'd spent one too many hours cooped up in a little broom closet of an editing bay, zipping through footage, making each other laugh with silly Avid editing tricks like splicing sound bites to make our subjects say stupid things, and talking with stupid openness ourselves about her shitty boyfriend, and my shitty marriage, and our shitty but totally spellbinding line of work.

There were old girlfriends or almost-hads, women I'd known *ten years* earlier; missed opportunities, blown crushes, and botched affections; relationships that had ended prematurely for unsatisfying reasons, that *deserved* another shot: Sydney, Jasmine, Rachel, Danielle—*Danielle,* who I'd recently heard was now living in Los Angeles, whom I still regretted not having boned back in my junior year when I had the chance!

And Zelda, a girl who'd once broken my heart and whom I now wanted desperately to track down, so that I could make her fall in love with me and then break her heart back.

And Sandrine, the stuck-up French broad whom I'd recently met in the waiting room of the L.A. French consulate, who thought I was some uncouth American *conard* until I whipped out the EC *passeport* I was there to renew, and chatted her up *en la langue maternelle,* and told her I was a big-shot *producteur de télévision américaine,* a fact that immediately sparked in her, or so it seemed to me, fantasies of postcoital Gitanes-puffing with me at her soonest opportunity.

And my agent's assistant, Jessica, whom I'd never met but sure *sounded* sexy on the phone.

And my old writer's assistant, Maalika, the Pants' racial opposite, a black chick with a black girl's name but the lithe body of a ballerina and a history of dating white lit-nerds like me . . .

There were so many women whom I intended to, in Steve's eloquent phrase, give my ding-dong—such a multitude of women: a whole seemingly eager coterie whom I'd kept close at hand, and an endless procession I had yet to encounter, charm, *know.* *So many women,* all with endearing new peculiarities and bad habits to reveal, who would ask for little more than a free meal, a rock show, a cocktail or three, me; who wanted to have *fun,* who *were* fun, to go places and do things without argument or debate or any fucking *conversation* at all, who would be aroused rather than antagonized by my hectic career, by the idea of seeing me when they see me, wanting nothing more, expecting even less.

So much lay ahead, so much for me to expose, see, touch, taste, discover, *experience*—so many momentary pleasures I'd been denied for too long, exploits it was now my right to rack up, discard, forget.

But I never got to do any of it, hardly a thing.

Because the man I expected to become—radiant with delight and possibility, unfettered, heedless, promiscuous beyond *measure*—was an infinite fucking illusion.

Because the man I was *about* to become was sick and pathetic and harrowingly small.

Small.

5.1

STEVE AND I, now the executive producers of *Seriously, Your Band Sucks!*—the MTV pilot for which the network had high hopes in the spring of '05—sat with our casting director, J.T., and his very cute assistant, Teresa, in a large cheesy-mod conference room in the network's sunlit Santa Monica offices. On a massive plasma TV on the far wall, J.T. was screening audition reels of various local rock acts hoping to be cast on our show.

Of course, the bands on the casting reels did not know the real title, or the real premise, of the show they were auditioning for. Our casting staff had told them that the series was a "new docudrama about America's most promising unsigned bands"—which had certainly piqued their interest. But, I ask you, why would two manipulative bastards like Steve and me, who'd made a career of pulling off mean-spirited pranks on unwitting reality players, make a boring-ass show like that?

What Steve and I were *really* plotting to do was orchestrate a surprise, Alcoholics Anonymous-inspired "rock 'n' roll intervention" on an incorrigibly crappy band who, despite failure after failure, were still holding on to their delusional dreams of rock stardom. Our chosen band of marks were going to show up at a rock venue somewhere in L.A., believing that they were about to perform a showcase gig for a group of top A & R execs, only to discover instead—to their shock and mortification—a gathering of their fed-up friends and family members, all of them, having been forced to attend one too many of the band's lousy pay-for-play gigs, prepared to confess to the group what they'd wanted to say for years: that the band didn't have a shot in hell of making it and seriously needed to move on with their lives.

It was, of course, a dirty trick to play on a group of vulnerable dreamers, just because their music licked donkey balls, but we were sure it was gonna be *gooood* TV.

"Their music blows, no doubt," I said about the band we were presently considering, an ensemble of post-grungy hacks who called themselves Deathknell. "And there's *nothing* more trite than having any version of the word 'Death' in your name—I mean: Death Cab for Cutie, . . . And You Will Know Us by the Trail of Dead, Death from Above 1979, Death by Stereo . . . Come on, fellas, log on to thesaurus.com! However, my concern is that they don't suck *enough*. They're too good at their instruments. I mean, even though what he's playing is complete doo-doo, that guitarist fuckin' *shreds*. And the singer actually sounds kinda like Lane Staley . . ."

Though our personal lives were poles apart, especially of late, Steve and I almost always saw eye to eye creatively: "Yeah, they're too good, and also *too nice*," he said. "I mean, we're about to *humiliate* these dudes, and it's only gonna be funny if they're cocky assholes who deserve it. With these guys the whole thing could end up being kind of a bummer."

The issue of finding deserving victims who justified the prank producer's nefarious intent was always a tough nut to crack. You wanted to find marks who had it coming, but you also wanted them to be likable and relatable as your stars—"rootability" is the strange word we use for it in the reality biz. It made casting our shows a delicate art, and put us—spiritually bankrupt purveyors of reality TV, of all people!—in the decidedly undeserved position of determining who among our potential cast members most warranted the strange and dubious form of retribution we were meting out.

"I still think the Summer Camp Rejects are our guys," I said, meaning an appallingly derivative O.C. act (in the mold of AFI or the All-American Rejects) who offended a punk-rock snob like me to the core and acted like they were God's gift to power pop to boot. "Those pud-whackers deserve this for sure. Steven?"

"They *do* suck hard . . . ," Steve concurred.

"Let's fuck 'em up!" I said.

Teresa giggled at my comment, as she had at several others. She was a cute, attitudinous Mexican chick in a black American Apparel hoodie, with *con leche* skin, big, pert titties, and a mess of thick, black hair that looked fun to brush—or yank, if she was into that kinda thing. For the halls of MTV—with its almost unparalleled density of young hotties—she was merely above average, but anywhere else in the world she was a *firme jaina* for sure.

After the meeting, as we were walking back to our production offices, I said to my would-be partner in tail chasing:

"Whudja think of Teresa? Think she has the Wieder Vibe?"

"She was lovin' you fo sho," Steve said. "I was getting *nothin'* from her—which is funny, 'cause usually the spicier ones go for me."

After meeting any attractive female, Steve and I invariably concluded that she either had the "Wieder Vibe" or the "Sobel Vibe"—meaning that she was perforce attracted to either one or the other of us, but never both and never—*certainly* never—neither.

"I'm gonna do it to her," I said.

"God bless," he said.

Back at our offices, with our pilot shoot coming fast upon us, we had a ton of shit to get done. There was a format to de-kink, a shooting script to write, field producers to hire, locations to lock, camera plans to design, and many other production details to finalize. But I'd already put in a very full week: On Monday I'd stayed up till three with Ms. K, putting in some serious garbage time by lying in her bed and suffering through the worst movie ever, *Garden State,* unable, like some hormonally hopped-up teen, to focus on anything other than her yoga-panted leg rubbing up against mine—a leg that, fortunately, I later got to de-pant and, uh, test the flexibility of; on Tuesday I'd driven down to Hermosa to hang with Jan at her bar after she was cut and buy multiple rounds of vodka grapefruits for her and all her Newport Beach-y girlfriends, and eventually take her home to the apartment she shared with the call girl I mentioned a few thousand words ago, who was not only *there* when we arrived but, late into the night, actually *followed* us—oh boy!—into Jan's unkempt bedroom, and after we'd all gotten pretty naked it seemed like a done deal that I would ball the two of them concurrently, un-til after some three-way smooching and petting Jan got weirded out and brought out a bag of potent weed, and we all smoked up and fell asleep in a cuddly pile (which was still pretty awesome); on Wednesday I'd planned to go to bed really early but ended up staying up till two drinking Chris's VSOP out of a shmancy Waterford snifter and playing *Vice City,* whose "Waste the Wife" mission I *finally* completed after thirty-odd feverish and deter-mined attempts; on Thursday I'd taken Michelle, my cute editor friend, on an excellent first date at a tapas joint and then to the Otheroom bar on Abbot Kinney, in whose cozy back lounge we wound up snuggling and making out till closing; and just that morning I'd gotten up way too early to retrieve from my realtor, a bubbly Pasadena blonde named Dana, the keys to the new 1BR I'd rented, and also cajole her into telling me where she, as did so many people in Hollywood, hyphenated as a bartender, so that I could drop by sometime and take her out for a patty melt or somethin' after work. After many thin insistences that she did not date clients, she more than willingly consented.

Man, *no wonder* I was wiped! And now, at six in the evening on a Friday and with a few solid hours of work ahead of us, all I really had the desire to do was fuck around on MySpace.

"Hey, check it out," I said to Steve, who was busy creating an act-by-act breakdown of the pilot on our whiteboard. Then all cheery: "I just got a new mes-s-age from So-fi-aaa . . . "

Sofia was an arty girl in New York City whom I'd met on MySpace but never in person. On a lark, I'd sent her a friend request, just because she was cute, twenty-four, and had listed— as had I—Robbe-Grillet's *The Erasers* among her favorite books. This had struck me as some kind of cosmic alignment: *What twenty-four-year-old hot chick digs Alain Robbe-Grillet?* Five days later, after a flurry of increasingly personal and revealing private messages—and a careful scouring of each other's pics to confirm that we were both acceptably attractive—we were locked in a torrid epistolary sex play, describing to each other, in inappropriate detail, the naughty things we planned to do when we finally met in the flesh.

"Sofia writes," I continued aloud. "She writes, in closing: 'I am getting in my bathtub now, *mon amour* . . .'"

I suddenly felt the air sucked out of the room. And then I looked over to my friend, and saw it: something in Steve had totally snapped. Clearly I'd taken one too many liberties with his time, his tolerance for my self-indulgent wannabe-Lothario ramblings.

"Look, dude," he said. "Are we staying late tonight to work or to talk about how much ass you're getting? 'Cuz I kinda got a family now, so if we're just gonna dick around here and waste time, I'd rather go home to my fiancée."

My *fiancée*. The word hit me like a sucker punch—quick, unanticipated, and leveling. It was bizarre to hear it come from Steve's mouth with such conviction, shorn of his usual marital misgivings.

"Whoa whoa," I said. "Are you being serious?"

"Dead serious."

"I'm not trying to rub it in your face—"

"You're not rubbing anything in my face," he said. "There's nothing to rub, Alan. I'm not single. I *was* single, I had a good time of it, and now I'm getting married. I'm trying to be a supportive friend, bro, but you're making it *so* hard! When you said you were planning to leave Sam, I told you I didn't think it was the greatest idea. I told you that your relationship was worth saving, to get into counseling and try to work it out. You didn't. And now—"

"Now *what*?"

Steve, when he turned it on, had an ability to deliver profoundly keen psychological insights—to encapsulate, with the breezy precision of a TV shrink, everything that was wrong with you and why. Not unlike my wife, my best friend had had a tough life—a broken home, serious financial hardship, a brother dead from congenital heart disease, family predicament after family predicament—and he had already put in ten-plus years of therapy to sort it out. Consummate goofball though he was much of the time, deep down the guy was bloody *mature,* so much more so than I.

"Now I can just see it," he went on. "It's like I told you. I love you like a brother, but let's face it, Al, you're a selfish prick. You admit it yourself! You *like* being that way. Your whole new thing, this whole new 'single guy' existence you've constructed, is all about *Alan*. And I just see you, I see you a few years down the road—you know what, not even a few years, less, *much* less—I see you living alone somewhere, sad and full of regret because you can't find again what you already fuckin' *had,* which is a woman who loves you and understands you and puts up with your *shit.*"

I was wounded by the comment, not least by its implication that Sam was the one who'd been putting up with *my* shit and not the other way around. Whose side was he on, anyway? I wanted to fire back. A flood of petty retorts filled my head: *How is it that I've never felt better in my life, and my best friend can't just be happy for me and have my back? Just because you're unhappy with your lame-ass life doesn't give you the right to project your misery onto me!* But obviously Steve had turned some major corner in his self-view and found a happier place for his marriage within it, and there was nothing I could say to restore his anguish even if I wanted to, which I kinda did.

"I'll be totally frank. I'm worried about you," he said. "*Very* worried. Partly for selfish reasons—because we're in business together—but also because, well . . . you're kind of a mess! For weeks I've been saying to myself: 'Well, he *just* left his wife. Let the guy have some fun.' But with every passing day it gets harder to hold my tongue. You're drunk almost every night of the week, showin' up late or not at all, running around with these girls who seem *fine,* but what the fuck are you *doing*? I'm sitting here, watching my best friend's life and going: 'Can this possibly be headed anywhere good?'"

I leaned back in my desk chair and crossed my arms poutily, like a little boy whose dessert was contingent on finishing a wholesome dinner he didn't want.

"All right all right," I said. "I'm sorry. I'll chill out. I promise. Now can we rain on someone *else's* parade? Please?"

A taut silence fell over us, as we turned our attention to the Summer Camp Rejects.

Fucker was right.

5.2

ONE OF THE GREAT BENEFITS of having spent ten-plus years of my life with Samantha, a brilliantly talented interior designer who just might have the greatest taste in the world, was that I obtained, by witnessing and financially backing her innumerable refurnishings of our home over the years, a rather impressive grasp of architecture, art, furniture, and textiles—a more commanding knowledge of the vocabulary and coveted objects of Twentieth Century Design than any straight dude should ever admit to.

And it was a skill that came in handy when, with the signing of my first-ever solo lease, my fantasy bachelor pad finally became a reality.

My new apartment was dope. It was a split-level one-bedroom on the top floor of a late-1920s Spanish building on North Fuller Avenue, a pleasant hilly street below Runyon Canyon. A cozy bedroom space was on the top level, up a narrow wrought-iron staircase and set behind a half wall open to the room below. A pair of arched windows in the living room framed a lilting oak that, through its sparse leaves—just emerging in the first of spring—let in a cool, soothing light. In the window ledges the previous tenant had left simple white terra-cotta planters teeming with robust pink and yellow houseleeks. The floors were wide-slatted—I loved that—and of dark wood, the walls a freshly painted pearl. The kitchen had recently been redone with cherryish cabinetry that kinda bugged me, but the stainless appliances were new, the closets spacious and refinished, and the bathroom all crisp white tile—with, along one wall, a nifty large Lucite-framed mirror that made the room seem twice as big and bright. There were many other pretty details: A tall, built-in shelf in the entranceway that held most of my books worth displaying, a chef's pantry that inspired me to buy lots of exotic spices, and a one-man terrace where I could grab a cigarette and watch cute girls power walk up to Runyon Canyon, their doggies in tow.

To avoid clutter—and go easy on the wallet—I'd decided to keep the place tastefully spare. I didn't have much furniture, and had few possessions of my own other than my ridiculous hi-fi stereo system and some other gadgetry, a heap of records and books, a few shoeboxes' worth of tchotchkes like my vintage toy Aston Martin DB5 from *Goldfinger,* and the kitchen crap Steve had lent me. After many weeks of tossing and turning on Steve's old stinky mattress, I'd finally ponied up and bought a Sonno memory-foam California king, 300 tc Inhabit bedding, and a pair of mirror-topped French Art Deco bedside tables. For the dining nook I'd purchased a small round maple table and seating from a Danish furniture store—not a name, but in the style of a Jens Risom—and a Robert Motherwell etching to hang above it. I desperately wanted a Ligne Roset Togo sofa for the living room, which cost a shitload, but instead decided to pick up a used B&B Italia leather Scarpa sofa at a furniture dealer's closeout in Silver Lake; and spend the difference on a wall-mounted LCD TV. At a Goodwill I'd gotten a really cool '70s-era smokedglass-and-chrome coffee table to accompany the sofa, as well as a large colorful antique kilm that needed a good cleaning but was a real find. In a corner by the window I'd placed the vintage Hovelskov Harp chair I'd swiped from my house when Sam wasn't home, because there was no fuckin' way I was gonna let her keep that.

I needed some potted plants and some art and design books, new kitchenware, a few appliances, and accessories. But I was pretty much set: *When it all came down, when I saw the thing that would send me into a sudden mental tailspin, when my mind fell overnight into the clutches of a neurotic obsession I feared I'd never understand, unravel, reverse—when my picture-perfect new life and everything in it abruptly fell to pieces, I was so fucking set.*

And you're not gonna believe what that thing was, either— that loathsome little *thing* that came out of nowhere to push me over the edge. Or maybe, knowing what you know about who I am—who I seem to *think* I am—you'll find it completely understandable, inferable, totally fucking transparent.

But now, as I write this in the early months of 2007, I can hardly fathom it. No, I just can't *believe* that less than two years ago I was sitting in a perfectly appointed apartment in Hollywood, on the brink of a hopeful bachelorhood, with plenty of cash in the bank and a Porsche 951 and cool new tattoos and a half-dozen girls on the call log and my whole life seemingly ahead of me and my troubled married past behind, and all I could think about was a stupid repulsive little thing not worth a nanosecond of second thought, that I should never have looked at in the first place.

Fred Durst's penis.

Though I know now that the seeds of my self-destruction were firmly in place long before I ever laid eyes on Fred's not-so-limp Bizkit, my precipitous downfall began in earnest on an evening in mid-April—just days after I'd moved into my sweet new pad—when I came across a blogged news blurb on Gawker. com. The offending piece read thus:

The Fred Durst Sex Tape You Never Wanted

Another day, another (yawn) scandal. Conveniently timed just after Paris Hilton's HackGate, some fool has taken it upon himself to "leak" a sex tape starring the one person you'd never want to see in a sex tape, Limp Bizkit frontman Fred Durst . . .

[O]ur inner porn critic would have to say that this video is completely and utterly disheartening—watching over two minutes of Fred Durst's unimpressive penis does little for our already fragile psyches. If you're feeling masochistic, hate life, and have given up on God, you're welcome to watch for yourself.

Having a voracious appetite for showbiz scuttlebutt— acquired during a previous career as a tabloid journalist—I can forgive myself for reading the blurb. But *why oh why* did I proceed to click on the link to the *video*—which, though it downloaded no viruses onto my hard drive, almost instantaneously planted in my skull, as if via some Gibsonian Internet-borne pathogen, a bizarre and afflictive thought pattern that would, within the space of weeks, ravage every corner of my mind.

The truth was, I didn't really care to see a doughy nü metal has-been screwing some, even worse, nü metal *groupie*. Fred Durst's oft-reviled miscegenation of pseudo-heavy funkified thrash and grotesquely soulless hip-hop might just be the worst concoction in the history of music—so offensive that I could hardly stand to look at his face, let alone his *fuck* face. Besides, having already seen in its entirety Paris Hilton's notorious night at the Bellagio with Rick Salomon and walked away deeply disappointed, I'd concluded that watching celebrities inexpertly hump on poorly shot DV—bereft of the directorial flare and silly precopulatory preambles of the gonzo porn I so relished—did little to get me going.

No, my sole impetus for watching that hacked video, which I totally *did,* twice, three times, replaying it helplessly over and again, was that I was seized by an insatiable curiosity about Fred Durst's dick. I just *had* to know its length, girth, overall heft—how it measured up against the Erik Everhards's of the world; and, more importantly, against my own. What, exactly, did Gawker's reporter mean by calling Fred's flesh rocket "unimpressive"—how long did people *expect* the barely five-foot-eight Fred's penis to be? And what exactly was "masochistic" about seeing a dumpy, pasty-white scourge on heavy music putting his allegedly teeny penis in a woman who, though tacitly skanky by virtue of being said penis's willing recipient, was probably hotter than any chick any of us dudes who detest Fred Durst had ever banged? If anything, wouldn't it be emboldening to see a regular schmo from Jacksonville, Florida, who'd figured out how to sell 30 million records and live the dream in a big big way, get the sweet tail he rightfully deserved? Was there not an inspirational message encoded in that haphazardly shot, super-low-rez footage—documentary evidence that if the lowest-of-the-low could do it, so, perhaps, could I?

But no. It was not emboldening, uplifting, or edifying in any sense. It made me sad, and agitated, and faintly ill; and it made me turn, instantaneously, the copious hatred I had for Limp Bizkit's frontman on myself.

Because, well, though I couldn't tell for certain, it appeared that Fred Durst—*Fred fucking Durst!*—had a bigger dick than I did.

And if Fred's penis was "unimpressive" and "disheartening"—an emasculate nub worth gawking at in ridicule and revulsion—then what did that make MINE?!

FUCK.

I couldn't stop: I watched the video a half-dozen times or more, masochistically soaking up every obscene detail: Fred's drooling, bearded visage in narcissistic down-the-barrel self-held close-up; his apathetic, this-happens-to-me-every-day thrusting against this poor, poor woman he had bent over a sofa; his fuzzy beer gut drooping slightly over her splayed ass; his alabaster, totally run-of-the-mill cock.

And when I could take it no longer, I found myself searching for *more*. I opened a new window and began obsessively scouring the Web for articles, blogs, bulletin posts for *anything* I could find written about that gruesome tape, in an effort to survey the broad public opinion on Fred Durst's schwanger. I just *had* to know: Did *everyone* who'd seen it think it was subpar, laughably small? Or were those people who hold Durst in disfavor merely using the fact that his penis wasn't massive—indeed, a Vienna sausage compared to Tommy Lee's notorious blood bomber—to give vent to their pent-up scorn and ill will?

Truthfully, there wasn't much to be found on the topic at all, suggesting that Fred Durst's penis, irrespective of its size, had made little cultural impact. But those who had seen it and taken the time to post a comment on it were just *ruthless*. I guess the guy deserved his fair share of vituperation, but fuckin' A: On sites like Stereogum, LiveDaily, CityRag, and ZUG, people were leveling against Fred a barrage of merciless penile put-downs that might as well have been directed at me: "He's hung like an infant." "He was grasping it daintily, like one might hold a tiny teacup." "An average woman's knuckle-span is 3 inches . . . Look at the part where she's blowing him. There's perhaps 1 inch more than her grip, making his cock a 4"er . . . well below an average of 6"." "Our generous calculations say he's packing 4.5 inches (hard)." "I don't even know how he can see his little dick over his big beer belly . . ."

The fact that Fred Durst's supposedly weeny wang appeared—*appeared*—to be bigger than mine should not have mattered one iota to me, nor should have the many disparaging remarks about it, which were obviously aimed more at big Fred than little. Besides, the shots aimed at Fred's penis were really not to be trusted at face value. For one, the repeated preposterous claims that Fred's penis was a very under-average four-or-so inches all but belied the general assertion that he was small. My penis, from what I remembered from the one or two times I'd measured it many years before, back in college, was in the six-plus range; so how could Fred's be less than *five?* Some commenters were apt to point out that Fred was getting the short end of the stick: "I don't know who you've been dating or what dicks you've seen," one levelheaded woman, marykate33, wrote. "Apparently 15-inchers, because Fred's penis is NOT small at all. He's lengthier than the average, which is more like 5" . . . He's at least 7"." Voices of reason like these reassured me that the rising chorus of Durst-haters raggin' on his package was all sound and penis envy.

But then again, even if I could concede that Durst's dick was average or better, what did all this mean with respect to *my own* size—because little Fred, remember, looked longer and beefier than little Alan. If Fred was indeed average, then *I* was—probably, dismayingly—*below* average; and if he was only *slightly* bigger than average, then I was merely average—*average! Alan Wieder, average!*—puncturing my lifelong belief that I was comfortably *above* the mean. And what if that axiom that I'd explained to a million reality TV cast members, that "the camera adds ten pounds," somehow worked *in reverse* for dicks—what if the camera made penises look *smaller* than they are in reality? This would mean that my penis would look *more miniscule* on video than it did in the flesh—and that, accordingly, Fred Durst's *actual* dick would be *bigger* than the one caught on tape, and hence *even bigger* than this puny thing between my legs to which I'd unfairly compared it, this nub of a cock just *lying there*, so soft and spiritless, disappearing now, shrinking into oblivion—*oh, no, not again!*—

After working myself into a total neurotic ferment, I decided there was only one way to put the matter to rest. I had to size up my manhood the old-fashioned way: To work up a respectable, porn-enhanced stiffy, lay it alongside a ruler, and *know* once and for all exactly where I stood—which, I was quite confident, was somewhere *above* the proverbial six inches. I had to shake off what I'd seen on that haunting video—to accept that there was no real way to know for sure how big Fred's dick was from that crude vantage, at that brief interval, via a medium that, I knew as well as anyone, was fraught with inaccuracy and distortion—and give myself over to cold, hard, empirical *fact*.

And so I did. I logged on to Richard's Realm, an online gallery of free XXX clips that I frequented, and prepared to put my dick to the stick, as they say. Among the sadder aspects of this self-evaluation was that the only thing I had in my new apartment to do the job was a Teenage Mutant Ninja Turtles ruler, a good-luck charm I'd had since elementary school that depicted Leonardo wielding two very (I couldn't help but notice) long

Ninjaken swords. The ruler ran six inches even, and I never, ever thought I'd measure my penis with it, but oh did I ever.

It wasn't easy to get an accurate first appraisal, not because the ruler was more suited to drawing isosceles triangles in a sixth-grade math workbook, but because my jittery cock was having a tough time staying hard under this kind of technical analysis. I had no trouble producing a decent hard-on, but then, as soon as I brought the little plastic TMNT-emblazoned ruler up to the side of my shaft, my dick went limper than a hospital French fry—terrified as it was, understandably, of the prospect of coming up shorter than a tool designed to fit snugly in a Trapper Keeper pencil case.

Finally, after a few aborted efforts, I calmed down. *Fuck it,* I thought. *It's just a dick. A dick I've had my whole life, a dick I always knew was not particularly large. And there's nothing I can do to change that now. It's fine:* **Fine.** *And none of the twenty-or-so chicks who've seen it, touched it, even sucked it, way up close— as close as anyone would ever want to come to a penis—has ever said or done anything to suggest that I have any cause for concern. Plus, I've* **measured it already:** *I already* **know** *that it's okay, more than okay. And it can only be bigger now than it was then: I kept growing taller till I was twenty-two, so surely my penis must have grown, too. Besides, for a guy who has as much going for him as I do, does it even fucking matter???*

I had a burst of confidence and—thanks to an appallingly rousing close-up of three Louisville Slugger-size cum cannons firing into the face of a North African neophyte—a solid surge down below. I quickly grabbed the ruler and placed it alongside my bobbing boner, pushing slightly into the fleshy pad at the base, careful not to let a single millimeter of shaft go unaccounted for. I grasped my dick firmly in one hand, the ruler in the other, and looked down, and noted the measurement, and looked up, and down again, and up, and down again, lest my eyes were deceiving me because holy shit: *I was even bigger than I thought I was.*

Bigger: Not smaller, but BIGGER.

My dick easily extended past the ruler's edge, by what looked like an inch or more! And if I shoved the ruler deeper into the fat, whoa! I *was* fine! *Better* than fine! Fuck yeah!!!

I was of course profoundly comforted by this discovery, at least momentarily. My penis was *not* below average, or even average at all. I had, as they say, "nothing to be ashamed of." The ladies wouldn't exactly be awestruck by my johnson, but they weren't gonna point and laugh at it, neither. They'd take my penis and take it gladly—indeed, they'd be *thrilled* to have my penis, not simply because it was better than nothing or even because the guy to whom it was attached was as consummately awesome as I—but because it was, in and of itself, statistically *larger than the majority* of those they'd felt, sucked, seen.

On a wave of happy relief, I stroked my now-erotically-charged wiener—its point served, its job well done—to completion. It took all of twelve seconds to finish, and afterward I lay on my back in my big, fluffy bed, my pubic mound slathered in cum, and counted my blessings because if things had gone the other way I'd have been so *fucked.*

Then I took a long, hot shower with some very aromatic aloe-infused Lever 2000, toweled off, and did something else I wouldn't have done if I weren't careening off some ego-dystonic deep end.

I stepped, fully nude, in front of the big mirror that hung on my bathroom wall, and for a good fifteen minutes, stood staring at my cock. I was absolutely transfixed, unable to tear my gaze away: up and down I looked, up and down, and down, and down, and down, and down, and down.

I scrutinized my cock from the front, the side, this angle, that, in various states of induced engorgement, pulling, stretching, pumping, probing, *looking*.

And the more I examined my penis before the mirror—that stupid fucking *mirror*—the less certain I felt about it. Whatever assurance I'd gained with my first measurement gave way to a fog of undermining doubts: *Was the average length of a dick **really** six inches? And by what methodology, exactly, was that figure obtained? And by whom?* It seemed there was no possible way of ascertaining whether the known average was anything more than a mythical figure devised to allay the insecurities of the inadequately endowed. Somehow, the part of my brain that just a few moments before had been sufficiently convinced that my schlong was satisfactory was now besieged by sinking suspicion, unable to *trust* any proverbial statistic, or even my own eyes.

I measured it again anyway: I tugged out another erection—weaker this time, but firm enough—and planted my ruler alongside it. And my initial discoveries held up: Checked and double-checked, even in its not-maximally-erect state, my dick surpassed the alleged average.

And I felt better, much better. For an hour, maybe more—until, on my way to work, my mind went to jelly again; and I could feel a strange thought taking hold, a thought that would soon deepen in persistence and intensity and malice, despite all statistical evidence that it was baseless, no matter how hard I tried to disprove it through measurements upon measurements, block it out, banish it from my mind, beat it back with logic that grew more useless, more impotent by the day.

That thought was: *My penis is small, too small, possibly the smallest in the world.*

And so began, with a fateful glimpse of Fred Durst's cock on a grainy video clip, a months-long and deeply pathological obsession with my penis—its length and girth, flaccid and erect, at rest and stretched to the point of agony.

In the first days it was kind of funny in a way: *This is so gay,* I laughed to myself, *so silly and faggy of me to be thinking about my dick—any dick—this much.* The part of me that could find the humor in almost anything viewed my penile preoccupation as a kind of ironic payback for my current vaginamania, comic retribution for having ditched my wife to become an out-and-out pussy hound.

But then, something happened that I didn't see coming: my mind went sideways, my vision warped and wavered, and a blackness fell over me unlike anything I'd ever known or overcome.

And in the grip of it, my penis—my ugly, loathsome, sickeningly small *penis*—seemed like the unfunniest thing in the world.

6.0

THE PROBLEM WAS, I couldn't get a fucking straight answer from anyone.

I had plummeted overnight into a web of deceit and disinformation, half-baked theories and two-faced truths; uncorroborated studies and skewed opinions stated as apodictic facts: an unending sprawl of data designed precisely to ensnare woefully insecure men who, at the edge of reason, were desperate to find that one incontestable piece of information that would restore their common sense, and sense of self.

Men like me, apparently.

I entered the vast wilderness of online penis info in hopes of determining one seemingly very simple thing: *How long, truly, is the average penis?*

That was it. That was all I wanted: to ascertain beyond a

doubt what the mean was and that I was *above* it, so that I could get on with my life fully assured that I had nothing to worry about; that in addition to having cooler taste in music and books and clothes and all the other bullshit by which I measured my self-worth, I had a bigger cock, too.

The truth is, it was not at all difficult to find trustworthy data confirming what I already essentially knew: that the average dick is, yes, roughly six inches long. In fact, according to the dozen or more credible articles, charts, and scientific studies I came across within two minutes of searching—on sites like AskMen.com, Slate, even WebMD—the average penis was actually just *under* six—5.87 inches, to be exact. Five point eight seven: even *shorter*—men, take courage!—than the universally acknowledged mean.

So from the outset I had everything I needed to know to put an end to the whole stupid issue. I was, indeed, statistically *above average,* even if not by much, proudly apart from the pitiable hordes of middling dicks.

Yet, for some reason, some part of me just could not accept these reassuring data as definitive. Instead, driven by a force I didn't understand, I kept clicking, and *clicking,* for hours, days, trying to drudge up any claim or morsel of evidence, however dubious, that *called the accepted average into question*—that forwarded the idea that the real average was in fact bigger, or smaller: Bigger, or smaller, smaller or bigger.

I don't know, honestly, what I hoped to prove: that the true average was more miniscule than people believed, which would make my own stats more impressive; or, more masochistically, that the mean was in fact *larger,* taking my wang down a peg and me along with it. One would presume the former, naturally— why in the world would I seek to substantiate my inferiority?—

but in fact it was both, or maybe neither. I looked for both possibilities with equal insatiability and rejected both with equal vehemence. I know now that what I sought—craved—was not any one definitive answer, but rather infinite slippage and inconstancy, a morass of irresolution into which I could descend, lose myself, and then emerge with proof that, if anything, there was no single indisputable number to which I or any part of me could be compared.

My confused and despairing online investigation really began to spiral when I came across a site entitled **"The Truth About Penis Size."** Adorned with a depiction of a harrowingly massive dong, this aggressive-toned and authoritative-seeming page issued the following troubling claims: 1) that contrary to popular opinion, the average penis was actually 6.67 inches erect—six point *six seven* inches, a number that struck me immediately as an exaggeration but was so *specific*, to the hundredth of a point, that surely it must have been derived from *some* kind of empirical study; 2) that the average girth was a fairly thick 5.22 inches, another size mine almost certainly did not surpass—girth, fuck, I had not even really considered *girth!* 3) that according to a recent survey, 74 percent of women have experienced a penis 8.5–10 inches long; 4) that 67 percent of women find a large penis more vaginally stimulating—and over *90 percent* find a big cock more *visually* stimulating—than an average or a smaller penis; 5) that more than 40 percent of women have dumped a boyfriend because his penis was too small; 6) that, therefore, anyone who tells you that women don't care about penis size is a LIAR, said like that, all caps; 7) *that, after reading all this, if you suspect you have a small penis, YOU PROBABLY DO;* 8) *that if you believe, whether it's true or not, that you have a small penis, no amount* *of reassurance from your partner can possibly convince you other-wise; 9) that*—you get the idea.

6.67, 5.22, 8.5–10, 74 percent, 67 percent: those confidence-destroying stats and figures are forever lodged in my brain, like bomb fragments. Now, I am more than obliged to mention that at the bottom of the page was a series of links and clickable ads for various penis-enlargement products—pills, pumps, propri-etary techniques, and the like. The report was obviously the fabrication of some opportunistic scare-tactician, a trumped-up study befitting the quack technologies it was blatantly hustling people into buying. But in my muddled mental state it didn't really matter. *Every* bit of information I came across was true un-til I could prove otherwise through some fresh finding, which I would in turn feel an uncontrollable urge to *refute* through some *new* piece of data, and so on, in a ceaseless cycle of verification and rebuttal, hopes buoyed one minute and dashed the next, compulsion and fleeting relief.

The numbers on that page were complete and utter nonsense, but their implication that I had a substandard *schmeckle* never-theless vexed me greatly. After a lifetime of never giving my ding-dong a second thought beyond whose and which orifices I hoped it would penetrate, I was now riveted by its raw physical-ity: this *thing* I held in my hand, its heft and hang, its volume as a function of length and circumference; where its length techni-cally began in that fuzzy intersection between shaft and "fat pad," as it's known in the community of penis obsessives (yes, there was such a thing, I'd soon learn), and at what point along the tip, precisely, it ended. When size suddenly matters on such a scale, every millimeter carries a measurable effect: a move, however microscopic, along a spectrum on which all of us men have been placed, whether we choose to acknowledge it or not.

Another flurry of doubts came on, punitive and vaguely paranoid introspections: *Could I have had a noticeably small penis my whole life and not known it? No chick has ever mocked or belittled my penis, true; but nor, it occurs to me now, has anyone ever **complimented** it, either. What are the twenty-or-so women who've seen it holding back, secretly thinking and whispering about me? What if the only reason it didn't seem small to me before was that I was a married man and had no reason to give a shit? And what about our present cultural time: does size matter more now than it did before the gargantuan beaver-batons of today's pornography demystified the big dick and made it an object of everyday expectation and overt desire?*

The idiotic notion rattled and repeated in my skull, over and over: *My penis is too small, too small, too small.* And variations on the theme: *My penis is too small flaccid. My penis is too small for my tall body. My penis is too small for sex.* And the most unacceptable of all: *My penis is too small for **Alan Wieder**, a guy who in every other sense—in mind, talent, looks, style, taste, attitude—is so fucking BIG.*

And then I went headlong in the other direction. I began searching, with equal resolve, for any and all articles that confirmed a *smaller* average. There were plenty. Within a couple hours I'd visited fifty or more informational sites that placed the average at 5.5 inches, 5.3, even as low as 5 flat—all of which quickly boosted my confidence, like a string of table-turning craps rolls. There was a site called "Penis Myths and Facts," at www.penis-website.com, an even-tempered report that thoughtfully deconstructed the myth that bigger is better; and put the average at 5.9 inches. There was a well-documented refutation of the famous Kinsey penis-length study from the '40s, which placed the average in the 6.3-inch zone; the study's results, this article pointed out, were inflated because Kinsey had *allowed the male subjects to survey themselves*, i.e., throw in a couple extra fractions of an inch for good measure. And there was the oft-cited LifeStyles Condoms study performed on a bunch of drunken spring breakers in Cancún in 2001 (also 5.9 inches); a 1996 study in the *Journal of Urology* (an encouragingly low 5.08!); another in the *International Journal of Impotence Research* (5.35); and endless further reports confirming that the so-called Truth About Penis Size (6.67 inches!) was a bunch of bullshit— that down below I was, indeed, *okay*.

But then, immediately afterward, I turned another 180 degrees: unable to accept the favorable data and move on, I scoured for larger figures that would supersede the smaller and cut me back down to size. They were harder to dig up, but I was absolutely tenacious, searching for three hours, more, another afternoon disappearing, night falling into a heap of numbers—6.4, 6.5, 6.6, 6.7, 6.8, 7.0—that left me right back where I'd started: *small*.

But that was only the half of it. Because there was a whole other source of ambiguity that wrecked any possibility of ever arriving at a verifiable figure: *There is no observable consensus, among doctors or anyone else, on the correct way to measure a cock.* I pored over another infinitude of sites—some new, some already well-entrenched in my browser history—in search of some standardized methodology. To no avail: some "experts" instruct one to place the ruler along the penis's side; while others insist that the official technique is actually to measure along the top, or "dorsal," side; while others favor measuring from underneath, beginning at the junction of scrotum and shaft. Some advise that one use a firm ruler, not unlike my Ninja Turtles six-incher, and some a tape measure; some say use a string or marked pencil or paper-towel tube or some other cock-compatible tool. Some urge shoving the measuring device deep into the pubic "fat pad" at the penis's base, a method that can add a half inch or more in length; some decry that very same technique as dishonorable and cheap, strictly forbidding any "pushing in." And some favor a mushy middle ground, directing the measurer to push slightly into the fat pad, leaving it to the dude to determine just *how* slightly—a method I found frustratingly vague.

And so, too, for girth. Wrap a tape measure around the base. No, measure just below the head. No, measure right at the middle. Measure at the visibly widest point, the narrowest. No, take the average of the two. No—

It was all so repulsive and pathetically sad—not so much the sites themselves or the petty differences among their schools of thought, but rather the fact that I was taking such pains to ascertain which of these degrading protocols I most trusted. Equally disturbing was the idea that in the absence of one ex cathedra measuring procedure, none of the hundreds of size surveys I'd so carefully studied carried any real weight. There was simply no way of telling which methods were used in which studies, and even if there were, there was no way of knowing—truly *knowing*—which technique would have generated the most legitimate results.

It was enough to drive a size-crazy guy even crazier. How could there be no one definitive penis study, a set of precise results beyond all contention? How could there be so many decimals of disagreement over this—with even medical science unable to forward a sanctioned methodology or single errorless statistic? This was not Roland Barthes's Eiffel Tower, a symbol full of semiotic indeterminacy, exploding with poetic insights and possible interpretations. This was not some epistemological black hole or unanswerable mystery of consciousness. This was a biological *thing,* an organ—not even a muscle, I recalled with chagrin, capable of change, *growth.* This was every dude's fixed constant, what we were stuck with till we called it quits. This was a cock.

The average human heart weighs eleven ounces and beats 100,000 times a day. The average human brain weighs three pounds. Nobody debates these facts.

How long, for fuck's sake, is the average penis?

The answer was right there the entire time, of course, but I couldn't see it. The answer was, *Who fucking cares?* But I did. I did.

My penis is too small, too small, too small.

I would spend many more hours searching the Web for an official measuring technique, till my eyes were bleary and blood-shot, till my wrists and fingers tingled from a developing case of carpal tunnel. I searched till I felt queasy and rotten inside, till my data-drunk brain heaved and convulsed in my skull. Then, with utter self-disgust, I searched some more. And when I had literally looked at *every single site* on the subject—no bullshit—I had an idea that, though completely fucking cockamamie, as it were, made perfect sense to me at the time.

The big breakthrough, which I believed would put the whole matter to bed, was this: *I need to measure my dick again. I need to measure it in a manner that gives my penis the **least** possible benefit of the doubt. That way, I will know my smallest possible measurement—my worst-case-scenario number. Then I must figure out the average of **all** the averages I've come across, and compare my **new** measurement to that totalized number. If my shortest measurement is bigger than the average-of-averages, or "grand average" as it's called in statistics, then I'll know for* *certain—beyond a scintilla of a doubt—that there is absolutely nothing wrong with my cock!*

And then I'll be okay. I'll be good to go. Really.

The most unforgiving way to measure an erect dick is to lay a firm ruler along its top side, allowing the ruler's bottom to rest against the abdomen at the base of the shaft *without*—and this is critical—*pressing into the fat pad*. There were, it seemed to me, a few big reasons why this method is flawed and unfair: namely that for many guys, there's a sizable chunk of usable dick that lies buried in that mushy pubic pad; that this *mons pubis,* as it's called, is mushier for some guys than others, meaning that the amount of chub nestled in chub varies widely from dude to dude; that measuring a penis along its side seems far more reasonable, given that women are more likely to glimpse a guy's schlong at a lateral angle than from the dead-on, top-down view maintained predominantly during hand-to-gland combat. Nevertheless, this dorsal method, for whatever half-cocked reason, is favored by most doctors and dick-size purists, and in my deranged mind I urgently, imperatively *needed* to know how the technique would affect—how much, precisely, it would *lower*—my already tenuous stats.

I was already becoming expert at this. Out came the porno, and the Ninja Turtles ruler, and after a good deal of fiddling, an erection that, though plenty firm, was completely sapped of any sexual sensation or urge. A bizarre feeling: it might as well have been a boner in a jar or on a cadaver, there merely to be evaluated in anthropometric terms, delimited, quantified. I could not help but observe, as I took great pains *not* to push into it, that my pubic fat pad was surprisingly deep and doughy for an otherwise lean and gangly guy, meaning that I was gonna lose at least three-quarters of an inch—*at least!*—to the anomalous settling of groin blubber with which I'd been so unjustly plagued.

Still, even at this severe disadvantage, my *schvontz,* as my grandpa Bernie used to call it, came in at a little *over* six inches: a few smidgens, perhaps a quarter-inch, past the end of the little ruler that was still—*thank God!*—inadequate to cover the entire length of my cock. And by my meticulous calculation, the grand average penis length was a mere 5.83, a probably bloated figure given that half the sample means did not account for fat-pad inflation. I did, yes, lose a healthy dick-chunk with the dorsal-side technique, but notwithstanding I had secured an unassailable position in *above-average territory,* in the worst-case scenario and beyond all question.

Or had I? No sooner had I put the ruler away than I was hit with another wave of equivocation and distrust: *Did I measure correctly? Did I note the correct measurement? Was I absolutely certain that I did not push in? Could I ever be absolutely certain that I was not pushing in?*

I had to confirm the measurement once more and I did, jotting down the number in a notebook: "6.2??"—like that, with two question marks beside it. I wasn't certain if the stat was accurate—Ha! As if I could have been certain of anything!—because I needed a *longer ruler* to determine *exactly how many millimeters* past six inches I was without pushing in, *if* indeed I *was* past six, *if* I could ever know for sure whether I'd pushed in, *if* pushing in—if *any* of this—even fucking mattered at all. Every single time the results were the same, and hence equally unverifiable: *6.2??* And again when I measured my dick a fourth and fifth and sixth and seventh time: same. And again: same. Six point two, maybe, or maybe not.

Or maybe not.

In one of the many psychotherapy sessions that were in my not-too-distant future, I would come to know about the Zeigarnik Effect: the theory, developed by the Russian psychologist Bluma Zeigarnik (continuing the work of her professor, Kurt Lewin), that humans tend to remember unfinished tasks better than finished ones. In the late '20s Dr. Zeigarnik was sitting in a café across from the University of Berlin, sippin' on a *Schwarzbier* over a nice *Schweinekotelett* (in my presently-very-hungry imagining, anyway), when she observed that her waiter could keep in his head, without writing anything down, an endless number of items that his customers had ordered—*until they paid*. As soon as the customers had paid, the waiter could no longer remember anything about their orders. Zeigarnik theorized that a psychic tension caused the waiter's brain to keep the data in working memory until the waiter-customer relationship was fully consummated. That *anxiety,* in essence, keeps the loop open, the information at play, and the waiter *determined* to complete the task at hand and, in so doing, reach a Gestaltian closure: That, in other words, irresolution incites obsession.

The theory, my shrink would explain, had great relevance to the current treatment of post-traumatic stress disorder. Many PTSD sufferers do not have in their active memory a complete and intelligible picture of the painful experience that triggered their illness. And until they are able to *tell their story*—to explain it verbally, or even comprehend it, as a coherent narrative—their unresolved stress will continue to drive them absolutely fucking cuckoo. Teach them how to tell their story, how it fits into the larger narrative of their life and its violent untoward disruption, and the PTSD-afflicted can finally neutralize their suffering, eventually storing it away in some cognitive recess where, deprioritized, its power over them fades.

I did not have post-traumatic stress disorder. But later, much later, with the benefit of understanding—of the effects of sudden loss and dislocation, of various long-unacknowledged fears, of the nature of obsession and the desperate things we do to indulge it, or thwart it—I'd find an angle, tell a story, make fun and move on.

But right now there was nothing even vaguely resembling a context for what I was thinking and feeling, merely a cascade of punishing ideas that, within another few days, would hijack my consciousness: *My penis is too small, too small, too small, too small. Too small how? And for whom? It's average. No, it's above average, no, it isn't, I didn't measure correctly, I pushed in, it's below average. The average is 5.8, 5.9, 6.1. I'm 6.2—6.2?? I'm 6.5! If I push in, I'm 7! I'm good. No, I'm below 6. No I'm not! Why would you say that? Oh, fuck it, Alan! Who cares? I don't care. I'm average. So? So? No, I'm not average. I'm above average. No, below. Wait, I measured! No, that didn't count. Did I push in? I did! I pushed in!!!*

My penis is too small, too small, too small.

And so it began to repeat over and over in a monomaniacal loop that started the moment I woke up and would not cease until I drank myself to sleep.

It was very fucking strange.

6.1

IT WAS AMAZING TO ME—unfathomable—how fast I fell away from reality: this thing I'd had so firmly in hand, over which I was even arrogant enough to claim a kind of professional mastery. How suddenly a few odd errant thoughts bloomed into full-blown obsession. How *helpless* I was to combat it—trying every tactic to turn back its inexorable advance, to do anything other than accept that I—a guy who'd never met a problem he couldn't fix, an outcome he couldn't *produce*—was too sick to actualize my stupid little dream of being a single guy—of working, making cash, meeting girls and fucking 'em, like that, like every other dude does, big fucking deal.

It was astounding how quickly—*within days!*—my new life withered and went away, like the incredible shrinking dick with which I believed I'd been cursed.

I could lie to you. I want to lie to you: I want so badly to tell you that my exploits as a newly single guy went on for a few more weeks or months, that my Year of the Cock was a spectacular seasons-crossing bender in which I drank historic quantities of whiskey and laid acres of pipe. I wish I could relate in ribald detail how I hit the L.A. bar and club scene full of swagger and smart talk, working my mature-slightly-older-guy mack on every pretty young thing who'd listen—boozing them up, bringing them home, breaking their hearts.

But that is not me. I wish I was that kind of cock, but I am not.

No. I, Alan Wieder, left my wife of two-plus years, on a rainy day in February 2005, explaining very little, saying very little. And by late April, I couldn't stop thinking about my penis.

Literally, couldn't stop thinking about my penis, all day and all night, no matter how hard I tried.

I didn't know what a psychotic break felt like. I still don't. I know what I've read in the *DSM-IV*: something about an "acute symptom-rich period" following a radical rupture in one's contact with reality. And I know a few people who've had one, supposedly. One summer when I was a young boy, a close cousin of

my parents began calling our house and telling us how worried
he was about us Wieders, even though we were in no apparent danger; and how much he *loved* us, in a way that seemed
really really weird; he was then sent somewhere to get well,
which he never really did. There was a college buddy who, one
Monday afternoon after a weekend of abusing his antidepressant
medication along with cocaine and heroin and alcohol, scribbled
an indecipherable text in blood on his dorm room wall and then
wandered into Morningside Park and smoked crack with a homeless man. The man later somehow got *my* number and called my
room to tell me he was holding this certain friend hostage and
was going to kill him unless I showed up at the corner of 135th
and Amsterdam with $500 in an envelope. My friend, too, was
never the same guy again after that day. There were a handful
of people—as there are in anyone's midst—who'd fallen apart,
who *could no longer function on their own,* who would always
need *help,* who couldn't *deal.*

*My wife couldn't really deal. I was always the one who could
deal.*

I didn't know what a psychotic break felt like, but I couldn't
help but wonder if I'd had one, or was in the middle of one.
You've had a psychotic break, my internal degreeless shrink kept
diagnosing. I felt as if I'd slipped through some mental fissure
into an adjacent mind-state from which I would never really return, within which I would for the rest of my life perceive my
cock—and myself, by extension—as substandard, mortally in-
ferior and unworthy. *My penis is too small, too small, too small.*
The thought became a pattern, and the pattern became a core
belief as powerful as any I'd ever held, deeply delusional though
it may have been. *My penis is too small, it just is, and no matter
what I do, no matter how much I accomplish in my lifetime, girls I*

sleep with, money I make, my penis will always be inadequate and defective, and so will I.

My penis is too small, too small, too small.

No it isn't.

Yes it is.

All day long.

How the fuck did this happen to me? With diminishing lucidity I tried to reason with myself, present a convincing case for reversing my warped thinking. *It's okay, Al,* I'd say soothingly. *This is normal. You're single again, so of course you would worry about the size of your dick. Who wouldn't? All guys fret over their size: a multi-billion-dollar industry's been built on this immemorial anxiety! Besides, your penis is merely average at the very worst, but definitely not below. Definitely not below: Just check the stats . . .*

But when cool-headed ratiocination failed again and again to stem the flow of obsessive thoughts, I raged, tore into myself: *What the fuck is wrong with you, you stupid fag? Grow the fuck up and stop thinking about this shit, right now!* And then I'd look at more Web sites, barraging my brain with yet more "averages"—5.5, 5.6, 5.7, 5.8, 5.9—in a futile effort to validate what I'd already proven a thousand times over, yet could never know for absolute certain: *That there wasn't a damn thing wrong with my cock.*

Just check the stats.

A search for some psychic shortfall or originating trauma that could explain this lunacy also yielded no curative insight. As far as I could tell I'd had a respectable, if not terribly wild or prolific, sexual history; besides, now I had all the time I needed to boost my numbers. I'd never had a complaint or castigation in the sack, and I had even received many compliments on how surprisingly gentle my lovemaking style was for so tall and gawky a guy. Apart from my postcollegiate malaise and a brief death obsession in my early twenties, a short-lived string of panic attacks around twenty-five, a scattering of manageable neuroses and Larry David-ish social hangups over the years—routine Jewboy stuff—I'd experienced virtually no significant psychological ordeals. True, Sam had been through her fair share of *tsuris,* and I too had suffered through her many psychodramatic turns, but it seemed improbable that any of it would've engendered a neurotic wiener fixation.

And my childhood: well . . . Jeannette Walls's it was not. I grew up a fairly well-to-do kid in a nice house on Miami Beach. My family was only mildly screwed up at best. Dad was a skinflint, had a touch of hypochondria, and frequently put his foot in his mouth. Mom was a bit of a nervous wreck and was always busting Dad's balls. My sister and I never had a whole lot in common. Our household was a little stricter than most of my friends'. Dad forced me to play clarinet and competitive tennis, and when I misbehaved he chased me around the house with that scary leather belt . . . Um . . . As Ian MacKaye once said, "Boo fucking hoo."

I'd never been a depressive type—not consciously, anyway—and so I hoped that what I was experiencing was simply aberrant and temporary, endurable. *I'll get over this. I just need to push through.* I remembered a time, back in my junior year of college, when a woman I was seriously dating confessed to me, in one of those nights of reckless postcoital honesty, that she'd slept with this absolute fucking douchelick with whom I'd shared a few classes; and how haunted I was by that revelation, unable to cease *imagining*—all day and all night for the remaining months she and I were together—every lurid detail of their stomach-wrenching hookup, until it was just unbearable to be with her and I confronted her about it like a ninny: "How could a girl as cool and awesome as you sleep with a guy like him?" I got past that obsession eventually—after she dumped me, true—and I had no doubt I would get past this, too: *This—this penis thing is nothing. It's silly. I'm not crazy. I'm neurotic. A little obsessive maybe, no, stop pathologizing it. I dwell on things. I'm not obsessing, I'm dwelling. So?*

I tried every means of halting the nagging thought in my head: *My penis is too small, too small, too small, too small.* I cranked up the volume on the hyperaggressive hip-hop so that I couldn't hear myself think. I started exercising like crazy, hoping that a continuous runner's high would mellow my runaway brain. I did Kundalini yoga, picked up meditation again, and started gobbling this stuff I found at a health food store called white chestnut, which claimed on the bottle to "remedy unwanted thoughts, worries, and mental arguments that are circling round and round in the head like a stuck gramophone record"—but, like everything else I tried, it didn't work for shit.

And I soldiered on in the Hollywood singles scene, going out, drinking like a fish, and chasing broads, even though I had absolutely no desire to do anything with any of them because I *couldn't, oh God no, not with this penis, it's too small, too small, too small.*

Late one drunken night at the Coach & Horses, in the minutes before the lovely Liza's last call at 1:15, I met this chick who was chunky but pretty enough, Ellie, Ellen I think it was, something. Or, I should say, *she* met *me*: I was yakked up and slumped over the bar and she—seeing that I was still there, where I'd been sitting like a lonely sack of shit since ten—approached me and said sweetly, "You seem so sad. Are you okay?" We talked for a total of five minutes before she whispered, "I think I want to fuck you"—and as any guy would have under the circumstances I immediately followed her out of the bar, thinking, *This is good. This is what I need to do: To fuck the shit out of some bar slut just to remind myself that I'm a man, and rid myself of this asinine worry once and for all.* But then we walked upstairs to her crappy apartment on Vista Street and sat on her crappy sofa and smoked hash out of a rotting apple, and when she took off her shirt and exposed her big floppy tits and attacked me I felt so disgusting and terrified, my dick so tiny and risible and useless, and like a schmuck I made the excuse that I was married and had to go home to my wife.

A few nights later at Barney's Beanery I drank a few pitchers and started chatting up one of the waitresses there, charming her just to see if I still could, taking her back to my place just to see if I still could, and as she sat in the living room waiting for me on my Italian designer sofa and listening to my $7,000 stereo I stood in the bathroom with my pants pulled down around my knees, staring into the mirror at my shriveled penis, mortified beyond belief, thinking, *I can't go through with this, I need to get her the fuck out of here, my dick is too fucking small.*

I met a girl at a hip wine bar in Santa Monica, a nice girl who was new in town and trying to land a job in reality television and, naturally, wanted to know *everything* about what I do as an *executive producer.* The more I drank and talked the more I started to feel myself again, joking, sharing stories from the road, laughing, making her laugh—briefly unconscious of how crazy I was as I walked her home down a quiet breezy street off Pacific. But as soon as we got to her door and she asked me inside—*wham!*—it was back again, *too small, too small, too small,* and I abruptly bid her good night with a dry feelingless kiss, telling her I had an early morning when in fact I had nothing to do the next day but look at more penis statistics on the Internet.

I must have been exuding some slobby sullen Bukowski-ish charm, because the more distraught and miserable I became, the more women I seemed to attract. To have crossed me in a bar during this period would be to see a guy who was clearly a sad, messy drunk but was workin' it to his advantage, who seemed heedless and uninhibited and all the things I strived to be but was not at all.

I tried to fight it, so hard, with everything I had. I kicked and screamed the whole way down the hill. I drank, and totally ignored my wife, and went out every night of the week with friends who had no idea what maniacal shit was raging inside my head, and hit on every girl in sight, and pretended that everything was A-OK.

But the feeling stayed with me, no matter how strenuously I tried to numb it or blot it out: *My penis is small, defective, it just is.* Rhizomelike, it seized hold of my brain, burrowing every which way, attaching itself to every thought and impulse, wildly, ineradicably. I'd try to destroy the thought, attack it from every rational angle—*Ha! If I really had a small penis, would regular condoms fit so snugly? Huh? Take that!* Then three new equally twisted notions would crop up: *My penis looks smaller than it did yesterday, and even smaller than it did the day before that. Even if my penis were average—it isn't, but if it **were**—you and I both know that "average" is not really average; average means 50 percent, a failing grade, deficient, small. Every orgasm I've ever induced must have been faked because no woman could ever have gotten off on such a dinky dick.*

All my logic failed because an obsessive thought, I would

learn, can't be reasoned with or refuted. By a paradoxical effect, the harder I tried to suppress the idea through mental argument, the more frequently and forcibly it returned.

I was going down in a hurry, and the only thing I could think of that might save me was time—*maybe*—and the compassion of a woman I'd never, *ever*, not in a million fucking years, give the pleasure of seeing me this way.

6.2

SHAME: it was a brand-new emotion for me.

I couldn't identify it at first. I was jogging up Runyon Canyon—sprinting straight uphill like a madman, trying to induce a mind-numbing endorphin rush—when an image popped into my head, an image that would cause me suddenly to heave and gasp and vomit in the grass. That would make me want to sink into the ground and disappear.

The image itself was totally ordinary, a fantasy otherwise too generic to mention: it was of me lying in a large white bed, my bed, waiting to receive oral sex from a woman. But the feeling it set off was seismic. As this anonymous woman in my imagination pulled down my boxer shorts and looked at my cock for the first time, sizing it up, this *feeling* rushed out from wherever it had been bottled up and grabbed me by the insides in a paroxysm of anger, abhorrence, revulsion, something.

Shame.

Until that moment, my penis obsession had been largely intellectual—carried along on a wave of ugly unwanted *thoughts*, cognitions that, though driving me to distraction, I could still contain, albeit through a near-constant mental dialogue. *My penis is small. No, it's not. Yes, it is.*

But now the effects had turned physiological, as if the toxic stuff in my head had spread into my blood. Now the thought of a woman seeing my penis—shit, even the thought of looking at *my own* penis in the mirror—made me choke and convulse. If I showered (which was becoming increasingly infrequent) I would dash out and immediately throw a towel around my waist, trying not to catch a glimpse of it. If I found myself touching it, I felt like gagging. I could not even pull my pong out and take a leak without this wretched *feeling* coursing through my stomach, my chest, my heart.

Steve had always made a joke that I was part cyborg, because there were a set of human states and emotions to which I'd seemed immune. Fatigue, hunger, and sickness were chief among them: he'd watched me buckle down and, with inhuman focus, plow through hellacious production after production, never giving way to anxiety or stress or exhaustion, getting through an eighteen-hour workday without a proper meal, expressing no regret over having to work through Thanksgiving and Christmas to meet our network schedule, no frustration with being forced to sit in a cramped little editing room for three straight days when an approaching airdate called for it. My partner was fond of describing our most recent production as "an eighteen-month anal rape," but to me it was *fun*. And there was also remorse: I felt absolutely *none* over the mean pranks we pulled on our unsuspecting reality participants, the relationships we sabotaged for entertainment's sake, the people we mocked and tortured and toyed with through our impeccably crafted show formats.

And there was compassion, too—never a strong suit of mine—and generosity: Steve was the kind of guy who'd give a job to an old friend with no production experience, just because he could; I was the opposite. *Fuck 'em,* I would think, *nobody ever helped **me**.*

I just didn't seem to give a shit about anyone or anything other than the people I liked and the things I liked to do. I was a *dick*—"You're a real dick, Alan Wieder," was Steve's mostly affectionate refrain—but that was an essential part of our team chemistry. He was the nice guy, the caring one who kibitzed with the PAs and knew everyone on the crew by first name; and I was the aloof a-hole who had better things to do.

As for shame: honestly, zero. I'd never been ashamed of anything in my whole damn life. I'd known embarrassment, sure, usually when I made an off-color joke that was taken the wrong way, or when I suddenly ran into someone whose phone calls I'd been dodging. But never shame. Never like *this.*

I'd loved Sam deeply, but when I left her, I'll be the first to admit: I felt *nothing* for her. I just didn't *care.* People would ask, *Don't you feel sad about leaving your wife?* Nope, don't care. *Aren't you at all concerned about Sam's well-being?* Nope, don't care. *Don't you feel guilty about dating other girls so soon?* Guilty? Me? Fuck no! Guilty about what? On some level, I guess I knew I couldn't maintain such flagrant disregard for our ten years of togetherness, that eventually I'd have to properly mourn the demise of my marriage, wade through a punishing divorce, suffer the melancholies of living alone, being alone, get on with my career, maybe meet someone else, deal with it. Eventually, maybe, but not now. For the time being I'd done enough. I'd cared enough. *So take your loss and guilt and shame and everything else I'm supposed to be experiencing*—"Did you hear that Alan left his wife, just upped and split, like that! Poor girl!"—*all that bullshit, and leave me the fuck alone.*

Now, a mere three months into my would-be swingin' bachelorhood, everything was gone or going away. Jan, the waitress down in Hermosa, was gone, because she'd gotten back together with her boyfriend. Breanne, Michelle, and Amber were gone, because I'd stopped calling. My libido, which had been raging with the vigor of a sixteen-year-old, was gone. The whole point of this whole grand postmarital journey was gone.

And the only thing I had left was my stupid little cock and the inescapable, miserable, unbearable *feeling* it had awakened.

Shame.

6.3

ACTUALLY, there was one other thing I'd held on to: my Souplantation girl, Ms. K.

Of the pathetically small handful of women who had the good fortune of spending time with me before I went nuts, Ms. K was the only one with whom I'd made anything resembling a real connection. I really liked this girl. At first she was just a low-level employee at the office whom I wanted to diddle, but then—too soon for either of us—I really, really liked her. At the time, I couldn't quite figure out exactly why. Yes, she was ridiculously cute and *fun* and so my type, and she had grown up only a few hours from where I was born and raised in Miami Beach. And yes, she had an affinity for booze and junky salad bars and a knack for opining on the pros and cons of various consumer products, which gave her three serious compatibility points right there. And she was also so earnest and unpretentious, as evidenced most clearly by the fact that she hated my sweet-ass whip.

But that was the skin-deep stuff. There was something else I liked about Ms. K, something much deeper that I couldn't quite put a finger on until I'd suddenly dropped out of her life, saying very little, explaining very little, too fucked in the head to be a friend or a lover or even a decent guy, to show a shred of manliness or dignity.

What I liked—perhaps loved—about her, I now know.

She was a lot like my wife.

The abrupt end of our relationship—our breakup, if you can even call it that—was the single strangest ordeal of my life. If it were happening on camera to one of my reality players, I might look on from the control room and comment gleefully, *You just can't write this shit!*—a common refrain that reality producers use to convince themselves that what they're doing is as aesthetically worthy as the scripted fare they'd prefer to be making.

Too bad the camera was pointed this-a-way, this time around.

At the time my strange thought-obsession began to take hold, Ms. K and I had been on ten or so dates and were really hitting it off. We'd pretty much covered the whole gamut of things worth seeing and doing in L.A. We'd eaten dinner at Chaya Venice and Sushi Roku and brunched at the Casa del Mar. We'd seen movies at the El Capitan and Hollywood Cinerama Dome. We'd gotten schickered at the Red Lion beer garden, the Dime, the Daily Pint, the Otheroom, Big Wang's, and 4100 Bar. We'd driven up the breezy Pacific Coast Highway and eaten at Gladstone's and spent the rest of the day at El Matador Beach; we'd visited the Getty Center and that local must-see oddball attraction, the Museum of Jurassic Technology. I'd taken her to Cheebo and the Coach

& Horses on multiple occasions. She'd even helped me pick out some new clothes at Loehmann's; with no woman before that, other than my consummately stylish wife, had I had the experience of emerging from a changing room and asking, "What do you think?"—and actually giving a shit what the broad had to say.

We'd spent a great deal of time together and had shared *a lot*. We'd reached the point where, when we weren't together, we were pretty much talking and texting all day long. With the other girls I was pursuing and taking out, I'd revealed nothing of myself other than those aspects that would better my chances of strippin' off their halter tops. I'd played the usual cards, already, after only a couple months on the dating scene, so lame and tired coming out of my mouth: I helped create *My Big Fat Obnoxious Fiancé,* one of the biggest reality hits in the last two years. I carried an EC passport, thanks to my having a French *maman.* I was once in a punk band. I was in possession of an extremely rare Mystery Diver toy from a 1966 box of Alpha Bits . . . But with Ms. K I felt compelled to open up about other things, things that might actually make me lose points in a different young woman's estimation.

Ms. K was a born let's-talk-about-it type, but not in an annoying way. Like Samantha, she had the innate desire and emotional acuity to understand the barricades, self-imposed or otherwise, that keep people from leading fulfilling lives. Of course, what I was capable of sharing during a time so devoid of self-awareness—so focused on drink and sex and *fun fun fun*—was hardly profound or soul-baring. But—like Sam—Ms. K was one of those people who, with brutal honesty, could show you aspects of yourself you were not prepared to see, but then glad you did.

She was a friend. She *was*.

We'd explored the possible reasons why I'd stayed with my wife for so long after Sam's father died, when the relationship was met with so many emotional and financial hardships. Ms. K seemed especially curious about this point. Beyond the fact that I loved Sam, why did I feel as if it was my responsibility to fix the things in her life that were broken and stand in for what was gone? And at what point did I decide that I was no longer capable of filling that role for her, and why?

I told Ms. K about my track record—my history of being with women who *depended* on me to help them navigate their screwy life circumstances, edit their papers, solve their *problems*.

"That's bullshit, Alan," she said. "*You* depended on *them*."

I'd told her how much it troubled me that my parents, after thirty-whatever years of marriage, seemed so loveless in each other's company—seemingly so bored and agitated by the fact that they were *still together* after a million-and-one hollow threats to leave, so far past the point where their respective quirks and hang-ups were cute in a certain light, or comforting, or at least tolerable. How they seemed incapable of addressing one another without erupting into argument and recrimination, without one of them saying, at some point, that their life together had been a big mistake.

"Do you honestly think that you and Sam were becoming like that, though?" Ms. K asked. "Because it doesn't seem that way to me."

"Really?" I said. "It does to me."

"Oh, Alan," she said, which was what she always said when she was about to call my b.s. "I think you *think* you're more cynical and angry about your marriage than you really are. But that's okay. That's what I like about you."

I'd told her about how much I admired and missed my grandpa Bernie, Dad's dad, how much I spent every single day thinking about him even though he'd died fifteen years earlier in 1991, when I was only seventeen and barely knew him; how fascinated I was with the things he'd said—"small change"—and done as a young man; how much I cherished the few objects he'd bequeathed me: a couple pocketknives, a monogrammed billfold, a gold Omega Constellation watch. Despite all the stories about what a badass he was in his day, how he'd come from Hungary with nineteen cents in his pocket and within twenty-five years owned a string of successful hotels in New York and Miami—*a millionaire!*—and how he'd greased local politicos and punched out this or that guy and got shit *done,* and how he'd also drunk and smoked and caroused, running through mistress after mistress—despite all that had been recounted, by the time I was old enough to know him he was a broken-down man, disabled from a car wreck some years before and now with a deepening case of emphysema, an invalid who could barely stand up from the sofa and walk to the door. My only real memories of him are of him *dying,* sitting in his leather recliner with a filterless Pall Mall 100 on his lips, too breathless to say my name, at such stark odds with the tough and unflagging character he'd apparently been.

"It's almost like you're trying to carry on his legacy, kinda," Ms. K said. "Like if you stand still and accept your life as this regular married schmo, you're betraying him somehow."

When she saw my new tattoos she wondered aloud: "Alan, do you think you're having an early midlife crisis?"

And she, too, had shared. Turned out the girl who'd once made me go "Wheeee!" had quite a complex inner life. For one, she was very troubled by the fact that she'd never been in love—inordinately bothered by it, I felt. It kept her up at nights, made her feel like there was something seriously *wrong* with her as a person.

"Jesus, you're only twenty-three," I said. "It's hard to meet a decent dude," leaving the *like me* implied.

It wasn't that, she said. She'd been with a few guys for whom she could perhaps have felt love, but as soon as she got close to them emotionally she became incapable of feeling anything for them physically. As soon as she liked a guy "like that," some switch went off inside her, and the thought of being with him sexually totally grossed her out.

"And I wasn't molested, if that's what you're wondering," she said glibly, but in fact what I was wondering was far more selfish.

In a moment of boozy candor she'd also revealed that at one time in her life, she'd been seriously overweight, and that she still visited a support group for a presently-under-control eating disorder. It was so hard to picture this petite sexy girl as the fatso she claimed once to have been, but it was true—she even showed me pictures of her tubbier former self to prove it.

So she was a fat kid, huh? So was I. *So was Sam.*

Interesting.

In the days leading up to our split-up, because of a combination of my increasingly busy production schedule and my deepening derangement, our multiple-daily-chat habit had been radically cut back. So when, on a Thursday afternoon—as I emerged from another useless healing meditation class at Golden Bridge Yoga—I received from her a cryptic and uncharacteristically chilly text message, bereft of her usual cutesy emoticons and such, I assumed the worst.

Hey oldman. Can we meet for dinner? Cafe Sushi 8p?

Uh-oh. It'd been more than a decade since anyone had broken up with me, and it had certainly never happened over text message, but it didn't take a genius to see that this was clearly a postmillennial preamble to getting dumped. And worse, the chick was angling to get some free spicy scallop handrolls out of the deal. The nerve! Even in my pathetic emotional state, I wasn't *that* much of a chump! So I fired back, trying to beat her to the punch:

Whaddya say we get it done with over coffee.

But then she surprised me:

Shut up. It's not bad. Promise. Just need to tell u some stuff. K?

Hmmm. Well at least at Café Sushi, a no-great-shakes joint on Beverly Boulevard in West Hollywood, I'd get away for seventy bucks or so including sake. I sucked it up.

K.

Now, by this point, several weeks after an eyeful of Fred Durst's nookie knocker first sent me spiraling, my penis obsession—and the shameful feelings it elicited—had deepened significantly. What had begun as a silly thought pinballing around in my head had now suffused my entire waking consciousness, intruding upon my every thought and action.

My penis is too small, too small, too small, too small, too small.

I will always, for the rest of my life, be stuck with this contemptible and worthlessly tiny cock.

ALL FUCKING DAY.

It felt like 85 percent of my brain—the only thing on which I could hang my self-esteem, in the absence of a dick—was unusable, swallowed up by a completely illogical idea that I had no clue how to silence; and the other 15 percent was busy beating back the thought's cancerous spread. Looking back now, I don't even know how I got through those days, frankly; how I found the wherewithal even to get out of bed and brush my teeth, let alone go to work and make TV.

And all the while, there was a new distraction to add to my already near-constant mental torment.

I'd started measuring my cock. I mean, a *lot*. Not only fretting, and wondering, and looking at data, and constantly running penis stats in my head—5.5, 5.7, 5.9, 6.2, 6.5, 6.7—but now also taking out a ruler and *measuring* it, repeatedly, *compulsively,* four, six, eight, twelve, twenty times a day. Each measurement yielded more or less the same result—within mere millimeters of deviation, depending on how solid a woody I'd cracked and how much or little I pushed into the fat pad—but still I found myself unable to reach any conclusion that would *stick*. An hour or less after each measurement, I could feel that statistic—like every other figure I'd tried to retain—losing credence, dematerializing, surrendering to an irrepressible urge to *measure again, no I shouldn't, yes I must.*

Finding a ruler I could trust with such a critical self-valuation was equally problematic. I had outgrown, so to speak, my Ninja Turtles ruler and had bought an old-fashioned wooden 12-inch so that I could determine *exactly* how many fractions of an inch over six inches, if any, I was. But then, when I'd read online somewhere that wooden rulers were considered generally inaccurate, I'd switched to one of those 12-inch plastic jobs designed to fit in a three-ring binder. Then, when *that* ruler had proven too stiff and sharp-edged to avoid pushing into the pubic mound (and hence corrupting my measurement), I'd switched to a soft tailor's tape ruler. Then, when *that* ruler had proven too *soft* to provide an accurate reading, I'd switched to a carpenter's tape measure. And then, still unsatisfied, I'd started measuring my din-gus with *all* of these instruments—carrying the whole ar-senal in my computer bag wherever I went, and pulling out whichever one suited my lunatic fancy on a particular dick-measuring occasion.

I was sizing up my penis flaccid and erect and semierect, at my apartment, at my office, in strange bathrooms, wherever I could fetch a moment alone; and recording the precise measure-ments, down to the tenth of an inch, in little notebooks, on busi-ness cards and credit card receipts, and in my cloudy head. Each time I did it I felt more devalued, more repugnant—and more compelled to *do it again*.

The stats, so many numbers scribbled on paper scraps, meant nothing. I know that now, beyond all doubt. It was not the num-bers but the *process* of culling them, writing them down, ques-tioning them, testing them, that kept me going—the sense of order and control afforded by the *practice* of even this terribly imprecise and self-abasing science, to a man whose life was spi-raling into the void.

Point being: By the time I'd agreed, on that May evening, to meet Ms. K at Café Sushi in Hollywood and hear whatever it was she had to say, I was completely fucking batshit.

It was raining hard that night and I couldn't find a park-ing spot anywhere near the restaurant, so when I showed up I was good and soaked and must have looked like a real yutz. Ms. K looked adorable, for her part, which was nothing new. She was already seated at a table near the sushi bar, wearing an auburn V-neck sweater and black mohair scarf, drinking green tea and watching one of the chefs chop up a big pile of softshell crabs.

"They make these things," she said upon seeing me. "They're called umbrellas."

Hers was hanging smartly on the back of her chair, and she was bone dry. I kissed her hello and sat down across from her, my blood speeding, my mind reeling. A good 20 percent of my brain was very eager to know what she wanted so urgently to tell me. And the other 80 was going, *My penis is too small, too small, too small, too small. No, it isn't. Yes, it is.*

I'll never forget this: The first thing I did upon sitting down was look at various objects around the restaurant, and wonder which of those items were *bigger* than my dick and which were *smaller*—as if my penis itself was now a measuring rod with which everything in my purview could be gauged. My thoughts just *went there* instantly, synaptically, my eyes darting around the room in a sequence of perceptual impulses I couldn't derail: *That sushi roll on that woman's plate is longer than my dick, and fatter. That soy sauce bottle on the table is shorter, and thinner at the neck. Those chopsticks are longer. That paring knife is longer. That soup spoon is shorter. That menu is two times as long, maybe three. That cucumber he's chopping . . .*

I took my hot towel and began vigorously rubbing my soggy head.

"How have you been?" Ms. K said. "We haven't *not* talked in two days in like, forever."

"Me? Good. Busy as hell," I said. I'd gotten a little better, each day, at keeping up the appearance of right-mindedness. "We shoot in a couple weeks. Cold sake or hot?"

"Think I'm sticking with tea tonight," she said. "Trying to cut back."

Tea? Ms. K? *After ten positively besotted outings together, she chooses **tonight** to get all temperance-society on me?*

"*Tea*-totaler," I joked, only because she liked puns, but this one zoomed over her head because her vocabulary wasn't great.

"There you go with your big words again," she said.

Our waiter—a wiry, tattooed Japanese dude with dreads—arrived, and before he took our order I wondered whether he had a bigger penis than I did. *He's Asian, and from what I've read Asian men are an average of 0.4 to 0.7 inches shorter than white men—0.4 to 0.7 shorter. 0.4 to 0.7. Black men are 0.5 to 0.9 bigger. Stop, Alan, please stop. 0.5 to 0.9. I am 6.2, no, 6.5, a little less, no, I pushed in, 6, no, under 6. Am I really under 6!?*

"I'll take a bottle of Genshu," I said, a 40-proof cold sake more often served as a cocktail liquor than a dinner accompaniment.

I asked Ms. K to order for us, as she'd insisted on doing the last time we'd gone out for sushi. But this time, as she rattled off items to our waiter, she hesitated, looking at me to approve each expenditure. I nodded at everything, not really listening—a $120 bill, easy—a chump after all.

She told me about her new job. She'd recently left the production company where we'd met and gotten a gig assisting an executive producer of a popular animated series, and she was happy to be done with unscripted TV.

"But you were so good at it," I said. "A sound-bite machine, from what I heard."

"Yeah, I guess," Ms. K said. "But my philosophy is, either you make reality TV or you watch it. You're a maker, Alan. You *get off* on it. I think, in the end, I'm more of a watcher. Suddenly I was like, I'm sitting in the edit bay for thirteen hours a day with the thousand pages of interview transcripts and all that *footage*—and meanwhile, I'm missing the whole *Bachelorette 3*! Life is too short."

I gave her an update on my pilot, *Seriously, Your Band Sucks!*

I told her that we'd finally settled on a band that were the appropriate blend of shitty and cocky. The group was totally amped that they'd been chosen for what they believed was a new MTV documentary, blithely unaware that we were secretly plotting to fly their friends and family members to L.A. to stage our intervention.

"Delicious," she said.

It was just *killing* me, to sit across this cute, witty young woman with whom I had such an easy rapport, in a cozy sushi restaurant on a rainy night in Hollywood—to have in my firm grasp everything I'd thought I could attain as a single guy, and more—and know that it was all tumbling away.

My penis is too small, too small, too small. It's not too small. It's average, above average, 6.5. No it isn't. It's below 6. It's small, tiny, defective, useless, worthless, it just is. If any woman were to see it I would just die.

The Genshu came first. I poured it roughly over a short glass filled with ice and pretended not to down it as fast as I did. The strong wine ran to my head and soothed it, but only slightly.

Ms. K refilled her tea from an earthen pot and added a sugar packet and cut the shit.

"So, no, Alan," Ms. K said. "I'm not here to tell you that I don't want to see you anymore."

As she said these words I felt a powerful urge to go to the bathroom and measure my dick, with one of the six or seven rulers I had in my computer bag, I wasn't sure which. *Later, I'll measure it later.*

"It's actually the opposite . . ." She trailed off, and then: "Gosh, I'm so nervous . . ."

I held out to her my refilled glass of Genshu, and when she declined I took another big gulp on her behalf. I hadn't eaten a bite all day and was feeling the booze—but beneath it still, the distinct and disquieting hum of *penis too small, too small, too small, it just IS . . .*

"You know how I've told you that I don't enjoy sex with someone I have genuine affection for?" she began.

"No, I don't seem to recall that," I said.

"Shut up. Well there's a reason for it. And I'm only telling you this because I like you soooo much, and feel more comfortable around you than anyone I've ever met."

My penis is small. If I stuck it in that glass it wouldn't even reach the bottom. That glass is, what—6.5? 6.2? If I stuck it into that jar of hot sauce it would slide right through the opening no problem, it's that narrow. Stop stop, fuck! The opening's circumference is 5 inches even, I'd say, maybe more; my penis is 4.75 in the middle, 5 at the base, above average by a hair, no, below. No!

"I'm serious," Ms. K said. "Almost no one out here knows this about me, because I wanted my life in L.A. to be about the *future*. I didn't want people to feel sorry for me, or give me a job, or be my friend because of weird shit that happened to me in the past. I left Florida to get the whole thing behind me, start fresh. But I feel like"—she began to tear up—"like we can't move forward till I tell you the truth."

No: Girls don't care about the size of a guy's dick. No. Yes, they do. Over 67 percent of women find a bigger cock more vaginally stimulating; over 90 percent more visually stimulating. Stop stop stop, please stop. Over 40 percent of women have dumped a man because his penis was too small. 40 percent! Too small, too small, too small. Wait, what am I saying, what kind of a lunatic am I that I'm citing a study clearly fabricated by some scumbag trying to con people into buying penis pumps! Women don't care, no! No!

Stop this now, Alan, fucking hell! Yes, they do care, they totally DO—

"When we met I told you that my parents were still together," she said. "I wasn't being honest."

One thing reality TV had taught Ms. K was how to milk a reveal, that was for sure.

"My dad was murdered when I was eighteen," she said.

The waiter arrived with a pretty array of cut rolls, a baked yellowtail collar, and a few other items for which I had absolutely zero appetite. *This dude over here definitely has a bigger cock than I do. I wonder if that stumpy guy sitting at the sushi bar with that hot chick has a bigger dick, too. I'm much taller than he is, but that doesn't mean anything. Well, it means something if there's an expectation. I'm tall, women will look at me and think I have a big penis, but I don't. That chick's all over him! If he has a small dick, he doesn't seem too worked up about it. Fuck it, fuck it, neither am I. Stop, stop. He must be big. I'm small, so small, the smallest here, I'm sure of it.*

Her dad was dead. Is that what she'd said? *Murdered. Murdered!*

"One day he went to work and never came home. We didn't know where he was. Nobody did for days—not the cops, nobody."

"Jesus," I said, a beat very late. "I'm sorry."

"A few days later he was found shot to death in a strange condo in Brandon. A bullet to the head. To the head! A neighbor reported the smell . . ." Now she was full-on crying, pushing her way through this terrible revelation of which I no longer had any right to be a protector. "Turns out he had this whole other life we didn't even know about: an apartment, a secret girlfriend, tons of gambling debt . . . I mean, we knew he was in construction; we weren't *idiots*. We knew he dealt with some shady people. He came home late a lot. But we never thought he could be into such bad shit that someone would want him *dead*—my fucking *dad!*—"

The small fraction of my brain that wasn't ruminating on my cock was thinking opportunistically: *So this girl's actually pretty screwed up, huh? The fun Ms. K, it turns out, is yet another in the long list of Calamity Janes I've fallen for? Good! I need a girl with issues right now, who will understand the crazy stuff that's going on inside **my** head. I can **help** her, **rescue** her. This is nothing, Alan, you're an old pro at this! Maybe you can help each other, work through it all, your shit and hers, **together** . . .*

"I didn't want to unload this on you," she said, "especially because of everything you'd gone through with your wife. Her dad dying when she was superyoung, just like me, leaving her mom and family behind with nothing—nothing but pain, turmoil . . . emptiness. When you told me that about Sam's dad, I kinda flipped. The *similarities*, Alan—it was just *freaky!* I couldn't stop *thinking* about it; I was up all night, thinking about it, over and over and over. And then there were other things: that she and I were both fat at one time and still struggle with that. And little details: She's obsessed with Madonna. I'm obsessed with Madonna. She keeps a list of things she likes in a journal. I keep a list in a journal. We're like the *same people*. Don't you think it's weird . . . ?"

My penis will never be bigger than it is right now, never. I will live with this small penis until I die, and when I die it will remain affixed to my rotting corpse, till it like the rest of me disintegrates to nothing and disappears, finally fucking disappears.

"And my point is," she said, "I don't think I can be intimate with men I actually *like,* because I'm terrified—I guess it's abandonment issues, I don't know, I'm still figuring it out; but I wanted to tell you the truth because—"

She suddenly halted. I sipped my Genshu, my 14 percent of available brain capacity trying desperately to wrap itself around what she'd just shared, to punch through the clutter and offer her some semieloquent condolence or emotional insight or cheering joke, *something.*

"You're not saying anything," she said. "Why do I feel like you're not really listening to me?"

"I am listening . . . it's just . . ."

It's just that my penis is too small, too small, too small.

"Just . . . ?"

"Do you think I have a small penis?" I asked.

Oh God. Oh God.

"Excuse me?" she said.

"Nothing, nothing."

"Do you have a small—what? What kind of shit is that to ask me?"

"Nothing, I—"

"I tell you that my father was shot in the head, and . . . What the fuck, Alan?"

Just then—*bam*—I had a vivid memory of something that had happened when I was twenty, summer after junior year, a year before I met Samantha. I was living in Manhattan with a woman, call her Helen, who was a few years older than I, maybe twenty-three or -four. This chick was hot, and smart, and *older*—did I mention? I'd met her on a flight into LaGuardia and somehow inveigled her into seeing *J'ai pas sommeil* with me at the Angelika Film Center. Largely because I seemed so cool and awesome for knowing enough to introduce her to the work of Claire Denis, we began hanging out often. Now the spring semester had ended and I was spending the summer living with her at her studio on Eighty-third and Columbus. It was a Saturday afternoon in July, and we were plopped on a bench on Central Park West in the withering heat. She was reading the *Village Voice* and I was eating a Good Humor Strawberry Shortcake Bar—I remembered it so clearly now; I was telling her she was fuckin' crazy for not liking the crunchy coating. She had no gustatory discernment, I said. I asked to see and touch her tongue, to make sure it wasn't made of tire rubber. *Let me see your tongue this instant!* I demanded. She was laughing. We'd made love that morning, and I'd actually made this *older* girl come like three times and felt like some stud. In a few hours I was planning to meet some tennis team buddies at the White Horse Tavern for burgers and beers. I had the planet spinning on my finger like "Sweet" Lou Dunbar would a tricolored basketball. I don't think I was in love, but I was so young and happy and full with the times that lay ahead and just lovin' being with this woman who, it was obvious, thought I was the cat's galoshes.

But then—then—Helen looked abysmally sad all of a sudden, like she'd gone away in her mind to a place where I was not. I'd blinked, and something between us had shifted, radically. I asked her what was wrong. Are you okay? I said. There was something she had to tell me, she said. And she wanted to tell me because she felt that she could tell me things, that I wasn't like most guys, that I was *sweet*, that I'd understand. Of course I'll understand, I said, my heart heaving. Tell me, tell me anything. Two years ago, she said, she passed out at a party, and two guys raped her. She woke up the next morning to discover she'd been raped. *Raped!?* I said. Raped, she said;

just like that, my girlfriend was a rape victim. She could not get past it no matter how hard she tried, she said; she'd been seeing a therapist two times a week and had joined a victims' support group, was speaking out at high schools about sexual abuse; but it stayed with her, not even a memory but this dark unfathomable imagining of what had happened to her while she was not even awake to reject the advances of these abominable boys.

As she began to cry I held her in my arms, close, tight. *My God, I'm so sorry,* I said. My role was clear, second nature at this point: to remain sturdy and unfazed and in control, to stop the hurt, to *cheer her up.* I'd been through it a dozen times already with different chicks. I'm gonna find those guys and chop their heads off, I said. I'm gonna hold 'em at gunpoint and make them gag on each others' cocks and then, midgag, decapitate both of 'em with a machete. They will die headless with each others' severed heads attached to their respective rigor-mortised penises. Okay, now *that's* a little scary, she said. She laughed through her tears a little and cozied up to me, burying her head into my chest, this sad sobbing haunted wounded needy girl. *Can you stay with me tonight?* she said, meaning could I cancel my plans for burgers and beers with Marc and Dave at the White Horse. Could I stay home with her instead and watch a movie, drink a glass or two of wine, *talk.* Of course, the thing to do was cancel my plans; of course. The woman had been raped! She *needed* me! And yet . . . I don't know. I so didn't *want* to cancel my plans. All I could think was, she was raped, mother*fuck,* I gotta deal with *this* now, *tonight,* when I'm supposed to go meet Marc and Dave for burgers and beers? Why me, always *me* with this shit? Why can't I just get laid like everyone else—why is it always so much bloody *work?*

What I was feeling then I could not name, but it blocked any possibility of compassion for Helen; though I appeared unconditionally supportive—a rock, as always—my heart was ice-cold. It was unexpressed anger and self-hate disguised as apathy, plain and simple, my shrink would later say; smothered rage at the sense that my happiness was once again being cut short, stripped away and replaced with the much lesser satisfaction derived from helping, understanding, *being there.* That whatever good befell me always came with a passel of *responsibilities* that, "sweet" guy that I was, I felt an unnatural obligation to fulfill. That somehow I always became a boyfriend before I got to be a boy. That I *was* seeking these women out for some reason, as Ms. K had pointed out, that I must have indeed depended on them—to assert my power and importance and manliness, shunt my own vulnerability—and not the other way around.

Of course I'll stay, I said to Helen—of course I did. *Whatever you need.*

And now here was Ms. K, another—the last, I decided—in a procession of women who'd unloaded their stupid fucking problems on me, *tonight* of all nights, without warning, when I had so much else to think about, and so little left to give.

My penis is too small, too small, too small. No it isn't. Yes it is. Stop. Stop!

"Why would you say something like that, Alan? Please explain."

"Okay," I said. "I'll tell you why. My wife's dad died seven years ago. He had a heart attack in some sad little back office when she—and I—were only twenty-three. And—big surprise—he left her, left *us,* with nothing, fuck, less than nothing. And it sucked, for her and for me, ever since. And now *your* dad

died, too, under even *more* unfortunate and disreputable circumstances. Great for you! Congratu-fucking-lations on being
equally if not more traumatized than Sam! We all have sorrow,
Ms. K! We all walk around with shit we can't solve or make go
away! I wish I had a bigger dick! So fucking what! This is life,
is it not? You want an explanation? What do you want? You
see a fucking time machine sitting beside me? You want me to
travel back to when your pops was alive, find a way to give him
a couple hundred grand to cover his debts, rub out the guys
who probably rightfully wanted him dead, help him clean up
his messy pathetic existence? Because truthfully, I'm not sure
what you want from me. I'm sitting here, listening, and try as
I might, I can't figure out *why* I should give a flying fuck about
any of this!"

"What?!" I'd never seen anyone so hurt by something I'd
said, not even my wife when I told her I was moving out. "You're
insane, Alan! Fuck you! Fuck you forever! How dare you say
something like that to me! I thought you were nice . . . !" and a
bunch of other shit I didn't really hear.

Ms. K stormed out of the restaurant, leaving her umbrella
behind, still hooked to the back of her empty chair. I thought
she'd return for it, march back in and grab it in a final huff, but
she didn't. And, another Genshu bottle later, I was oddly thankful for it as I paid the $105 bill and headed into the rain. *Good
riddance. Eff her.*

I made it all of five blocks before I parked in a spot on Santa
Monica Boulevard and sat there for two hours in the downpour,
in my stupid overpriced piece-of-shit Porsche that didn't even
have a working windshield defroster—*A vintage Porsche! What
the fuck was I thinking!?*—banging my fists on the wheel and
crying like a little bitch.

Then I drove back to my apartment, took out my collection of rulers, and spent the rest of the night measuring my dick.

6.4

MEANWHILE, Sobel and I had a show to deliver.

We had a lot riding on *Seriously, Your Band Sucks!* The high professional stakes were at stark odds with the lowliness of the show's premise. Over our five years in the reality genre, Steve and I had earned a reputation as the mad architects behind a number of successful formats, but few networks yet saw us as full-service executive producers who could produce a *series* on our own, soup to nuts; and we wanted to hit this one out of the park. Besides which, our producing contract on the show was such that if MTV liked the pilot and ordered, say, twenty half-hours, we stood to make cake like Duncan Hines, as Killa Cam likes to say. We'd been paired with an extremely experienced in-house MTV producer, a seen-it-all-done-it-all veteran of MTV-gen channel fodder, who was there to sign off on key decisions, steer us through the network political maze, and keep us from fucking anything up too badly. But he had several other shows under his oversight at the same time, leaving me and Sobel with more final-word responsibility, from casting to final cut, than we'd ever had.

Under normal circumstances, of course, I'd have been a pig in doo-doo. The opportunity to produce our own pilot— to cast, shoot, and frame-fuck it to our hearts' content; to execute our specific vision and prove our mettle as full-fledged showrunners—was the ultimate prize, the thing every young reality TV producer is playing for. But when 94 percent of your brain is far more wrapped up in the quality of your pecker than in the finished product, giving the requisite attention and focus to the infinite number of decisions that go into even something as patently silly as *Seriously* is a distressing, debilitating, and all-around miserable endeavor.

The show needed both Steve's and my brains in a big way, not because the prank on which it hinged was difficult to pull off, or the thematics of the show challenging to articulate on screen. It was a simple concept: We tell a crappy band they're about to perform before a group of big-time record execs—that this is their big break—and surprise!, there are no record execs, and this is not their big break at all, nope!, actually, their friends and family have all gathered together to tell them that their band gargles balls. That was pretty much the extent of it. But the show needed our joint attention because, well, Steve and I did everything better *as a team*. Our brand, such as it was, was built on our friendship, the power of our comedic back-and-forth and combined thinking. MTV had bought the show because they liked *us*—everyone around town liked *us*. *Seriously* was a Wieder/Sobel show—we'd conceived it together, sold it in the room together.

And now Wieder was checked the fuck out.

My penis is so small, so small, you couldn't even see it in a microscope. No, that's ridiculous, it's over six inches, above average. I should cut it off with this pair of scissors and be rid of it once and for all; it's as good as nonexistent anyway. That would be better, no, worse, no, better, no, worse. Stop, oh please Alan, just stop.

All day long.

Every morning I showed up to work, sat next to my producing partner, popped open my laptop, and did what I needed to do to prepare for the shoot. We signed off on call sheets, transportation plans, locations, budgets and revised budgets; hired producers, associate producers, sound guys, camera assists, that cute quirky craft services chick we always used who made the great low-carb breakfast burritos. We fiddled with the script over and over till it was just so, presented and re-presented our format to the network honchos till it was locked. We interviewed the band and their conspiring family members, then re-interviewed everybody on better cameras. Every hour or two I snuck away into whatever bathroom was nearby and measured my cock, and recorded the measurements on a secret page in my production notebook—6.4, 6.3, 6.1—and cursed myself, and felt my heart fill with self-loathing and dread, and drank straight whiskey from a flask I hid in my jacket to numb the thoughts that raged through my head like a poisoned river: *My penis is too small, too small, it just is.* We got through it—I got through it, somehow, one day at a time, just barely.

The halls of MTV positively crawled with attractive and overtly available young women who flirted with me hard, probably more out of professional interest than extracurricular. Their navel shirts and come-hither stares made me recoil from myself; their contact made me want to completely *disappear.*

How I hid my condition from my coworkers, a scattering of network bosses, and from my best friend most of all, I'm not certain. Either by dint of my superhuman ability to mask unceasing mental torment, or because people are generally oblivious to any unceasing mental torment other than their own, no one—not a damn soul—ever had any inkling what I was going through. Whom would I tell, to whom could

I open up about something as ridiculous and embarrassing as the fact that I was despairing over my perfectly acceptable dick? By this point I'd ruthlessly ignored my wife for four straight months, so calling her out of the blue to seek help with my sudden pathological penis panic was about as much an option as reaching out to the president of MTV. Ms. K and I, safe to say, had had our final heart-to-heart at Café Sushi. I had not yet met the shrink who would, months later, lead me out of this wilderness. My maman and dad, Stephanie, my mild-mannered suburban sister . . . there was just no way. That left only Steve, really, who, it seemed, had more than enough on his plate. Not only was he getting hitched in a couple months—a far more legitimate source of anxiety than mine—but whether he was aware of it or not, he was also carrying the lion's share of our production duties. I didn't want to dump the fact that I was possibly having a nervous breakdown on him, too, not now.

Forty-eight hours before our shoot, as we munched on take-in Daily Grill Chinese chicken salads and talked through the choreography of our Big Reveal, I decided to test the waters, just to hear if my problem sounded as absurd when vocalized as it did in my bollixed brain.

"Dude," I said, "lemme ask you something."

"Sure," Steve said.

"Have you ever worried about the size of your cock?"

"Nope," he said. "Just about the vaginas it's shreddin'."

"Seriously," I said, prompting Steve to put a finger to his lips and lean toward me with a facetiously sober "I'm listening" face.

"It's weird," I soft-pedaled. "Since leaving Sam, I just . . . I find myself thinking about it a lot. Ya know? Like, I'm not *that* worried about it, but I think about it a lot more than I used to."

"Do you have a small wiener?" Steve asked bluntly. "You're so tall, I always thought you had a real trouser snake down there."

"No . . . I mean, it's like six and a half?"

"Six and a half." 6.5. No, I pushed in, it's 6.3, 6.1, less, less. Did I push in? I pushed in, I totally pushed in, I need to remeasure. I will, not now, later.

"Well, fuckin' A, Wieder. Six and a *half*? You're *fine*. Let it go, bro. Chicks don't care about that shit. I gotta tell ya, I'm not sure if I even clear six, and I don't wanna know, truthfully."

"You don't want to know?"

"Nah. I've never had any complaints. Well, one, but she was a slutbag. And anyway, I'm getting married. Marita obviously thinks I got a big enough rod, so—at this point in life—does it really fuckin' matter?"

I left it at that. My best friend was getting married. He was getting okay with it, more okay by the day. He possibly had an underaverage cock and, as a married man, would no longer have cause to give it a second thought. I wanted to know more: When was his last measurement? By what method did he measure—along the side? the dorsal surface? from underneath?—and did he, heaven forbid, *push in!?* But to probe further would seem either vaguely gay or kinda creepy and probably both, so I dropped the subject.

With another good friend I'll call Scott, who'd once felt close enough to me to confide that he suffered from congenital depression and was currently taking a stiff daily dose of Lexapro, I felt comfortable enough in kind to have this conversation.

"Hey Scott, I was wondering: You told me you'd been clinically depressed . . . But have you ever suffered from obsessive thinking? Because I think I might be having a bout of it, and I'm not sure what to do."

"Are you kidding?" Scott said. "I *totally* have an obsessive thought disorder."

"Really?" I felt a surge of relief, because Scott also happened to be a wildly successful producer who owned a sweet (and quite well-decorated) house in Beverlywood and a new Benz and seemed to get laid a lot and, Lexapro-popping aside, have a generally pretty awesome life.

"Oh my God . . . I obsess about shit constantly, all the time," he said. "Like the other night, I was literally up at four in the morning and couldn't go back to sleep because I was worried I'd bought the wrong lawn furniture. I'd just spent like ten grand on these Lucca chaises and lounge chairs, and I was like, *Fuck,* I shoulda gone with the Knoll. And I just couldn't stop thinking about it, for *hours*: Lucca, Knoll, Lucca, Knoll, Lucca, Knoll."

"Wow," I said, deflating.

"What kind of stuff do you worry about?" he said, after a beat.

"You know . . . same kinda shit."

Scott was neurotic. Steve was neurotic. I, Alan, was fucked up, possibly psychotic, deeply OCDd, *crazy.* And there was no bigger drag, I could say from firsthand experience, than a crazy person, than someone who needed *help.*

What I was experiencing was incommunicable, not merely because of its all-consuming extremeness but also because, well, the origin of all my shame and implacable worry was itself absurd, silly, something you had no choice but to make light of. All dudes fret over their dicks, sure they do, but the large majority of them just make a joke about it and then move on to thinking about what chick to stick it in.

When another friend of mine saw my arm tattoos, he asked me: "Do you think your tattoo artist could design a drop shadow around my dick and balls, to make 'em look bigger?"

I laughed. He laughed. After all, what's a guy supposed to do? Worry about it all fucking day?

6.5

OKAY, FELLAS," our host said. "I'm gonna stop ya right there. That's enough, thanks. Could you please come off the stage? We're gonna have a little powwow."

Our power-pop trio of marks, the Summer Camp Rejects, were stunned and confused and aghast. They'd just taken the stage like the rock stars they believed they were on the brink of becoming, and torn into their earachingly awful single "Vicious Circle," which if they actually *knew* anything about punk rock they'd know that there's a pretty well-known (at least to me) I'd say '82 track *and* record by the same title by Indiana punk legends the Zero Boys—the band had just seized the stage and started rockin' out when, midway through their first song, we'd pulled the plug and left them standing there in front of their silenced rig going, *What the fuck???*

Then, just below the stage, a mosh pit of hired-audience extras parted like a biblical body of water, revealing behind them a neat Narcotics Anonymous-intervention-style circle of chairs filled by concerned-looking family members and close friends prepared to speak their minds. At the head of the "intervention circle" were three empty seats for the three offending band members the assembled had gathered to confront. In a comedic touch, in the center of the arrangement we'd set a crappy coffee table on which there sat an urn of fresh coffee, a box of Yum Yum donuts, and a Kleenex dispenser.

"Holy shit," the bassist, Dustin, said from the stage. "Is that my mom?"

"What's going on?" the singer/guitarist, Matt, said into the dead mike. "No fuckin' way, my sister, my *guitar teacher!?* What the—?"

Behind a large bank of monitors some distance from the stage—"Video Village," in production-speak—I was directing our multicamera coverage. The entire time I sat there my mind was ablaze with self-flagellating thoughts—*My penis is so small, no, average, no, below, it's worthless, I'm worthless, I want to cut it off and die, God just take me now, stop my heart, I'm ready*— but I managed to call cameras through the haze, which I suppose doesn't exactly speak to the difficulty of reality directing.

"Camera A, push in on Dustin's mom," I told my operator, trying to grab the live reaction of the bassist's mother, who'd traveled all the way from West Virginia to tell her son personally how concerned she was about his band's prospects, or lack thereof. "Tighter, tighter. Camera B, widen out and gimme a two-shot of Guitar Teacher and Mom together, wider, right there, yup . . ."

Steve rapped my shoulder gleefully as if to say, "Here we go, bro!"

Once the band had come offstage and taken their designated seats, our host, Sum 41 drummer Steve "Stevo" Jocz—whom the network had forced us to cast, despite my numerous vehement protests that he was unqualified to emcee our show because his band was arguably as shitty and derivative as the one he was about to deem unsalvagably sucky—continued with the Big Reveal over which Sobel and I had so labored. Unlike his musical output, Stevo's hosting skills weren't terrible.

"Guys, you've probably figured out by now that this is not your big break. This is an intervention," he said to the band. "We've gathered your closest family and friends this evening to let you know that, well, you guys have a serious problem."

First thing I noticed was that Damian, the band's beefy, shirtless, tatted-out drummer, looked like he was gonna jump out of his chair and punch someone in the teeth—namely the two executive producers who'd conned him into being a part of this stupid show, if he had any idea where to find us.

"Camera C, single on Damian," I said in Video Village, safely ensconced in a huddle of producers, engineers, and network brass. "Camera E, gimme another angle on 'em. Tighter, dude's superpissed, tighter."

But nobody was gonna punch nobody, I knew well from experience. *American Idol* had taught this generation that being at the center of any reality TV segment—even one designed to mock and humiliate them—would probably be good for business in the end.

"It's your music. It's your style. It's your stage presence," Stevo went on. "Bottom line, fellas: your band sucks. Seriously. And it's hurting you. And more importantly, it's hurting everybody in this room."

At this absurdly sentimental overture, which we'd modeled after the transcript of an actual NA intervention, everyone behind the monitors suppressed their laughter, not wanting to make our obvious ridicule of the band any more overt. The band nodded resignedly, seeming to accept that if their loved ones had gone to such lengths to confront them about their musical pursuits, maybe there was some truth to what they had to say—which, make no mistake, there *was*.

Stevo said: "All we ask is that you keep an open mind and listen to these people, because they wouldn't be here if they didn't care about you a great deal . . . and also dislike your band quite a bit as well. They've each put their concerns in the form of a personal letter. Grandma, why don't you start?"

The family members, starting with drummer Damian's seventy-six-year-old grandmother, each pulled out letters they'd written and rehearsed beforehand—further extending our drug-intervention conceit—and unleashed their torrent of heartfelt criticisms, which I edited in my head as we went.

"Damian, I don't want to see you working at Jamba Juice for the rest of your life," Grandma said. And the yuk-yuk we'd prepared for her: "Plus, your Good Charlotte-wannabe sound is, like, *so* two years ago."

"I agree with Grandma, son," Damian's pop said. "You've always been a very smart boy. . . . It's time to get a real job and start really thinking about your future, because one thing's for sure: the Summer Camp Rejects ain't it."

"You guys need to spend less time partyin' yer asses off, and more time practicin'," Guitar Teacher (himself a onetime member of a failed metal band) chipped in. "A helluva lot more."

"Matty, you need to stop smoking and take some *serious* voice lessons," the frontman's older sister said. "You're my brother and I love you to death, but you sound like Kermit the Frog with strep throat!"

"Damn, Sis, yer *killin'* me here," Matt replied.

As the family continued to lay into the band, the singer

shifted in his seat, smiling through his evident mortification. The bassist dropped his head in his hands in undisguised dismay. Drummer Damian, who took the biggest beating, got kinda lachrymose as he watched his dreams of rock stardom go up in smoke, not unlike the mushroom cloud tattooed on his shirtless chest.

"Thanks for sharing, everybody," Stevo capped off, when everyone had said their piece.

It was mean. It was funny. It was a total fucking train wreck. It was everything the show wanted to be—pure reality *gold*.

But I didn't give two shits about any of it, because I was too busy thinking about you-know-what.

"Camera C, stay on Damian," I said. "Push in, somebody push in, we got tears."

7.0

VEGAS WAS A DUMB IDEA, from the beginning to the end. A man named Finian, "Fin" for short, a kick-ass editor and an absolute party animal with whom Steve and I had worked on a bunch of projects, and whom we'd now hired to cut our pilot, got the urge the moment we finished our first cut.

"Let's fuckin' drive to Vegas right now," he said to me and Sobel as the DVD burner was finalizing the review copy we would send upstairs to our MTV execs.

It was the middle of the night, like 2 or 3 a.m. on a Thursday. If we left immediately, Fin proposed, we'd be able to reach the Strip by sunup, crash for a few hours, spend the day chillin' by the pool, and go from there. He had a crapload of Vegas hookups and could get us cheap rooms at THEhotel at Mandalay Bay, comped booze, and ins at all the clubs where

Steve and I had been turned away at the door on numerous previous Vegas visits.

It was actually a terrific idea in principle. We'd been working like dogs to get the first cut done before the weekend, had finished a day early, and now wouldn't get network notes till Monday at the earliest. Fin had just broken up with his longtime girlfriend, Myara, and was on a mission to do some damage. I was single, too, and, as far as anyone could tell, up for some good old-fashioned Vegas misbehavin'. As for Steve, well, he too thought the notion of a spur-of-the-moment Vegas trip was a no-brainer, even though he had no intention of even asking his fiancée if he could go.

"Fellas, I wish you the very best in your bacchanalian festivities," Steve said, assuming *I* was on board, which I guess I was. "But the future in-laws are coming to visit us this weekend and take us to a prewedding dinner, and I believe I'm expected to be present."

So we went, just Fin and I. We swung by our respective apartments in Hollywood, picked up a couple changes of clothes and grooming items, and set off in Fin's tricked-out black '05 Escalade.

"Let's bounce, homie," Fin said as I climbed in.

Though he was essentially a pasty-white film geek from Cape Cod, Fin was the editor's equivalent of a rock star. He'd gotten a rep in the unscripted world as a super-fast Avid cutter with a hyperkinetic style and natural musical ear, who could bring to even the lamest reality segment the spry movement and watchability of a movie trailer. It was simply amazing to watch his fingers balletically bang along the Avid's multicolored keyboard—fingers across which he'd tattooed the words "E-D-I-T L-I-F-E"—like some crazy electropunk percussionist. Only in his mid-twenties, he received daily offers to cut stuff and was making serious scrilla—more than me and Sobel combined—and he had the flashy tastes to match, from the Rollie he wore on his wrist, to the twenty-four-inch black Rozzi rims he'd just put on his gas-guzzling behemoth of a car.

The Escalade raced like a bullet train along the open I-15, windows down, blasting Death from Above 1979's *You're a Woman, I'm a Machine*—a little groovy for my tastes, but one of '05's more interesting records—over the bellowing night wind. Fin had the hood of his black Addict sweatshirt pulled over his head and one Winston cigarette after another dangling from his lips, not saying a word, his eyes focused miles down the deserted road, on *getting there.* In the noise-filled silence between us, I sipped Don Julio tequila from my flask, watched the miles of Mojave whip past, and, yes, thought about my cock.

We stopped only once, at a gnarly Arco station in Yermo, where I tried to measure my erection in a bathroom stall, but when I couldn't work up an adequate hard-on in that acutely malodorous and unseemly surrounding, I settled for measuring its flaccid length in a fully stretched state. And I mean *fully stretched.* I yanked and tugged my limp dick along the plastic ruler till the poor thing ached and stung and could be yanked and tugged no more. The result was 6.7, give or take a fraction of an inch, and resolved absolutely nothing.

And as we hit the surreally lit Strip, I wondered to myself, *Vegas? Now? What the fuck am I thinking???*

I guess I believed that subjecting myself to Sin City would be forcibly restorative, would somehow reset, by the overriding power of its sexcess, the fractured male psyche that had given rise to my bizarre penis anxiety. Vegas would impel me to think *with* my dick again rather than *about* it, would leave me no opening to do otherwise. *I would party it out of my system:* I'd drink and do a bunch of Ecstasy until my thoughts were quiet enough, then pick up some chick and take her up to my hotel room, and *force myself* to recognize that my cock is an instrument of pleasure, not self-assessment. I was becoming more and more depressed and had not the remotest urge to drink or drug or gamble or fuck or do anything Vegas-y, but I would do it anyway; I would beat my brain into submission and fucking conquer this thing once and for all, and return to Los Angeles my old self again.

Yeah, that plan didn't go so well.

Thank god the hotel had Wi-Fi access in the rooms, because the first thing I did after settling in was pop my Sony laptop and log on to a site on which I'd been spending a disturbing amount of time of late: Oh God, it hurts even to say it—I can't believe I'm telling you *any* of this shit—Cinemale.

Cinemale.com is a stupendously gay Web site that catalogues nude shots of male celebrities—essentially a Mr. Skin for dudes who'd rather look at famous penis than boobs and bush. The site boasts hundreds of full-frontal pix of male stars, and, well, I've seen every last one of 'em. This, now, was my new thing: *looking at dicks on the Internet*—quote unquote normal dicks, i.e., dicks not belonging to men who use them professionally.

You see, at some point during all this craziness it had dawned on me that the reason for my penile preoccupation was perhaps that I had a distorted mental image of what the majority of male members look like. Even though I'd been an athlete my entire life and had spent plenty of time in locker rooms, I'd always made a point of not really checking out other dudes' peckers. This meant that pretty much the only ones I'd seen had been the donkey schlongs of Anabolic, Vivid Video, mrchewsasianbeaver.com, and the like—hardly the healthiest frame of reference. So, as a corrective measure, I'd begun scanning the Web for pictures of regular joes' johnsons on yet another endless barrage of sites. By the time I went with Fin to Vegas I'd already looked at more cock than a gay urologist and was still going strong.

The funniest penis site I'd come across was Nobscan, on which users post scanned images of their comically scanner-lid-flattened cocks, à la the arse-in-the-photocopier office prank of yore. There was also the very dick-rich gay cult fave, www.ratemycock.com, which is essentially a "HOT or NOT" for dongs, where people can assign point values (according to a complex ratings system) to an endless concatenation of user-posted penises. And then there was perhaps the most repulsive of the bunch, The Soft-Hard Gallery, or SHaG, a site whose expressed mission is to prove that there's no predictable correlation between flaccid length and erect length, to show that on average, "growers" and "show-ers" wind up at the same absolute size. On SHaG, men of various dick sizes post JPG's of their penises in their completely flaccid states and beside them, by way of comparison, exact-same-angled photos of their cocks at full mast. Alongside these ickily candid images, the men also post their ages, height and weight stats, flaccid and erect lengths (typically measured from the side), and some brief personal comment about their puds—usually exposing their deep insecurities about it—to which the SHaG Webmaster always replies with a piece of helpful advice or encouragement. For example, with an anonymous six-five, twenty-one-year-old Londoner whose shriveled and extremely hirsute 3-incher grew to a very solid and statuesque 7.2, the WM had this exchange:

User: Hi. Great site. Keep it up (no pun intended!). I have had sex with five women, two of whom remarked that my cock was bigger than average. If I could choose my own cock size I would choose 9" length by 7" around.

W.M: You're already 2 inches above average! It's interesting how even men with big equipment sometimes wish for more. Maybe guys who have 4 or 5 inches should take note and realize that if they had your 7 inches, they, like you, might still wish for more! The wishes and anxieties men have regarding size do not follow any logic as far as I can see. I guess a little wishing can be harmless as long as you keep it in perspective.

But Cinemale—oh, *Cinemale*—offered a whole new level of immersion in cock. Celebrity penis lore was not totally unfamiliar to me when I happened upon the site. I'd of course already gotten intimately familiar with Fred Durst's dinger. I'd also heard some famous men, most notably Howard Stern and Eminem, publicly lament the small size of their dicks; and my hip-hop hero Cam'ron repeatedly boast (big surprise) about the proportions of his. There was that story I'd heard in college about F. Scott Fitzgerald: that he was so insecure about the size of his penis that he once asked his confidant Ernest Hemingway to retire with him to the toilet to inspect it, which Ernest did, telling Scotty (none too reassuringly) that his dick was "normal." Living in L.A., one could not avoid the rumors that Colin Farrell, George Clooney, David Duchovny, Bruce Willis, and others had earned places alongside the likes of "Uncle Milty" Berle and John Wayne on the "Hung Hollywood" list. I'd also recently come across a thing called The Penis Chart at the hard-rock fansite metalsludge.com—where women who've allegedly fucked famous rockers dish on the size of their tools, heh heh—and learned that even Gene Simmons was purportedly six inches tops. *Gene the Nazarene,* average!

But here, on Cinemale—*here* was living physical *proof,* in the form of good-quality nudie-shot movie screen grabs and paparazzi photos, of the endowments of various leading men—what, exactly, they were packin' beneath their $20-million-a-picture-perfect exteriors. My hope, of course, was that I'd find solace in the discovery that some of these famously studly and badass dudes had average or below-average packages; and it causes me no small amount of further embarrassment to say that I was so eager to browse Cinemale's extensive library that I actually forked over thirty-five bucks for a thirty-day membership—*twice.* But I more or less got my money's worth: to my shock and temporary relief, I found that a lot of male stars I admired had what appeared to be *even smaller penises than mine* (at least flaccid)! Antonio Banderas (who went full frontal in some Spanish flick early in his career), Viggo Mortensen (who dropped trou in *The Indian Runner*), the then newly minted Bond Daniel Craig (from the obscure 1998 biopic *Love Is the Devil*), Richard Gere, Sting, even Brad Pitt—all of them and many others, it seemed, were no better hung than Alan Wieder.

I would look at these images over and over, and then compare them to my own dick in the mirror, and put myself through the wringer in an effort to draw from this deranged exercise an antidotal dose of common sense: *Dude: Gérard fucking Depardieu has a smaller* bistouquette *than you do! He obviously made it work for him! You think he sat around feeling sorry for himself? No! He was too busy bangin' the shit out of Carole Bouquet! You, Alan, like 80 percent of the male population, have a comme ci, comme ça cock— c'est la vie! Nobody's perfect! Now snap the fuck out of it!!!*

I was several hours deep into my online penis gazing, intensely scrutinizing Cillian Murphy's limp mickey as it appears in the opening scene of *28 Days Later*—*bigger than mine, no, smaller, no, bigger, no, smaller*—when my cell buzzed. It was Fin, who was well rested from a siesta and ready to paint the town red. I had not yet slept a wink since arriving in Vegas and felt dizzy and nauseous, my eyeballs spiraling.

"Weedz!" Fin said when I picked up. "I'm at the Moorea Beach Club. I left your name at the door and just ordered you a mojito. Come fuck wit ya boy."

The Moorea was the European-style, meaning topless, private pool at the Mandalay Bay. I'd been there once before, as a guest of a hotshot DreamWorks exec friend. Being granted access to it meant not necessarily that you were a player, but that you knew *somebody*, even if it was just the towel boy.

Separated from the Mandalay's fake-beach mob scene by a tall, frosted glass wall, the Moorea is about as pristine an oasis as you can find in Vegas, a genuinely tranquil enclave where buoyant-breasted chicks bob around in the pool and lay about crisp daybeds, the drinks are strong and well mixed, and the whole scene seems to be on the brink of descending into a saturnalia of multihole copulation. Naturally, it would have been a fantastic place for me to pick up—that is, if I had a usable cock.

I took a shower and threw on some grey linen pants, a great-lookin' short-sleeve Thomas Pink button-up, and of course my Rolex. I wandered down through the casino toward the pool, grabbing a double Red Label along the way.

Everything was okay, and so not.

When I reached the Moorea Fin was sitting shirtless in a big puffy chaise, sipping an icy mojito with an even frostier chain around his neck, talking up a very cute stripper.

"Wuddup, Weedz," he said. He graciously took my empty

whiskey glass and swapped it with a drink that, it should be noted, was Hemingway's favorite.

"Yo."

"I was just tellin' Vanya here that we worked together on *My Big Fat Obnoxious Boss*," he said, referring to *Obnoxious Fiancé*'s underappreciated and quickly canceled sequel, another very mean show in which we'd fooled twelve unsuspecting business-people into competing for a position with a fake CEO at a fake corporation—essentially, *The Apprentice* as an extended prank.

"It was a very good show," Vanya said, with an obvious Russian accent. "Nobody watched it, but it was funny."

"Большое спасибо," I said to her, taking her cheap-French-tipped hand.

"Вы говорите?" she said.

"Я плхо говорю по-русскп," I said.

"Whoa whoa, cut that shit out," Fin said. "I been workin' hard here, professor. You can't just mosey over and fuck it all up just 'cuz you speak pinko."

Vanya laughed. "Where did you learn to speak Russian?" she said.

The truth was, Samantha had spent a year of high school living in Moscow as a foreign exchange student and had taught me fifteen or so phrases—which, it seemed, was more than enough.

"I don't really speak. My grandmother is from St. Petersberg," I said, which was true, too. "Her father was an advisor to the tsar."

"A rich kid, eh?" she said.

"*Nyet*. They lost everything in the революция. She lives in Paris now."

I still had it, my whole pseudococky bullshit rap. Inside, I was a raging mess, but that portion of my brain that knew how to charm women was somehow, I don't know how, still firing on all cylinders, still equipped—cursed, perhaps—to attract the very thing that now repulsed me to the core.

"Your friend would like my friend," Vanya said to Fin. "She is smart, graduate student at UNLV. She dances with me."

"Yeah, she sounds like his type," Fin said, shooting me a friendly but forceful "back the fuck off" look. Little did he know how little he had to worry about.

My penis is too small, too small, too small, too small.

No it isn't. Yes it is.

Vanya grabbed her teensy stripper-y handbag and abruptly stood up. I will make no attempt to describe her physique with paltry words. Behind her a VIP's view of the Mandalay's glittering gilded-windowed façade lent her a strangely angelic bearing.

"Okay, I gotta go to work," she said. "I'll see you boys later?"

"How do you say 'absofuckinglutely' in Ruski?" Fin said.

Vanya laughed again—ultimately, my pal had her in the bag—and strutted an imaginary stage out of there. *Da svidaniya.* Watching her go I felt another surge of disgust and dejection as I considered all the pretty things like Vanya that had drifted, seemingly forever, beyond my reach. I lay in a chaise beside Fin and stared at the sun through shut lids, my mind a seething ball of self-hate. I tried to shake it: I took a dip in the pool and swum a few vigorous laps, then ordered another mojito and sipped it in the Jacuzzi, losing hope in a hurry.

"Wanna shoot some guns before dinner?" Fin said when I got out of the pool.

"Sure."

In a few hours we got freshened up and drove to The Gun

Store on East Tropicana Avenue, a small building so cluttered with high-powered firearms that it has the feel of a weapons cache for some coming revolution. Our instructor, a heavy-goggled, no-nonsense ex-Nevada Highway Patrol cop, gave us a quick safety spiel and led us into the fray.

Now, for those of you who have ever been to a gun range and worried that the dude blamming the big 4-5 next to you might be a total fucking lunatic, here I stand as an alarming case in point. Except instead of a long-barreled revolver, this time the crazy man was toting an AK-47.

Fin and I decided to stick to full-auto, which neither of us had ever shot before. We bought two dozen paper targets and sampled the store's mind-blowing fleet: Colt M16 carbine, M249 Minimi, Uzi 9mm, MP40 "Schmeisser," M3A1 "Grease Gun," and finally the infamous Автомат Калашникова образца 1947 года.

The Diplomats young gun Hell "Ruger" Rell has a song called "Line of Fire," in which he rhapsodizes about the virtues of— and samples, very loudly—the death-dealing sounds issued by the different automatic weapons in his personal arsenal. It's perhaps the most visceral and murderous rap of its kind, but it offers no sense of the sheer merkage of these guns, their terrible coupling of speed and hostility.

I turned a paper bank robber and Adolf Hitler into a flurry of black-and-white confetti. Fin, a far better shot than I, surgically removed Osama bin Laden's humorless face with a precise blast of 5.45 mm's. At like a buck a bullet, plus rental fees, we were blowing change at a rate of about twenty bucks a second.

"Myara would be *soooo* mad if she knew I was doing this," Fin said, proudly retrieving his obliterated Osama from the target-pulley. "She *hates* guns."

Although my penis thoughts continued at roughly the same rapidfire rate as the weapons we gripped, I must say I felt a little better as I popped off those automatic rounds. The fact that I showed enough strength not to turn a rifle on myself and splatter my brains against the wall gave me confidence somehow, that I wasn't yet completely ballistic, that I might just shoot my way out of this.

"Hey, can we fire a bazooka?" Fin asked our instructor, who didn't seem too amused.

7.1

WE WERE AT THE SPEARMINT RHINO for all of two minutes before Fin tracked down Vanya by the bar off the main tipping stage and disappeared with her into a private cabana—"Later, homie"—the last I'd see of him till we drove back to L.A.

I was already drunk as shit—too tanked to focus on my dick or anything else, really. I ordered a neat triple bourbon and took a seat beside some other dudes off one of the go-go stages, where a dancer with tats and punky blonde dreads—ordinarily my favorite type—twisted and spun as beguilingly as she could in her small allotted surface area. I watched her, absently tossing crumpled singles onto her stage, trying desperately to *feel* something—in my pants, anywhere—as I descended into an alcoholic stupor reminiscent of Ben Sanderson, Nic Cage's suicide-by-booze-bent character in *Leaving Las Vegas.*

I was a sitting duck. A million and one girls came by to say hi, wiggle their thonged *tuchuses,* and coax a private dance out of me. I deflected them all—*no thanks, my penis is too small*—until—

"Alec?"

"Alan," I said.

"Hi, I'm Nicole. Vanya sent me over."

She was thin and quite tall, I'd say five-eight, with shoulder-length, ironed-straight red hair and a freckled smart face resembling a twenty-something Julianne Moore. She wore a black pleated miniskirt, some kinda intricate lace-up bodystocking thing, nipple-blocking suspenders, and a pair of square-framed hornrims. Vanya had said she was a grad student, and clearly the chick was running with the naughty-bookworm thing.

"Hi," I said.

"So . . . Vanya said you were a documentarian?"

"Um, not exactly. I produce reality shows."

"I'm sorry," she said, smiling.

"Alessandra Stanley over here."

"Ale-who?"

"Never mind. What do you like to watch?"

"I don't have a TV," she said. God, I hate it when people say that. "I read a lot. I'm getting my Ph.D. in anthropology."

"An anthro grad student with no TV. I take it popular culture isn't your primary area of research?"

"Clever boy. Let's switch glasses."

She tried mine, her eyes going all squinty. I tried hers: she was blind as a bat—just, I noted, like my wife.

"These are soooo wimpy," she said. "I can't see shit with these."

Hmm, I thought, *at least she wouldn't be able to see my dick.*

"I can't see shit with yours, either, Ms. Magoo."

"Hee," she said. She drew close as we reswapped eyeglass

frames, and I got a good whiff of that vanilla "eau de stripper" that even the more cultured dancers, it seemed, were required to slather on.

"So . . . what else do you like to do, Alan, aside from hang out at strip clubs?"

I dunno. Collect cereal toys. Jog. Measure my cock.

"I'm into punk rock and rap," I said. "And . . . uh . . . Native American ethnohistory."

"Really?" She got all excited.

"No. Not at all."

"Hee hee," came her cute li'l laugh. "You're kinda funny."

"*Kinda* funny?"

"No, you're just funny," she conceded.

"Whew!" I wiped my hand across my brow in a show of relief. "So Nicole . . . what do *you* like to do, aside from stick your nose in a book and hang out at strip clubs?"

"Lemme dance for you and I'll tell ya."

Oomph. Dance for me.

There seemed to be real chemistry between us, but at the end of the day the question was, was I gonna drop some dollas or what. It stopped me in my tracks. I'd just begun kibitzing with this woman and forgetting myself and, for a few minutes, *not thinking about my cock*—and now, through my boozy haze, the thought returned in a blitz: *My penis is too small. She'll feel it through my pants and laugh, she'll be able to tell instantly how small it is—she's a pro!—it's so small but no it's not, it's average, above, below, above, below—fuck, fuck, FUCK—*

"Okay," I said. "Lemme just get another drink—"

"Don't worry, I'll order you one, ya big alky. Come on."

She dragged me by my shirt collar to a curtained-off nook in a back room, where I blew two bills, then another two, on consecutive half-hour topless private dry-humps. As she grinded me and waved her big fake titties in my face I was vaguely sickened and hyperconscious of my penis, but I did manage to pop real wood (that is, an involuntary erection rather than one I'd manu- ally worked up for the purposes of measurement)—a fact which, devoid as I'd lately been of any sexual urge, I found immensely uplifting. Nicole said nothing of my size, good or bad, which I let slide, or tried to.

I'd caught her at the end of her shift, so we talked and drank in the private room for a while afterward. I asked her if Nicole was her real name and, if it was, why she used it instead of a stage name like "Ocean" or "Anastasia," like most Rhino girls. "It's my real name because I'm not ashamed of what I do," she said, after which there was a good five minutes of nebbishy "I didn't mean it that way" backtracking on my part, which she seemed to find endearing.

I asked her if she used the money she made stripping to fund anthropological expeditions to the Andes and shit like that.

"Not so much," she said. "I have two kids."

"Two kids! With a body like that—*two* kids! You should, like, write a fitness book or somethin'."

"You're so sweet," she said, tracing her pretty finger down the side of my face.

She had a three-year-old boy and a six-year-old daughter and was raising them on her own, she said, because Daddy sounded like a real scumnut.

"Want me to kick his ass for you?" I said. "I *am* a purple belt in Tae Kwon Do."

"Hee . . . Do you have a girlfriend?"

"Actually," I found myself saying, to my great surprise, "I'm kinda married."

"*Kinda* married?"

"No, I'm just married."

We laughed. "Well—truth is, we're separated right now," I added.

"Oh," she said. "I'm sorry."

I gave her the *Reader's Digest* version: I met my wife when we were basically kids. We fell madly in love. Things got very difficult in her life, and then, by extension, in mine. But we stuck through it, for a long time, and eventually got married— here in Vegas, of all places. And then, three years later, years of unmet expectations and unresolved hurt had caught up with us, and we—I—called it quits.

"I can't believe you were married downtown, like two miles from here," she said. She rubbed my leg either seductively or sympathetically, I couldn't tell which. "That must be so weird for you."

I hadn't really thought about it at all, truthfully, but when she put it that way, I supposed it did seem kinda strange. Less than three years before, Sam and I were married in Las Vegas. We'd been planning a whole big wedding in Florida—had even sent out two hundred "Save the Dates"—but then, when we realized we couldn't afford the kind of affair we wanted, we called the whole thing off and drove to Clark County on a moment's notice. We arrived at the courthouse at 11 p.m. on a Friday, an hour before closing; we exchanged loving vows in front of whatever clerk was on shift and signed the documents, with a security guard doubling as our witness and photographer. We exchanged rings made of aluminum foil and snapped pictures of each other holding up "Just Married" license plates; and then checked into a suite at the Venetian for three of the happiest nights of my life.

And now I was here, nine whiskeys in, spilling the story of that marriage's undoing to some stripper, who admittedly was the most thoughtful and higher-educated stripper I'd ever encountered.

"Can I ask your advice on something?" I said.

"Sure," she said.

"This is gonna sound totally strange. But I've been having this problem lately . . ."

I just spit it out: either because I'd just spent $600 on her and felt like she owed me one—or because I knew I'd never see her again—probably both—I told her all about the little psychological problem I'd been having with my cock, from Fred Durst to Gérard Depardieu.

"Well . . . you felt okay to me," she said. She held out her hand, with her fingers outspread, and indicated the length between the tip of her thumb and the tip of her middle finger. "As long as you're from about here . . . to here, you're solid."

I stared at the space between her two fingertips and tried to compare my own size. Bigger? Smaller? Bigger. Smaller. *I need to get to a bathroom—*

"Do you want me to just look at it and tell you?" she said.

"Um," I said.

"Pull down your pants. But do it quick, 'cause if my boss sees me my ass is grass."

I quickly yanked down my drawers. The way she'd been kinda snuggling up against me, I still had a pretty bouncy boner going.

"Whoa, easy, cowboy," she said.

"Well?"

She put on her thick academic specs and examined it. I felt like throwing up.

"Oh you're fine. Totally normal," she said, just as Hemingway had to Fitzgerald.

"Really?" I said, relieved, disappointed, confused, not believing her one bit.

"Really. But don't think I'm gonna fuck you now," she said. "You're married."

7.2

ON THE DRIVE HOME, Fin took it slow and talked a mile a minute. He'd spent the last forty-eight hours holed up in his room with Vanya and—rightfully, I supposed—was pretty fuckin' psyched about it.

"I think I might be in love with her," Fin said, after regaling me with every last detail of the fucking and sucking that had gone down. "I mean, she's like the *total opposite* of Myara—"

"A Russian-born Vegas stripper versus a bookish (albeit very sexy) freelance writer from Beverly Hills—yeah, I'd say."

"I know it's crazy. But holy shit, Weedz, you really have *no idea* how awesome that was. I mean, the things we *did* to each other . . ."

"That's great, dude," I said.

"We gotta go back next week!"

After my relatively pleasant experience with Nicole—and after her reassuring words about my penis—I suppose I should have felt a little better, on my way back to sanity. *A professional stripper looked right at my erect dick and told me it was okay. What more do you want, Alan? Fuck it, for the love of God, fuck it all to hell!*

But instead I felt like crawling into a hole and drinking myself to death.

My mind fulminated worse than ever with catastrophic thoughts about my penis, myself, my life such as it had become. A screaming hangover didn't help things. I stared into the open desert, hoping its unadulterated beauty could somehow cleanse my festering mind. I wanted to bolt into the sandy expanse and run and run until my breath ceased, and my tumbling dead body rotted in the sun.

That night, back at my apartment, I completely stopped sleeping—like, *really* stopped sleeping. For the rest of my story I will not sleep, not a nod, not a wink, other than via drugs or booze. I stayed up all night thinking about my dick, running numbers in my head, stats, conjectures I'd seen on Web sites of dubious authorship—6, 6.5, 5.8, 5.7, 6—getting nowhere and going absolutely fucking mad. I remember that I was reading *Moby-Dick* at the time—one of the few books I brought with me when I left my wife, because with her out of my life I'd finally have time to finish it!—and I lay in bed till all hours trying to make sense of Melville's minutely descriptive and massively metaphorical prose with my addled head, reading a page or two and then not having any inkling what I'd just read. All that stuck were the *sizes* of things—the "rather small" *Pequod,* the "fortress"-like Daggoo, the surpassing hugeness of the white whale.

Smaller, bigger, smaller, bigger.

*Moby fucking **Dick,** of all books to tackle right now.*

Sleepless day after day went by. I did not call my wife. I went to work a zombie and came home and drank on my sofa till I collapsed into a semiconscious waking nightmare of unshakable thoughts. I snuck into random bathrooms and measured and remeasured my cock. I stood naked in front of the mirror and stared and stared until, at wit's end, I pulled the mirror off the bathroom wall and stuck it in the closet. Then I took the mirror out of the closet, hung it back on the wall, and stared some more. I angrily snapped my rulers in half, threw them in the trash; then went to Staples and bought a whole new array.

I despised myself more than anyone in the world. I still could not bring myself to tell anyone what I was thinking and doing behind closed doors. It took all my wherewithal to think about anything *else*. If Steve or anyone noticed my somber expression and asked me whether I was okay, I just said that I was a little depressed, but fine. That seemed to deflect concern: of course I was depressed; my ten-year relationship had come undone. I knew that I probably needed the help of a therapist, that there must have been some subconscious root to all this that I could not unearth by myself. But all my perceivably normal life I'd never had the greatest opinion of psychotherapy. It just took so *long*, if it even worked at all. I'd gone to a shrink for eight months in my mid-twenties to treat recurring panic episodes, and the problem only worsened until I left his care and it went away seemingly on its own. *What's a therapist gonna tell me? That my cock is normal, that I have nothing to worry about or be ashamed of? I already know that, Doc. I'm well fucking aware of it, thanks.*

So I dove into self-help: Over the next weeks—in something of a last stand—I launched a bizarre and disorienting war against my glitched-up psyche. I became determined to fight this thing tooth and nail, as obsessively committed to defeating as I was to perpetuating it. My penile misapprehension was *foreign*, I decided, a temporary illness, a virulent pathogenic outsider. I believed that if I could eradicate it through some quick fix, I could recapture my otherwise sturdy self-image and resume my carefree bachelorhood as speedily as the affliction had come on. I held out hope—till the very last minute—that I would get on top of it, that I would make a speedy and full recovery and *win*.

I tried an array of self-healing techniques—some legitimate, some totally *farkakte*—enough to fill a whole 'nother book with my various trials and unremitting errors. I tried *everything*, anything that had even the slightest chance of magically lifting the shameful and paralyzing emotions surrounding my dingus. I haunted the self-improvement and psychology sections of various Borders and Barnes & Noble stores across Los Angeles, poring over every in-print pop-psych workbook on anxiety, obsessive thinking, obsessive-compulsive disorder, and body dysmorphic disorder. I read a half-dozen "Unleashing Her G-Spot"-type books, figuring that if maybe I acquired some special techniques for using my present cock I would somehow obviate my terrible longing for a bigger one. I tried three different kinds of yoga, somatic experiencing, neurolinguistic programming, biofeedback, and several other forms of mind-body healing. I paid $300 for an online anxiety cure called Change That's Right Now—a cultish, CD-based self-empowering program that promised freedom from all of one's worries within twenty-four hours and felt more than a little frighteningly Scientological. Eckhart Tolle's opening revelation in *The Power of Now*—that one afternoon he had an epiphany that cured him of a lifetime of misery—recharged my hope that I, too, could be freed from my mental disease through some miraculous insight that I just had to *find*. I ejected Cam'ron and Hell Rell from the car CD changer—not an easy thing for me to do—and put in Tara Brach's *Radical Acceptance* guided meditations (and, yes, rode around town in my gas-guzzling Porsche trying to induce a sudden state of enlightenment). I gobbled handfuls of L-Theanine, GABA, SAM-e, white chestnut, and a half-dozen other homeopathic "relaxants," none of which did a damn thing.

One Saturday I visited a world-famous "hypno-regressionist" in Santa Barbara to undergo a deep-memory process and, I hoped, expose some long-buried trauma that might have given rise to my strange obsession—and then spent the next three days processing his revelation that apparently, in a prior, fifteenth-century existence, I was responsible for killing hundreds of civilians in a Saint Bartholomew's Day-like public massacre. After much self-searching, and three successive $150 visits to that quack, I failed to make any epiphanic connection.

Jesus Christ, I even attended *an organized nudist BBQ*. Yup, I drove out to San Diego's Black's Beach—a famed illicit nudist hangout that the local police turn a blind eye to—and went publicly in the buff for the first time in my life. Hoping to root out my bodily shame via one liberating afternoon among free-ballin' naturists, I stripped off my shorts and boxers and joined a weekly picnic held by the Black's Beach Bares, a group of diehard clothing-optional beachgoers. I introduced myself to the saggy-sacced, bushy-vagged gathering, had a burger and a couple Corona Lights, and strutted my stuff as confidently as I could. *See, look at me, I have an average dick and I'm fine with it. Now toss me that muthafuckin' Frisbee.*

But nothing I tried worked. *Not a thing.* With every attempt to extinguish my illogical cognitions, they became only more malicious and debilitating. I found myself at a total loss, falling the fuck apart; weeks of failed attempts at self-assuagement had left me exhausted, hopeless, and as fixated as ever on my schmeckle. I felt that I would better cope with losing a limb, or a stroke, or terminal cancer—no joke.

And finally, at the apex of my vulnerability and suffering, I fell prey to that most dubious of sales pitches.

Yup: penis enlargement.

Penis enlargement—or, as it's known in the godforsaken community of males whose ranks I was about to enter, "P.E."

To the men reading this, I don't know if I'd say, "It can happen to you," but it sure as shit happened to me.

I bought it, and bought it hard.

8.0

WHAT I STILL THINK ABOUT—what still keeps me up at night and chills me to the bone—is how badly I could have fucked up my dick. I could have damaged it beyond all functionality, rendered it *truly* unusable, bloodless, dead to the world.

I did it to myself: no one but me. Following a regimen prescribed by a madman I rubbed, stretched, squeezed, tugged, twisted, and bent my penis till it was terrifyingly sore and my piss came out in a wobbly and painful trickle. Till its head was covered in strange purple spots that my comrades in P.E. advised me to ignore, calling them "just blood spots and nothing to worry about." Till the poor thing was raw and blistered, the veins at the surface thrombosed, taut and hard as guitar strings. Till I could barely get it up.

I came so fucking close.

Penis enlargement, I can now say from firsthand experience, is indeed a scam. I do not mean, however, that it doesn't work. I may give some vulnerable blokes the wrong impression by saying this, but the regimen I followed actually *did* make my dick almost an inch longer in eight weeks—believe it or not—and I do think that the man who created the program, though a ruthless opportunist and serious oddball, has a product that more or less lives up to its claims. What I mean is that penis enlargement is predicated on the fallacious idea that its potential physical and psychological rewards far outweigh its risks, that the life-changing gains in confidence and self-esteem yielded by P.E. are worth every penny and every painful pull. Actually, the exact opposite is true. The physical hazards of P.E. are immeasurable and the psychological upside so puny relative to the gruesome and soul-destroying work it requires.

Following the program I did, you can gain an inch if you really dedicate yourself to it, two inches if you're a bit of a lunatic, maybe more—along with likely irreparable neurological or vascular damage—if you're a total fucking nutbag. But if you're at all like me, you'll be no happier with your slightly bigger pong because the guy attached to it will feel even smaller and more worthless than he did before.

Here, then, is the reality: you *can* increase the size of your cock. Everybody says you can't, but you can. I did. But if you have a relatively normal-size penis (anywhere in the five-to-seven-inch range erect) and think you need to start a P.E. program of any kind, there is something terribly wrong with you. You are a sick, twisted fuck—take it from me—and need help pronto. Call me, Facebook me, e-mail, something—*let's talk*—but whatever you do, I beseech you: do not do what I did and start tuggin' maniacally on your pecker.

When I turned to P.E. I found that there were countless providers of goods and services but a surprisingly limited gamut of accepted options—none of which inspired much hope. And even with my remaining 4 percent of functioning brain, I somehow retained enough sense to steer clear of most of them. There's herbal pills and ointments, of course, which everybody knows don't do shit and which I especially knew—after my recent failed homeopathic trials—had about as much chance of growing my cock as I did of Scarlett Johansson magically appearing to suck it. I saved my dough. There's all sorts of *devices*—vacuum pumps, mechanical extenders, traction and hanging weight systems—sad, medieval-looking, and notoriously genital-mutilating contraptions with which, after considerable deliberation, I fortunately decided not to experiment. And then there's phallic-lengthening surgery, a fairly common but by no means routine or recommended procedure involving *severing the suspensory ligaments above the*—no fucking way.

But then there was what's known as *natural penis enlargement*. It was a newer and clearly more trusted trend in P.E. because it was *device- and surgery-free*. In fact, the sales approach of nearly every natural P.E. program is rooted in the open acknowledgment that pills and creams are bullshit and that pumps and surgery are provably hazardous—that, unlike its competitors, natural enlargement is "safe" and "effective," even "comfortable." The big hook of natural enlargement is that it involves little more than a series of seemingly simple "stretching exercises" and requires no implements other than those two with which every man's cock is already amply familiar: his front paws.

As a further selling point, natural P.E.'s repertoire of

exercises are all derived from a penis-lengthening technique, called jelqing, that the men of certain Arab cultures have purportedly been performing for thousands of years. Jelqing essentially consists of forming an "OK" sign with each hand and using them to stroke one's penis in a continuous, somewhat onanistic milking motion, repeatedly forcing blood from the base of the dinger to the tip. According to the supporting literature, this repetitive displacement of a larger-than-normal amount of blood into the penis' *corpus cavernosa* gradually increases the spongy cylinder's overall capacity and, in the process, also extends the ligaments, skin, and fibrous sheath, or *tunica albuginea,* that hold a dude's works together. What's more, the programs almost universally promise not only bigger but *better, healthier* boners too. Says the dime-a-dozen site www.massivemember.com:

> Our all-natural exercises help to actually break down the cell walls of the Corpus Cavernosa by forcing blood into the erectile tissue in a safe, controlled manner. Each time this is done, the cells are expanded beyond their normal limitations. The human body then repairs the cells, making them larger and stronger to withstand the increased flow of blood generated by the exercises . . . Over the course of a few weeks, the constant breakdown and rebuilding of cells within the Corpus Cavernosa equates to a noticeable increase in size of the penis.
>
> Using our specially developed exercises and techniques . . . will not only exercise and enlarge the penis, but will also improve overall blood circulation . . . , improve the strength and control of your ejaculations, and boost your sexual endurance so that you can last as long as you want.
>
> And best of all . . . It's completely risk-free!

Looking back on it now, the fact that I actually found promise in P.E.'s pseudomedical jargon and alleged ancient origins makes me laugh. But at the time, in my desperate and diminished mental state, P.E. truly seemed to be a wholesome and trustworthy pathway to a better cock and, concomitantly, life. *Hmm,* I thought. *These **natural** exercises, **these** might be worth a shot. "Stretching exercises"—what could be wrong with a little cock calisthenics, eh? For thousands of years, evidently, men of swarthy persuasions like me have been yanking their yogurt shooters according to this methodology. How can a practice so historic, virtually biblical, be at all dangerous? The penis is not a muscle, however, and can't be pumped up like a glute or a trap? Bah! A minor detail!*

The first site I joined was www.penishealth.com, which offered a 7-minute daily "workout" promising a longer and thicker winkie in a matter of weeks. Go to the site and you might see how a sad sliver of a man might fall for its dry and clinical-looking presentation, its caduceus-adorned site logo. PenisHealth prides itself on the fact that it's backed by "not just one, but *two* medical endorsements from professional, qualified doctors." *Not just one, but two:* the numbers instantly lodged themselves in my mind, alongside all the other figures that had obliterated my reason. *Not one, two.* "Both doctors were so impressed by our amazing program that they wanted to provide their full backing and support. This is what makes our program credible as well as *in*credible." It was a convincing-enough sell. True, upon closer inspection it turned out that one of the supporting doctors was merely a doctor of psychology, and the other had an unpronounceable name and, judging from his portrait, looked like he ran a small medical practice in Borat's home village, but I'm not gonna soft-pedal: I was snared; $49.95 later, I was downloading instructional clips from the site's member section and feeling like a fucking loser of the highest caliber.

But something about PenisHealth didn't instill confidence that it was *the* site that would furnish me with my new and improved wee-wee—insofar, of course, as *any* of these sites could offer such hope. PenisHealth's how-to videos were decently shot and lucid and well-organized. It's a fine product, for what it is. But such was my paralyzing self-doubt that I could no more accept that the site I'd just paid fifty bucks to join was satisfactory than I could settle on the length of an average cock, my own or otherwise. And no sooner had I become a member of PenisHealth than I was back on the Web searching for another alternative, evaluating every possible natural P.E. program in all of cyberspace, for hours and hours on end.

Then I came across a site run by a guy called Doublelongdaddy.

Doublelongdaddy, a.k.a. DLD, a.k.a. Mike Salvini, is a superskeezy dude from Massachusetts who claims to have doubled his penis size over a three-year period, from six and change to nearly *twelve* inches, through a five-phase regimen he personally designed and now sells through his pay site, www.MattersofSize. com. Salvini has become nothing short of a penis-enlargement guru and is an absolute marketing virtuoso. He also happens to be a self-professed agoraphobic obsessive-compulsive body-dysmorphic-disorder sufferer who measures his cock multiple times daily—a detail that at the time made me only further identify with him and his deranged crusade. "MoS" is by far the most impressive of online natural-P.E. destinations: a sprawling global community of over 100,000 members (including the now-inactive yours truly)—a veritable army of insecure wusses who have united to conquer their short, narrow, curved, or otherwise dissatisfying wangs.[1] When I came along in the Year of the Cock, DLD had just gotten some significant mainstream press—profiles in *Salon, Esquire, Wired*—and was about to distribute a glossy instructional DVD. He seemed to be as legitimate a figure in the super-shady world of P.E. as one could ever hope to find, the one guy who might actually devoutly believe in the bunk he hawks.

So I bought it. I forked over another fifty bucks and joined Matters of Size, figuring if this DLD guy lived up to only a fraction of his audacious sales pledge—*"2–4 inch gains in just ten minutes a day, or 200% of your money back!"*—it would be money well invested. With a heady mixture of delirious hope and grotesque shame, I logged on to the members area and surveyed the patented "5-phase program" that had supposedly transformed DLD's once-average pecker into a spunk cannon rivaling Captain Stabbin's. One thing DLD was surely not lying about was the *present* size of his cock: the guru himself demonstrates his techniques in the videos that guide you through the program—and his penis is absolutely *whopping*. Not only that, but it also bears a five-inch stretch mark along the undershaft—a scar that DLD is quick to flaunt as indisputable, if quite ghastly, proof of the biology-defying gains that you, too, will achieve if you follow his lead.

The jelqing-derived exercises in DLD's regimen are half-baked and gruesome-sounding, with decidedly visceral names like the "Bundled A-Stretch Blaster," "Girth Buster," "Supra Slammer," "Isolated Compression Squeeze," and "Slow Squash Jelq"—the latter being an intricate technique involv-

---

[1] It's worth noting that as far as I could tell, the vast majority of MoS's members had penises well within the average range of five to seven inches.

ing firmly clamping one's fully erect penis at the base with one hand, and pressing down hard on the cock—"squashing" it—with the other. And as I looked over the descriptions and clips of the various techniques I had visions of my dick turning purple and falling off within days, like in that classic Buddy Hackett bit.

But any misgivings I had were allayed once I visited the site's "Penis Enlargement Forum," where DLD's thousands of devotees gather to share "workout tips," post their gains, and chat with the man himself. It was terrifying, and deeply sad, and totally *irresistible:* There was a whole community of men of all ages, all over the world—too vast and numerous to be DLD's shills— all claiming to be lengthening and thickening their cocks with every vigorous daily workout, by an inch, an inch and a quarter, two, swearing by the program, praising DLD as a mad genius who'd changed their lives—and urging apprehensive newcomers, or "noobs," to stick to the program, and have faith, because it *works:*

> **Gimme9   Registered User   Join Date: May 2005**
> **Thread: Erections after p.e.**
>
> Hey all, I'm new to PE and am starting DLD's noob routine. But I have a question: A lot of people here are complaining about worse erection quality after PE, that it's harder to get erect and stay erect. Is this true?
>
> **tonsiljammer   Registered User   Join Date: May 2004**
> **RE: Erections after p.e.**
>
> hey Gimme9 i been doin PE hardcore for a little over a year and i would say my erections have been better and more frequent since i got on the program . . . also they last longer even after i bust my nut (all over my gf's tits, LOL).

Start May 4, 2004   As of June 18, 2005

BPEL 5.8 in   BPEL 6.6 in (7 here i come fuck yeah!)

NBPEL 5 in   NBPEL 5.8 in

FSL 5.5 in   FSL 6.3 in

EGMS 4.6 in   EG 5.2 in

FGMS 3.7 in²   FG 4 in

I CAN'T STOP I WON'T STOP I CAN'T STOP I WON'T STOP I CAN'T STOP I WON'T STOP!

I hear ya, bro. Neither can I.

SnakeCharmer99   Registered User   Join Date: Feb 2005 Thread: How long is TOO long?

What do y'all think is a realistic length goal for me, given my stats? I know girls can take a lot of girth (7+ from what I hear), but what is the ideal length? I want a length that will come close to bottoming out without actually bottoming out. What about guys like DLD—over 10"? Can they go balls deep? I have a few Lex Steele vids—he might be the biggest ever, and I haven't found one vid where the woman he's pounding can't take it all. I know I've got a ways to go to reach my goal but for now I'm just trying to decide what that goal should be.

Stats:

2/25/05 BPEL: 6 7/8" / EGMS: 5 1/2"

4/25/05 BPEL: 7 1/16" / EGMS: 5 1/2"

6/25/05 BPEL: 7 1/16" / EGMS: 5 1/2"

My goal is 8.25" NBPEL and 6.5" EGMS.

---

[2]BPEL, NBPEL, FSL, EGMS, FGMS: Abbreviations, commonly used in P.E., for "Bone-Pressed Erect Length," "Non-Bone-Pressed Erect Length," "Flaccid Stretched Length," "Erect Girth Mid-Shaft," and "Flaccid Girth Mid-Shaft."

My fat pad is currently 1.5" thick, so I guess I need to do some situps or something. LOL.

*ONE-POINT-FIVE inches of pubic-mound blubber? It's gonna take a little more than a few crunches to slim down **that** fat pad, lardo!*

DickNinja   Registered User   Join Date: March 2004
RE: How long is TOO long?

Wuddup SnakeCharmer. I would say with your stats you'll top out somewhere round 7 3/4"—8" in NBPEL, which is huge! No reason why if you stay on course and do some abwork to slim down that fat pad you won't hit that goal. Most women would find it difficult to take over 8 anyhoo. BTW I've got a couple of Lex videos and he doesn't go balls deep in any of em. Only a small % of chicks (nasty cum-dumpsters) would actually enjoy a cock that big.

Start (8th April '04):	Current (6th May '05):
BPFL - 3.7"	BPFL - 4.5"
FG - 3.75"	FG - 4.25"
BPEL - 6.5"	BPEL - 7.25"
EG - 4.5"	EG - 5"
	11.53% Total (Erect) Increase

Short Term Goal: 7.5" BPEL x 5.5" EGMS
Medium Term Goal: 8" BPEL x 5.5" EGMS
Long Term Goal: 9" BPEL x 6" EGMS

BPEL, NBPEL, FSL, EGMS, FG: Bone-Pressed Erect Length, Non-Bone-Pressed Erect Length, Flaccid Stretched Length, Erect Girth Mid-Shaft, Flaccid Girth . . . Another thing that drew me in was the exhaustive rigor of MoS's measuring practices. DLD's disciples are encouraged to counter (or perhaps embrace) the maddening ambiguity of penis size assessment—the impossibility of ever knowing the "correct" measuring technique—by sizing up their puds *every possible way:* soft, hard, soft-but-stretched (yow!), pushing into the fat pad ("bone-pressed") and not ("non-bone-pressed"), etcetera. It was an obsessive thinker's wet dream: here was a methodology that legitimized and codified the desire to *measure everything,* the repetitive urge to resolve doubts about one's measurements with endless further measurements. There were a few defined rules that kept a dude from spiraling into an all-out paralysis of wenus-analysis: members' members were to be measured without exception from the top or dorsal side; during fat-pad-inclusive measurements, one must be sure to push the ruler *all the way in,* till hitting the pubic bone; girth was to be taken at the penis's widest point, and so on. But the larger intent of MoS's measuring policies was clearly to perpetuate the anxious uncertainty of those men who would *never* be happy with what they discovered when they took out their rulers and took stock of their cocks, no matter how they did it or how many times they did.

Men, apparently, like me.

8.1

I CHOSE THE USERNAME "frenchfryguy" because I thought it sounded funny and affected an air of comic indifference— *Ha ha, I'm trying an online penis-enlargement program, what a gas!*—but there was hardly any irony to the fierce pummeling my cock was about to sustain.

No joke: I was actually *doing* this.

Having meticulously measured my dick according to the standard MoS parameters—and then remeasured it ten more times, just to be sure I'd done it correctly—and recorded the figures in a fresh notepad I'd bought specially for the purpose, I posted my first entry on the Penis Enlargement Forum on June 29, 2005:

> **frenchfryguy   Registered User   Join Date: June 2005**
> **New thread: Wuddup fellas**
>
> Hey fellas, I'm a 31-year-old in L.A. My pork sword and I are about to embark on DLD's noob routine. Starting stats below. Any advice for a nervous novice???
>
> *As of June 25, 2005*
> BPEL: 6.8" / NBPEL: 6.2"
> BPFSL: 6.5" / NBPFSL: 6.1"
> EGMS: 5" / FGMS: 3.3"

Within five minutes came a string of helpful replies from three of my new P.E. brethren, who clearly spent all fucking day logged on to this meshuga bulletin board:

> **peternorth   Gold Level Member   Join Date: Dec 2003**
> **RE: Wuddup fellas**
>
> hey fry-guy, decent starting stats! remember warm-ups and warm-downs keep your cock loose and the blood flowing and are key to avoiding blood clots. do at least 5 mins with a warm wet towel or heating pad before your routine, and after. get up earlier or go to bed later to give yourself the xtra time. welcome and stick with it!

MY GOAL: 9x6

"If you build it, she will cum."

cash-n-prizes Registered User   Join Date: Jan 2004
RE: Wuddup fellas

take it slow at first, french fry, tortoise and the hare . . .
remember what DLD says, "Size happens inch by inch."

2x6   Registered User   Join Date: Dec 2004
RE: Wuddup fellas

Welcome aboard frenchfryguy! Rock out with your
cock out!

I decided I wanted 7.5 in NBPEL, 8.25 in BPEL, and 5.25 in EGMS: a reasonable goal, I felt, given that I'd need only an inch and a quarter gain—of the up-to-4 in DLD's pledge—to hit it. *An inch and a quarter,* that was it. Despite my weeks of self-flagellation over my size, that was all I felt I needed, ultimately, to make my dick long enough to *stop thinking about it.*

7.5, I thought. *At 7.5, everything will be okay.*

Still, I knew that in the world of P.E., which deals in teensy-weensy fractions, adding a *whole inch* would be an enormous and perhaps impossible feat. Just think about it: as a percentage of my starting length, it would be a *16 percent increase* in a size that all good medical science firmly says is unchangeable to begin with. Even more daunting was the fact that there was absolutely no way of knowing how *long* it would take me to achieve my possibly quixotic gains. One of the more agonizing facts about P.E.—one of DLD's big points of emphasis—is that everyone responds to it differently. According to the stats of my fellow P.E.'ers, some dedicated practitioners could register a permanent—"cemented," in the lingo—one-inch gain in as quickly as six weeks, while others might grow a quarter-inch in six months, and others a few measly millimeters in a *year*.

Of course, if I thought about any of this for too long—about the sheer harebrainedness of penis enlargement, natural or otherwise—I plummeted into incapacitating dubiety and despair. And, rest assured, I thought about it a *fuckload*. But I also truly believed I had no other option and nothing, really, to lose. The only alternative was to accept the cock I had, to embrace indefinitely its punishing *lack*, to live and die in the inescapable little cell to which it had sentenced me. It was either that or pop a bunch of Seconals and dive off the Santa Monica Pier, which I can't say I totally ruled out.

And so, extreme odds and x-factors be damned, I dove headlong into MoS's program, my only hope. With a new set of figures swirling around in my head in a ferment of fuzzy logic—*6.25 to 7.5 inches in NBPEL, 8.25 inches in BPEL because my fat pad's 3/4 inch; if I can lose fifteen pounds I'll probably drop 1/4 inch or more from the fat pad and won't have to gain as much in NBPEL, maybe just an inch, less. From 6.25 to 7.5 inches, a difference of 1.25 inch, maybe less, that's nothing. That is, if I measured correctly. Did I measure correctly? Did I push in when I shouldn't have? I did. I didn't. I did. Fuck—* I began DLD's noob routine. My twice-daily ritual was this. Every morning before I went to work, and every night as I drank myself numb, I ran a hot bath, sat in it for about ten minutes to warm up my cock and balls and futilely attempt to relax, and performed the series of kooky yanks and two-fisted jelq maneuvers outlined in Phase One. I remember the regimen by heart: Firmly tug your flaccid shaft straight out and hold it there for thirty seconds, then out and to the left and hold for another thirty, then out and to the right; then twirl it in a rotary motion fifteen times like a helicopter propeller. Then tug it straight *up* for thirty, up and to the right, up and to the left, upward rotary. Then straight down, down and to the left, to the right, downward rotary. Pull it all the way back between the butt cheeks and hold for thirty seconds—that was a *really* weird one—left, hold, switch hands, right, hold. Repeat stretches three times, firmer each time, till you really feel the burn in the "ligs" at the base.

Then onto jelqs: 600 two-second lubricated reps with your cock 80 percent erect, followed by a five-minute hot-soak warm-down, 100 quick Kegel squeezes and then another 50 slow, till your PC muscle "screams."

The supposedly seven-to-ten-minute workout took more like thirty-five to complete, when you factored in the warm-up and warm-down time. It didn't feel terribly harmful—at first, anyway—but was staggeringly humiliating; and as I did it, I told myself over and over that it was ridiculous and grotesque, that my dick was *fine,* that I couldn't possibly be one of those piteous dupes out there trying some cockamamie online method to grow his penis. But after each workout was finished, I did actually feel *better,* hopeful, the mild euphoria borne of relieved compulsion.

My post-P.E. penis twitched and throbbed in the mirror, veiny and raw and flushed with blood: Fuller, stronger . . . *bigger?*

No. No.

For the next eight weeks—*eight weeks,* about which I remember almost nothing else—I stuck to DLD's program. I followed my master's prescription to a tee, my faith in him increasing with every new bulletin-board boast of miraculous gains. Salvini advised his students to cease measuring their penises daily, as the frustrating torpor of their growth could hurt their motivation, so I did. He recommended taking baby aspirin daily to thin the blood and reduce the risk of clotting, so I did. In week five, when the head of my penis became covered with scary red-purple dots and I posted my concerns about it on the Members Forum, DLD himself replied that the spots were merely from "small capillaries bursting" and would go away in twenty-four to forty-eight hours, don't worry, keep going—so I did. In week six, when two bloodless veins protruded along my shaft and stiffened—seemingly thrombosed—DLD again assuaged my worry: They're not veins, he said, they're only clotted lymphatic vessels. Take a brief break, keep your penis warm, and keep going. So I did.

I probably pulled on my pisser more during that two-month period than I had in all my previous twenty years of pretty regular meat beating. After my morning penis routine I'd go about my day, working with Steve, developing and pitching new reality show concepts, sitting in production meetings and editing rooms, lunching with colleagues, ignoring my wife, pretending I was happy and fine as I secretly counted down the hours till I could go back to my apartment and put my cock through the wringer again. At nights I drank alone in bars and drifted home shitty and tried to eat a little something but had no appetite, and got back in the bathtub to yank at my poor aching penis before I crawled into bed and tossed and turned till whatever bottle sitting by my bedside was nearly gone and I blacked out till morning.

And then—then—on the first morning of week nine, per DLD's instruction, "frenchfryguy" checked his progress and—with a Staedler 12-inch flexible architect's ruler—remeasured his erect penis.

Whoa whoa—

Did I push in? I did. No, no.

I measured again.

And again.

And again.

And again.

And again.

Holy shit.

My cock had grown! I mean, *really* grown—by seven-eighths of an inch! I was only a *half inch* from my goal—already! My penis was *bigger*—blistered and bruised and barely erect from eight weeks of maltreatment, but *BIGGER—by almost an INCH!* Science said no fucking way. Accepted medicine said no fucking way, urologically impossible. But after only eight weeks on DLD's program, there it was, indisputable mathematical *proof,* again and again. The program worked, dudes! It was the most repugnant and terrible and ignominious and reckless thing I could ever have done to myself, but holy fucking shit it fucking totally worked!!!

I immediately logged on to MoS and posted to the Members Forum:

frenchfryguy   Registered User   Join Date: June 2005
New thread: Two-month results

Fellas! My eight-week stats are in! My head (so to speak) is exploding with joy. Doublelongdaddy, you fucking rule!

As of June 29, 2005   *As of August 31, 2005*
BPEL: 6.8" / NBPEL: 6.2"   BPEL: 7.6" / NBPEL: 7.0"
BPFSL: 6.5" / NBPFSL: 6.1" BPFSL: 7.3" / NBPFSL: 6.9"
EGMS: 5" / FGMS: 3.3"   EGMS: 5" / FGMS: 3.3"

Lonelybone Registered User   Join Date: Jan 2005
RE: Two-month results

AWESOME!!! CONGRATS FRENCHFRYGUY!!! Hearing
that kinda shit is what keeps me going . . .

tonsiljammer   Registered User   Join Date: May 2004
RE: Two-month results

SICK gains, dude! Noobs, I hope you're reading this!

DLD   Diamond Member   Join Date: June 2003
RE: Two-month results

Niiiice! From shoestring fry to steak-cut! Keep up the good
work and move on to Phase Two!
-doublelongdaddy-
"Size Happens Inch by Inch."

Words can't capture the elation, the instantaneous restoration of all my previous cocksureness and ten times that. I felt a surge of relief and joy unlike anything I'd ever experienced. I was so happy I didn't know what to do with myself: I took a nice hot shower and drove to Arnie Morton's steakhouse and sat in a big empty booth, alone, and celebrated, treating myself to a $200 lunch. Then I hit the Coach & Horses happy hour, flirted up a storm, snagged a coupla chicks' numbers and even the unapproachably hot bartender Liza's e-mail address. I hopped in my 951 and got on the 10 West interstate shit-drunk and rode all the way to Malibu in the late afternoon, blasting Cassidy's *I'm A Hustla* album, with its infectious Swizzy title track. I took a six of Negra Modelo to Matador beach and lay in the sand staring at the sky till sun touched ocean, feeling like the world was once again my oyster. *Look out, muthafuckas, Wieder and his new-and-improved cock are, as the Dipset say, back in the buildin'!*

And as night came on, I got that *urge* that can be satisfied by only one thing. I called who else but my new comrade-in-arms, Fin.

"Dude," I said. "Let's drive to Vegas right now!"

"Um," Fin said glumly. "Sorry, homes, but I can't . . ."

"Why?"

"I kinda got back together with Myara," he said.

8.2

THE VERY NEXT MORNING, I woke up more fucked in the head than ever.

Oddly, though, I didn't give a shit about the size of my dick anymore—even though I hadn't yet hit my 7.5-inch goal. I lay in bed, waiting for the thought to kick in, as it always did two seconds after I opened my eyes—*My penis is too small, too small, too small*—but this time, nothing. I was good down there, it seemed, or fine, for the time being anyway. *My penis is okay. Am I okay? I'm okay. Good. Good!* In fact I could scarcely even *remember* being so worked up about my cock, why or how I could have been waylaid by something so patently silly.

But in the black hole that collapsed fixation had left, there came an irruption of thoughts that were far weirder, uglier—*crazier*.

Like a flash flood: My mind was suddenly inundated with what I can only describe as the twisted introspections of another, far more troubled and self-hating man, not me, no, not anyone I even recognized. It started with my hands: I looked down at them, held them up to the light, and they looked *differ-*

ent somehow: shorter, stubbier-fingered, thicker in the knuckles, weaker, backward, not like they were, *not right*. It occurred to me—no, I was suddenly, dreadfully, convinced that *they were not my hands*. Whose hands were they? *I can't use these, I can't type with these, I can't play guitar with these, I can't do anything with these—*

These are not my hands.

Then, as I stepped into the bathroom and gazed into the mirror, I was struck with another wave of dissociative doubt: *Is that my hair? No. I had much more hair yesterday, or did I have less?* More. Less. More. Less. Something's different. *What's different?*

Before the mirror I carefully inspected my hands, my hair, my hands, my hair, for an hour, two, more, immobilized by deepening psychosomatic confusion and disorientation. I could feel my mind and body *splitting apart,* the fissure between unleashing a torrent of mortifying thoughts. *I'm losing my hair, no, that's ridiculous, my hair's thicker than ever.* Pulling back the hairline, I had more hair: *Look how thick it is!* Releasing, less: *I'll be bald within a year. It's thicker. No, thinner. Different. My hands are different. Something's wrong with my hands!* Holding them out horizontally, my fingers seemed longer and leaner than before; vertically, shorter and fatter; against my chest, deformed, stumpy-nailed; against my thigh, substantial and tough, a man's fingers. Long, short, thick, stumpy, slender, strong, weak. Weak, thick, slender, strong, short, long, stumpy. My right hand looked smaller than the left, the left smaller than the right. No one self-perception stuck, and all of them seemed *equally unacceptable.* I dreaded the prospect of actually having to *use* my hands for anything, because I was mortally terrified that *they were not mine, that they would not work.*

I stripped off my boxer shorts and T-shirt and stood naked

in front of that pitiless glass, seized by white fear, surveying the whole length of me. My entire body felt fragmented and foreign, a heap of alien parts that had been attached to me as some sort of punitive measure, violently defective and *wrong*.

This body is not mine, no, it can't be: I'm perfect.

The hair on my head was wispy and evanescent, on my chest a barbaric thicket. My nose was craggy and gibbous, my stomach shapeless, my arms and legs spindly, a weakling's. My penis was terribly tiny now, a little baby's penis, not usable, worthless, incapable of giving a woman pleasure, me pleasure, nonexistent. I felt cold and sickly ashamed: *I'll never hold a woman again, never make love again, never be loved again, not with this body, no. I am repulsive, hideous, untouchable. My hair, my hands, my cock. My cock, my hands, my hair.* I felt that any one of my perceived somatic imperfections was enough to destroy me; I couldn't fathom how I or *anyone* with even a single flaw—let alone as many as I had—would be able to continue on, live life, be happy.

And then came the onrush of something, a funny feeling that had been shadowing me, it seemed now, my entire life, at once unknown and utterly familiar: *Death*. It came on not as a hollow apprehension or prenotion but a *certainty*, something that was *already here*, in my stomach, over my shoulder, in my head, in my blood: *I'm dying*, I thought, *I have Death running through me now. I'll be dead in days, a week, two max. There's no way I'm going to live through this, whatever this is. It's my time: I am going to die, and die soon.*

And then—then—a flood of *regrets*: strange, knifelike shards of remorse and shame over things that had happened months before, a year, ten years, twelve, twenty-five; and over some things that had never happened at all. Things that I'd forgotten completely or that hadn't crossed my mind in so long, things I thought I'd grown past or had never given a second thought. Out of nowhere I recalled this one time when I was maybe eight years old and I intentionally stepped on the head of a lizard, crushing it dead with a grisly pop; and I felt again the guilt and self-disgust I'd felt then, but now its resurgence was so devastating that I couldn't bear it. I remembered that camera op I'd let go three shows ago; he was cantankerous, something about him was disruptive and off and he questioned my decisions one too many times and I fired him on the spot, because I wanted to, because I could; and as he packed up his gear and walked off the set everyone could see that this grown man was crying. Where was he now? Did he ever work again? Did he go home that night and off himself—*because of me*? I remembered all the *lies* I'd told people in my life—to friends, family, countless reality cast members—most of them, as untruths go, so white, and there were not nearly enough to amount to any kind of disturbing pattern or pathology; but now even the most innocent of them seemed unpardonable, murderous. I remembered all my poor ex-girlfriends, the one who'd been raped and the one who cried in my arms incessantly and the cutter and the alcoholic and the bulimic and all the others I'd tried to help but had *let down*—and I remembered my wife, Sam, how I'd abandoned her after ten years without a warning or a hopeful word.

I thought, too, of all the times I'd felt happy, consciously *happy*—winning my first tennis tournament, falling in love for the first time in New York City, playing onstage in a punk-rock band, selling my first television show, that awesome road trip from Miami to New Orleans with the two cute Cuban girls before college—and I felt I *never deserved any of it*.

I thought of Sam's father's death, that I was somehow responsible; that when my own father died, it would be because of me.

I felt my mother dying, Steve dying, my wife dying, everybody in the world *dying*, right now, because of me, for my defects, for my sins.

What common sense remained tried to push through this tide of excruciating illogic: *These are just thoughts, Alan, empty ideations, distorted and unreal, errant and untrue. None of this is real.* Some part of me knew that it was all just noise, cognitive garbage, that it would fade eventually, that I wasn't nuts. I still maintained that there was some logical cause for what I was thinking and feeling, an identifiable incident at the root of it all that I could locate, unpack, disarm. Shit, there *had* to be! People—people who've led otherwise normal, relatively mentally healthy lives don't just wake up one day with their sanity deep-sixed, do they? There had to be a *reason* for this, and hence some rationale that would make all of it go away—if I could just *find* it, resolve it.

*I walked out on my wife, yes. Maybe I shouldn't have, probably not, certainly not the way I did. We could have tried counseling, as Steve had advised me to do, tried to work things out. Hadn't I owed her that much, in sickness and in health? Perhaps I'd held her responsible for things that weren't her fault; and perhaps she was more appreciative of me than I, for purely selfish reasons, wanted to recognize. I was her husband. I married her. It was immature of me to leave without proper cause or explanation. It was **wrong**, clearly. But—but was it, though? I was bitter and angry and had every right to be. Much of what had come between us was not her fault, but it wasn't mine either! I'd given her—no no, she'd **taken**—so much! I was her husband but, in the end, just a man. Just a man!*

A man who mistreats people for a living, arguably. Okay, maybe that was it. Bad karma, coming back to haunt me. I'd preyed on the frailties of people who just wanted to be on TV. In exchange for their fifteen minutes I'd handed them a big steaming pile of shit and asked them to eat it and tell me all about it afterward, in a clean sound bite that I could cut to time. No? No! Fuck that, no. These people were vain and willing to do anything for some screen time and lucky to have been cast on my shows. They signed the contracts. They knew the rules. I mean, come on, this was reality fucking TV!

What the fuck was it then, behind all this lunacy? What repressed memory or unrepented mistake had spilled forth from some mental recess to shove my life into the abyss?

I fell to the bathroom floor, a worthless pile of flesh and bones. I felt *so small*: a human speck with a heart like a ball bearing and a dick like a fleck of dust.

All I could think to do was crawl into a warm bath and exercise.

7.5, I thought. *At 7.5, everything will be okay.*

9.0

DRUGS. I NEEDED SOME DRUGS, PRONTO.

Pretty late in the game, I realize, I finally dragged my ass out on a Monday morning to see a psychiatrist. Through a friend, the doc had come highly recommended: a Harvard M.D. with a psychotherapeutically probing mind. But my hope was less to *talk* than to score some psychopharmacological magic bullet—a wonder drug that would miraculously spot-heal that one sick nerve center or fractured part of my psyche at the root of my madness.

I'd spent the whole weekend—and I mean the *whole* weekend—studying the available treatments for obsessive-compulsive disorder. Of course, no one other than I had actually officially *diagnosed* me with OCD, but I had it—distressing recurrent thoughts, neutralizing rituals, an awareness that my cognitions were warped—I was *sure* of it. There were two basic approaches to treating my condition: cognitive behavioral therapy, a therapist-guided technique that involved cultivating the patient's ability to replace his unwanted and obsessive thoughts with more benign and supportive ones; and drug therapy, the use of selective serotonin reuptake inhibitors, or SSRIs—Prozac, Paxil, Zoloft, and the like—to boost serotonin's effect in the brain and, in so doing, cool your monomaniacal thoughts and mellow you the fuck out.

Yeah, yeah, those. Gimme some of those.

It's worth noting that, during my highly amateurish online medical research, I also came across the notorious NSFW full-frontal shots of Jude Law—caught in the buff by paparazzi while changing into a bathing suit at his mother's house in Vaudelnay, France—that were bouncing around many an e-mail box in August 2005. Jude's cock, it turned out, was no great shakes—and because he'd recently incurred much public contempt by porking his nanny behind Sienna Miller's back, the tabs and gossip blogs were now having a field day with the exposure of Jude's rather modest fish 'n' chips. THE WORLD LAUGHS AT JUDE LAW'S NANNY-POKING STICK, read *Defamer*'s top-story headline. The *New York Post* went with NUDE JUDE'S NOT A HUGE ISSUE. The *Superficial* eschewed all wordplay and went for the jugular: JUDE LAW HAS A SMALL PENIS.

But it gave me little Schadenfreude to see Jude's spotted dick (English food reference) become the butt of such vituperative ridicule. Truth was, Jude was about the same size flaccid as yours truly. I maybe had him beat by a half inch in length, tops. As for girth—well, dude had some serious hoodage, so it was a tough call . . .

But *anyway:* I didn't think getting pills would be a problem.

I *needed* them, after all. I was a mess, obviously, borderline non-functional, ten times more fucked up than anyone I knew on meds. I'd barely eaten in two weeks, lost fifteen pounds, and hadn't had a dry night's sleep in months. The guy would put me on *something:* All psychiatrists do is write scripts, right? They talk to you for a few minutes—*Are you sleeping? Depressed? Feeling suicidal?*—and boom, here ya go, here's a six-week supply of Lexapro, Wellbutrin, here are some samples, and we'll up the dose if it ain't doing the trick.

On the drive out to the headshrinker's Brentwood office I must have checked my hair in the rearview a hundred times. I looked into the mirror: *More hair than I had previously.* Back down at the road and up again at the glass: *Less hair.* On the steering wheel my hands were longer, shorter, fatter, thinner, tougher, weaker than they were the last time I'd checked.

Dr. Goodson was tall and preppy and had a telegenic office of quintessentially midcentury decor: Milo Baughman desk, clean slat shelves lined with psychology tomes and other books, and a gorgeous Kagan sofa on which I slumped, staring at him, not knowing where to begin.

"So what's going on?" he said.

Oh boy.

It took me an hour fifteen to get through it all: my relationship history, my abrupt departure, my brief dating period, my dick, my dick stretches, my insomnia, my repetitive thoughts of self-annihilation, my complete mind-body brainlock.

"Hmmm," Dr. Goodson said. "Interesting."

Glad I'm so interesting to you, Doc. How nice. You can write all about me in your next article in the American Journal of Psychiatry. *Now gimme some fuckin' drugs, bitch!*

I said, "I've been reading a lot about OCD, and—"

259

"I don't think it's that," he stopped me, all like, *I'm the one doing the evaluating here, bub*.

"Well what is it then?"

"I'm not certain," he said. "Have you ever been alone before, living by yourself?"

"Not really. I met my wife in my last year of college. We got pretty serious right away and . . . I guess we've pretty much been living together ever since."

"Do you miss her?"

"Since I've been sick I have . . . like, I *need* her—like, there's no one else in the world I could turn to right now. But not because I want to *be* with her."

"You're angry," he said. "I can feel it from here."

Never was I more aware of how fucking uncomfortable beautiful furniture is.

"I am angry, yes. But it doesn't *feel* like it. I mean, most guys get angry and toss furniture or step out into traffic and bash someone's headlight, or start a bar brawl, *something*. How does anger drive me to measure my dick thirty times a day or believe my hands are someone else's?"

"The bodily fragmentation is highly unusual, but the underlying problematic is quite common," he said. "It's a loss of selfhood: a lack of a conception of yourself as a whole person, a man. The penis—well, all guys fret over that to varying degrees. The hands are an extension of your penis. They're metaphors for a larger issue of inadequate self-identity. Without Sam you are less of a person, even if when you were with her you felt like you were *more* of a person than she. Realizing this, consciously or unconsciously, can make someone very frustrated and angry. Do you understand what I mean?"

I did, intellectually. I thought of Jacques Lacan's mirror

phase—the theory I'd studied in one of my college critical stud-ies classes, which posits that a prelinguistic baby, at some point between six and eighteen months, will see his reflection in the mirror and be hurtled into an identity-shattering crisis of mis-recognition before emerging from the bits and pieces of this *méconnaissance* as an integrated whole. But I was long past my eighteenth month of life, and Dr. Goodson seemed to have had enough of my self-analysis for one day.

"Sure," I said.

"We're out of time," he said. "I'd like to see you again in a couple days."

He took out an Rx pad and began scribbling. I perked up.

"For now I'm going to write you a prescription for Xanax, just to help you sleep."

"No Lexapro?" I said, bummed.

"No."

"Celebrex?"

"Only if you have arthritis." Dr. Goodson smiled. "I think you mean Celexa, and sorry, Alan, no. I don't think anti-depressants will do much for you right now, frankly. Plus the suicidal and morbid thoughts will only worsen with SSRIs. Get some sleep. Force yourself to do everything you liked to do before you felt yourself slipping away. And stop with the mea-surements, and the dick exercises, and everything else. Just *stop*—doctor's orders. The thoughts are only reinforced by the behaviors."

I took his script and sat back in the sofa, terrified to leave.

"I also want you to try an exercise," he said. "You're a writer, right? I want you to take a piece of paper and divide it into two columns. On the left, write down your automatic thoughts exactly as they sound in your mind: 'My penis is too small,' what have you. Then, on the right side, write a rational response to each thought, one that corrects the distortion: 'My penis is well within the average range, and while some girls might prefer a bigger penis, the size of my penis will not in any way prevent me from having a perfectly satisfying sex life.' Got it?"

"Great, just what I need, more exercises," I said.

"You're going to be fine, Alan," he said. "Really."

Well it sure as shit didn't feel like it. I filled my Xanax prescription that afternoon, trying to be hopeful about the prospect of working through my thoughts and feelings, bringing my relationship to a more harmonious close, learning to live with the things about myself I didn't like and couldn't change. The pills did help me sleep, and eat, and function, and get by: I gobbled up the twenty-day supply in about four, and then was back to hard booze and a batch of Percocet I swiped from Steve's medicine cabinet till I could get the blue footballs refilled.

It was such a strange time. Steve and I had turned in our finished pilot to MTV and were between projects; our production deal at Fremantle was such that we got paid whether we showed up at the offices or not, so for a few weeks we didn't. Steve used the time to make final preparations for his wedding and disappear to Hawaii with the wife-to-be. And I wandered Los Angeles in a wilderness, drinking, popping pills, every corner of my mind colonized by unsettling ideas, becoming more unglued by the day.

I really tried to get well. I made the effort. I stepped up my yoga practice and Zen-meditated twice a day. I reread Tara Brach's *Radical Acceptance* and Dr. David Burns's *Ten Days to Self-Esteem* and Larry Rosenberg's *Living in the Light of Death*.

I forced myself to see friends and movies and concerts and do what the doctor said. I completely stopped measuring and stretching and even touching my dick for any other purpose than to wash it or take a piss, which was just *torture*. I saw Dr. Goodson again, and again, and again—opening up about my family and my marriage and my anxious sexuality, uncovering things, making connections—and actually did his stupid double-column thought chart religiously. I found myself entirely capable of writing eloquent, well-reasoned responses to my internal critic's illogical aspersions: "My hands are the same hands I've always had. They're probably on the small and pudgy side for my height, but they're quite masculine and not unsightly in any way, and have certainly never interfered with my sexual pursuits." I was able to say, *Fuck you, mind, I'm way stronger than you, way smarter than you: I don't accept you; I will work through you. Bring it on.*

But none of it really mattered, when even a glimpse of my naked body in the mirror made me want to die.

I was working hard on myself but not feeling a lick better. My mind boiled over with harrowing images and ideas. I totally dropped off the map. People called—Steve, Chris, my mom and dad, the studio VP Steve and I reported to—wondering where I was, if I was okay, they hadn't heard from me in a bit; I was home with a really bad flu, I said, and would be back on my feet in a week or two. But I was already catastrophizing. The doctor and I had only just scratched the surface. This affliction of mine, whatever it was called, would take months—maybe *years*—to sort out. We'd talked about the importance of *numbers* in my life, the various ways in which my worth had been statistically assessed: the numerous aptitude tests I took as a very young boy, when my parents were convinced I was a genius; my constantly fluctuating state tennis ranking, 19, 30, 41, 23; my all-important precollegiate percentiles. And size, too, particularly the close attention my family had paid to my *bodily* proportions: their neurotic worry about my preteen chubbiness, and then their marvel at a high-school growth spurt that my dad proudly charted on the back of my bedroom door—5'7", 5'9", 6'2", 6'3", 6'4".

We'd also touched on my father's hypochondria—his compulsive need for exercise and constant unnecessary dieting, his tendency to assign pathological labels to his everyday aches and pains: His heart didn't flutter; he had an *atrial fibrillation, bradycardia, ectopic beats,* something else he'd pulled from his medical dictionary. His shoulder didn't just hurt; the MRI showed *adhesive capsulitis,* a *herniated disc.* By all appearances Dad was a hale and fit man—in better shape than probably all my friends' fathers—but in his own eyes he was ailing and decrepit and could drop dead at any moment.

And yes, my mother was also an overprotective worrywart, loving and responsible but *proper* as hell—*French,* after all. Steve always remembered my home as a place of rigid order, a minefield of heirlooms and antiques where he'd been constantly afraid he might break something and incur Mom's wrath.

And yes, Samantha was in many ways like my mother: punctilious, and consummately tasteful, and *measured.* And now that I thought about it my father was also obsessed with cocks—he repeatedly joked, "You've got a huge dong, just like your old man, right, son?"—and hands, too. Dad would put his hand up against mine a hundred times to see whose was bigger—'bout the same—

Point being, there was *stuff* there. No, I wasn't emotionally or physically abused, I wasn't neglected, my family wasn't terribly dysfunctional—but there was perhaps enough of a history there to create a logical framework for my shattered state of mind. But Dr. Goodson and I were only just beginning our work. This was a *process*; it would be God knew how long before I felt well enough to go to work, interact with people, resume a normal life. In the meantime I would be exposed as a madman and professionally disgraced and Steve—*oh, Steve, old pal, I'm sorry, you bet on the wrong horse.* I was as good as broke, homeless, asking my parents to let me come home to Florida for a few months, my mom to cook me dinner, sitting on the couch afterward with the two of them eating sugar-free ice cream pops every night, watching *Anderson Cooper 360°*, a bloody fucking invalid, because it was either that or move back in with my wife, which I would *never, ever* do. *Neverrrrr* . . .

9.1

THE IDEA OF PLANNING Steve's bachelor party made me want to prepare a final cocktail of bleach and ammonia and end it all.

But it was also the very thing that kept me from doing it.

The party was so much *work,* more than I felt capable of taking on. I'd reached a point where it required all my strength and concentration just to take a shower or boil an egg. How I would now coordinate a *twelve-man prewedding excursion*—how I would handle the umpteen phone calls and e-mails back and forth, booking restaurants and activities and so-long-single-life surprises—I had no fucking idea. Who knew that after the dozen million-dollar-an-episode spectacles I'd produced without

breaking a sweat, this little party, a weekend of organized silli-
ness and male abandon and *fun,* would be the event that finally
did me in.

But the party was also my undeniable *responsibility*—that
thing with which I could cope so instinctually, for which I had
an inexhaustible reserve of energy and focus. My sense of duty
toward my friend, even in—perhaps *especially* in—the face of
my reckless self-disregard was enough, thank God, to keep my
mind on the task at hand. I was Steve's best friend and business
partner and best man by leagues. He was *counting* on me—the
only person in the world, it seemed, who still was—and fuck if
I was gonna bail on him now. If I was going to kill myself—and
I couldn't say for sure that I wasn't—it would have to wait till
a few days after his *I do*s, till the poor guy was on some island
somewhere on his honeymoon, far removed, for a few weeks
anyway, from the terrible news that would befall those few remaining people who loved me.

As for the event itself: Steve had made it clear that he didn't
want a big, besotted affair in Vegas with a platoon of strippers
who would tie him to a chair and fuck each other with beer bottles and double-headed dildos. Like, he *really really* didn't want
that; he wasn't merely saying so to exonerate himself of any
filthy activities that he secretly hoped his buddies were plotting
behind his back. "No strippers, dude," he said to me. "Please,
I'm serious, *don't.*" It was an odd thing for him to insist upon,
because if there ever was a man who you'd think *would* want
that type of premarital shebang, it was my congenitally pervy
pal Steve. But his reluctance to have the customary debauch-
erous dudefest had nothing to do with his wanting to avoid
any eleventh-hour guilt-inducing slipup or fresh-titty-inducing
case of cold feet. On the contrary: He was just happy, finally

happy, to be getting married and was, well, just not interested in all that stuff. He had nothing to get out of his system, no final thong-removal-with-his-teeth or jeans-creaming lap dance. He was headed into marriage desiring nothing more than the chance—gay as it sounds—to share his last moments of bachelorhood with a few close buddies.

What Steve specifically had in mind was a weekend getaway in a cabin on Big Bear Lake, in the mountains east of L.A.: steaks on the grill, cigars, a couple bottles of Johnnie Walker Blue, maybe a fishing trip after which we would cook our day's catch. It came as a shock to the invitees: not only a night with no boobies and beaver, but a *whole weekend?* Some were simply incredulous: "Sobel doesn't want strippers? Yeah right, Wieder," one of Steve's longtime buds e-mailed me back. "What kind of insanity are you *really* planning?"

I put on my producing hat and put the event together. Bright and early on a Saturday the whole gang met for breakfast, at Du-par's Restaurant on Ventura Boulevard in the Valley, and hit the road in a small cavalcade of cars. A race began on the 10 East freeway, with Steve and me—in the brand-new '05 Mustang GT he'd bought himself as a prewedding gift—quickly seizing the lead and holding it till we hit the 330 North through Running Springs—when Marc came out of nowhere and took us in his sweet SLK, giving us the finger as he zipped past.

"Motherfucker!" Steve shouted, having the time of his life.

By midday everyone had arrived at the cabin I'd rented and was drinking himself senseless. On good stuff, too: I'd gone all-out on the booze: bottles of Johnnie Blue and Dalwhinnie 15-Year, Rémy XO, Don Eduardo Silver tequila, and—best of all—a fridgeful of big-mouth bottles of Mickey's malt liquor. There were also good smokes: a humidored assortment of Romeo y Julieta Viejos, Cusano 18s, Don Diego preludes, one small-batch Vegas Miami for Sobel, and a big bag of blue kush. And while everyone by this point was quite convinced that there would, in fact, be no late-night skankery—unless we made a spur-of-the-moment decision to scrounge up some local gals from whatever seedy strip club was in the vicinity—the guys couldn't help but marvel at the five-bedroom cabin's many amenities: gas grill, Ping Pong and foosball tables, Jacuzzi, satellite big-screen and DVD player, even an impressive collection of air rifles. Not to mention, one of Steve's dear friends, who has asked to remain unnamed, had the good sense to bring along his disturbingly comprehensive collection of *Barely Legal* DVDs.

I'd produced our location perfectly, no doubt—shit, even *I* couldn't help but take my triple Dalwhinnie onto the back porch, take a seat on the steps overlooking the lake, and forget for a moment that my penis was microbial, my hands and hair hideous, my life a complete shambles.

In the later afternoon we went out on a fifteen-foot pontoon and didn't so much catch as effortlessly reel in a bunch of bass and rainbow trout that our guide had trolled. Upon our return the boys dispersed to drink and smoke up on the upper-level balcony and bat around Ping Pong balls and shoot air guns and watch porno. Steve and I were put in charge of the grill.

We stood out in the yard trying to figure out how to turn the gas on, fat, smoking Dominicans between our teeth.

"You having a good time?" I said.

"Dude, the *best*," he said. "*Exactly* what I wanted. You think everyone's having fun, though? I mean, I guess in hindsight a coupla naked sluts woulda been no big deal."

"It's not too late. Vegas is only four or five hours away. I gotta coupla Spearmint girls I can call."

I sipped my Dalwhinnie, wishing that were the slightest bit true. I spotted my fingers on my glass: *Not my hands.*

"I'm sure you do," he said. "Ah-*ha,* here we go——"

He figured out that the gas cylinder's valve wasn't connected to the grill. He hooked up a tube to the manifold, fiddled with some knobs, turned a dial, and——

"Boom," he said, very proud of himself, as rows of clear blue flame appeared beneath the grill plate. "Blue flames are good. Means the gas is burning hot and cleanly. If the flame's too yellow it means that not enough air is mixing with the gas as it enters the burner."

"Good to know . . . Dad," I said.

"*Feh,* what do you know about BBQing," he said. "You and Sam used a Smokey fuckin' Joe."

He spatulaed some gunk off the grill surface, puffed his cigar, and stared up at the reddening sky above the lake.

I segued into my obligatory Best Man Check-In. "So . . . How ya feelin' about the whole marriage thing? Last-minute jitters?"

"Ya know, Al? I'm feeling pretty fucking good." He choked a little on the smoke. "I never woulda thought so, but here I am, not flippin' at *all.* I still got a month to go, though, so we'll see . . ."

"Bah."

He laid the fish filets our guide had expertly skinned and deboned on the hot grill. The tender meat smoked and popped.

"I mean, who am I kiddin', right?" he went on. "I can kick and scream all I want, but, in the end, I know I'm not going anywhere. What am I gonna do, leave Marita and start over now, get another bachelor pad, start chasin' strange? Oy. That's the *last* thing I wanna do. I mean, it's different for you, Al. You *enjoy* going to bars and talkin' to bimbos and . . . playing the game."

"Right," I said. "Right."

"But for me, marriage is a *relief*. I gotta tell ya, I'm kinda *tired* of chicks . . . Especially L.A. chicks. Every girl you even *look at* in this town thinks you want to bang her. They all give you this *attitude,* like, 'I know you wanna fuck me. I know you want my pussy.' Now I can show 'em my wedding ring and be all like, 'You know what, bitch? I already *got* a pussy. And I fucked it so good she's keepin' me around forever!'"

Now *I* was hacking up smoke. "That's fuckin' funny."

"Yeah? Think there's a bit there?" He made a mental addition to the tight-five that he was constantly refining in his head.

Sobel was clearly over-justifying to save face; he and I knew that his premarital panic and muddlement had long dissipated. His wedding venue was booked, invitations mass-mailed, cake-icing flavor decided upon—and, after all his moaning and groaning, my friend was totally psyched to be marrying his longtime girlfriend. He'd recognized—with 98.7 percent certainty—that he and Marita were inextricably bound, that he cherished her and needed her, that it was time to grow up, start a family and open an IRA, swallow the idea that he was going to get old one day and that it'd be better to do it alongside a woman he loved, a wife. And his acceptance of these facts had come not with self-pity or resignation but rather a true wisdom and sanguineness that I, in my now-hapless state, envied profoundly. Where before I'd sneered at Steve's garden-variety suffering, basked in my sudden freedom from marriage, its vexations and vapid woes, now I wished I had the courage to share his average-guy aspirations, his ability to embrace—

and even find the humor in—*reality*, the hand it had dealt him for better or for worse, marriage, family, age, sickness, death.

I'd wager some serious dough that I had the worst night's sleep in the history of somnolence that night.

It had been a good party. I'd done my job very well. We men had fished and feasted and polished off many bottles of good liquor. We'd lit a fire and joked and shared memories and teased the living shit out of Steve. And around 3 a.m., as most of the guys stayed up in the living room to watch a movie called *See Her Squirt Vol. 6,* I crept off to bed feeling like I might actually catch a few honest Zs. I brushed my teeth, put on some flannel PJ bottoms and my comfy hole-ridden Slayer tee, crawled into a cramped-but-cozy bottom bunk in one of the bedrooms, and closed my beyond-tired eyes.

And then, just as I drifted off, it came on: another wave—the most awful yet—of thoughts, feelings, images, ideations; and I lay wide awake in a fit of panic and dread. It was kind of like Bergman's gothic horror film *Hour of the Wolf,* about the sleepless artist who's slowly ravaged by the demons and other creatures who haunt his tortured imagination—except waaayyy worse than that. Again I felt and witnessed my body *coming apart,* vivisected—my hands, my feet, my hair, my eyes, my heart, my lungs, my penis—every part of my corpus detached, dead, disintegrating. I held my hands up in the moonlight coming through the window; my silhouetted fingers were strange and hateful and wanted me dead. I had an urge to cause myself unspeakable hurt: to gouge out my eyes, pull out my hair, set myself on fire. I thought, *I should get up, go for a walk in the night air and shake this off*—but I was bedridden, palsied. *I can't go anywhere. These are not my hands, not my legs, not my feet.* I lay frozen and afraid, violent thoughts attacking me on all sides like angry Promethean birds.

My hands, my cock, my feet, my hair, my eyes, my lungs, my heart.

My hair, my hands, my lungs, my heart, my eyes, my feet, my cock.

I am dying, everybody is dying right now, because of me.

At five or so I heard my shit-drunk roommates stumble into the room, climb into their bunks, and pass out unthinkingly, without a word.

At six I quickly polished off a bottle of whiskey and then dashed back into bed, hoping the inrush of booze would finally push me down.

At seven the sun was up and so, still, was I. The birds were singing in the trees and I hated them.

At ten everyone was still asleep as I sat in the living room, drunk as ever, wondering—again—if that day would be my last.

9.2

BUT NO: I didn't do myself in. Instead, pathetic sack of shit that I was, I finally called my wife.

I buzzed Sam's cell phone the moment I returned to L.A.— after nearly six months of pretending that she didn't exist. It rang three times and went to voice mail.

Then I called again, and again, and again.

Bitch, pick up . . . pick the fuck up!!!

Please?

Nuthin'.

I hadn't the foggiest idea where she was or whom she was with or what she was doing. *She's over me by now,* I thought, *she's seeing someone else for sure. They're already buying a duplex together in Silver Lake or some other neighborhood that would have been a great place for us to start a family, had I not been such a self-absorbed work-obsessed a-hole; it's got 13-foot ceilings and downtown views and a charming private garden, and he's fucking her harder and better than I ever did, than I ever could now with my noodle-limp nervous wreck of a thimble-size dick and these calamitous thoughts coursing through my brain that I just can't FUCKING STOP.*

Two hours later—easily the two longest of my life—I heard the opening drum solo of the Youth Brigade song "I Hate My Life": *Dum-ditty-dum-ditty-dum-ditty-dum-ditty-dum*—

I picked up on the first ring, panting: "Sam?"

"Hello," she said.

There was a leaden silence over the line. I tried to be cool—to disguise my intense fear that she wanted nothing to do with me anymore—but I—I just *couldn't*—

"I'm sorry," I started spilling. "I know I've been—"

She laughed viciously. "Sorry? You're *sorry*? Sorry about what?"

She's sucking his eight-and-a-half-inch cock with a vengeance, taking the whole thing, tickling his balls, sticking a finger up his asshole, guzzling his cum just to spite me, that much is irreversible.

"I love you and miss you," I said. "I want to see you. I know I haven't exactly let you know that—the furthest thing from

273

it—but I know, now, what a huge mistake I made and I . . ."
went on for another minute or so, selfishly, pathetically rambling, *spilling*.

"We should probably talk about this in person," she said.
"Mishima tomorrow after work, say seven?"

"Okay."

Mishima was one of our old favorites, a brightly lit, no-frills
Japanese diner on Third Street & La Cienega where we used to
go all the time. She would always order the Soba Seaweed Salad
and a side of steamed black cod, and I'd usually get the Katsudon. We'd had a lot of fun there. It was nestled in an anonymous
strip mall and rarely crowded, a great place to meet at six on a
Friday (before I got too busy with work to do so) and recap our
weeks before catching a 7:30 movie at the Bev Connection. It
happily reminded us of a Vietnamese joint we used to frequent
on Eighty-sixth and Broadway when we lived on the Upper West
Side. I didn't know whether it was a good or terrible sign that
Sam picked Mishima—and picked it, I couldn't help but notice,
with such unwonted *decisiveness*. Did she view it as a place to
relive an old tradition, recharge our affection for the life we'd
shared—or merely as a neutral setting of equal comfort and familiarity to each of us, where we'd be on even footing and could
meet halfway, negotiate?

I arrived at 6:30, so that I could guzzle a large Sapporo before Samantha arrived, and grabbed a table along the empty
banquette on the far wall. I looked out the window and noticed, for the first time, that just across Third Street stood
the beige stucco structure that housed—yup—Souplantation.
The restaurant's tacky green neon sign flickered, *Ha ha, ha
ha, ya putz*.

Oh *my*: when Sam pulled into the parking lot, in the midnight-blue Audi wagon we'd bought together just after we'd wed, I started to weep like no man ever has or should.

My penis is so small, so small, oh God please give me another chance with her, I'm begging.

She entered the restaurant and spotted her sweating, convulsing, whimpering excuse for a husband way in the back. I forced back my tears with all my might: *Come on, ya big fag, keep it together!* Upon seeing me she offered up a small reflexive smile and then swallowed it whole.

"Hello Sam!" the hostess greeted her sweet, familiar face.

She was wearing her long gunmetal-grey Comme Des Garçons raincoat and had dyed her hair dark brown. She looked extremely tired and thin, but very beautiful. She calmly took a seat across from me and picked up the large glossy menu with her left hand, revealing immediately, pointedly, that she was not wearing her wedding band.

"Black cod bento?" I sniveled.

"Nah, think I'm gonna get sushi."

"I like the hair. Same color as when we met—"

"Stop, Alan," she said. "Please, just *stop*."

The waiter came over and took our order: assorted hand rolls and a Kirin Light for her, white udon noodles in broth for me— the only thing I could imagine stomaching.

Then—before I could say anything else loving, restorative, hope-instilling—she said: "Alan, I've hired a lawyer and I'm filing for divorce. First, I'd like to keep the apartment . . ."

Ruh-roh.

I was truly, if undeservedly, shocked: Divorce! *Divorce! Mais ce n'est pas possible!* Divorcing *ME, Alan,* her devoted husband who was so good to her for so long before he so *briefly* and *temporarily* fucked up big-time!

Divorce, after ten-plus wonderful years together, after every-thing I'd done for her, all the tough times we'd been through *together?*

"Don't you think that's a little extreme, honey-bun?" I said, knowing full well what a miserable, manipulative wretch I was for calling her that.

"Honey-bun?" she exploded. *"HONEY-BUN?!"*

"I'm sorry, you don't understand, I'm not well right now—"

"No no no. Just shut up. Just shut the fuck up! Okay? I don't want to hear *anything* from you. Believe me, by this point I'm used to not hearing from you! My God, what the fuck were you *thinking,* Alan? It was one thing to walk out on your wife—okay, we were having serious problems, many of which I fully acknowledge were my fault—but to *not even pick up the phone* and see how I was doing after you left! Was I okay? Did I need anything? Was I even fucking *alive?!* After a month I thought, okay, I put way too much pressure on him, with all my family drama he's been through a lot, he needs a little time on his own, he'll come around. After two I thought, okay, he's still angry, he has a right to be, maybe this'll be good for us. After three—if you checked any of the hundred thousand messages I left—you *knew* I was on the verge of *killing myself* and still *nothing,* not even a fucking *phone call!* I was like, could I have married a man this fucking selfish? Was he *always* capable of acting so savagely? I guess so. And when I realized that—what a complete fucking prick you are, Alan, through and through—I moved on! I found the strength and moved on!"

"I was sick," I was full-on bawling now. "I was sick when I left. I didn't know it then, but I know it now and I need you—"

"Sick! Oooh, you were *sick,* poor *baaaby.* I'm sooo sorry. I didn't know you were *sick.* Were you *sick* when you were running around town drunk with God knows how many different girls, having a jolly ol' time with some young slut at El Carmen taqueria?"

"What? Girls! What? No!"

" 'Wha? No! Girls? Who, me?' Come on, Alan! Do you honestly think I didn't *know* where you were and what you were doing? Did you think I wouldn't check our joint credit card statements and see all those meals that were clearly for two people, at Casa del Mar, Sasabune, Cheebo! Don't tell me you took Steve to *Cheebo!!!*"

Shit! Deny, deny, deny—

"What? No, I had some business dinners but that's—"

"Business dinners . . . hmmm. That's interesting. Because I logged on to your online Verizon account and saw the ten different numbers you were calling and text-messaging, often within hours—*minutes*—of these supposed 'business' dinners. There was one number in particular, with an 813 area code, you called a *lot*—how the fuck did you meet a girl in Tampa?"

She had me in a hammerlock. *Oh no, no, no, no—the cell phone—shit!—what a total schmuck I am!*

"Stop lying to me, Alan! You lied through your teeth when you said you wanted to marry me, and you're lying again now! You asked me to set up that cell account for you last summer when you were shooting in Chicago! I still have the password—Jesus Christ, I *chose* the fucking password! I saw the numbers you were dialing—I dialed them myself! I heard the voices of the home-wrecking sluts you were sleeping with, or doing God knows what with. But you know what's funny? At least they had the courtesy to *pick up* when I called!!!"

"Sam, I—"

"Do you think I am a complete fucking idiot?"

"No, of course not—"

"Yes you do! You, Alan Wieder, are a genius, and everyone else is a big fucking moron!"

She got up from the table and put on her coat.

"I'm sorry, Alan," she said. "I love you, I *loved* you, but our marriage, our life together, is over. Forever. I'm divorcing you. I wanted to mediate, to have an actual *conversation* and see whether there was hope for us to either try again, or at least settle the matter amicably—I wanted us to be *us,* to walk away as good friends if we had to at all, but *now!*—now, there's just no way."

As a last stab I tried going in the other direction, to play hardball rather than play on her sympathy, which I'd obviously bled dry.

"Okay," I said. "I wanted to try to work things out, but if that's the way it's gotta be, I guess I understand."

She made for the door—coldly, spitefully, in clear requital for my own now-clearly-idiotic plot to leave her.

"Pick up when I call," she said, her eyes welling but unafraid. "And don't worry, it'll be just *business*—so you should be able to deal."

And with that—just as Ms. K had—my wife stormed out of the restaurant, sticking me with a table full of untouched Japanese food and yet another fucking bill.

Bitch, come back here right now.

Come back, you fucking cunt!

Please?

I am so fucking fucked!!!

9.3

I SAT IN DR. GOODSON'S OFFICE, surveying the spines of the impressively eclectic and erudite collection of books that lined his shelves: Oliver Sacks's *Awakenings, Psychodynamic Psychiatry in Clinical Practice, The Diaries of Paul Klee, The Man Without Qualities,* Mark Twain's *Collected Tales, The Clinical Manual to Psychosomatic Medicine, Scandinavian Design,* Gaston Bachelard's *The Psychoanalysis of Fire,* whoa, Maurice Blanchot's *The Space of Literature*—?

"What were you expecting her to say?" the doctor asked.

I thought of the effort it would take to answer this question and let out a big melodramatic sigh.

"I dunno, Doc. I just figured, after all she'd put me through—not *she* personally, but I mean . . . I mean, after all the familial hardships I'd helped her through, the financial support I'd given her over the years, the love and support I showed her for so long relative to the short time I've been away, that I still had some currency in the bank with her . . . that she—"

"—that she still *owes* you something."

"Is that totally ridiculous of me?"

"Well, yes and no. I've noticed you have a tendency to think of relationships, of your marriage in particular, in financial terms—profit and loss, plus and minus columns. It's true that in a healthy relationship there should be a relatively equitable give-and-take—over time, anyway—but this 'currency' you describe can be a perilously faulty measure. How can you think the money you've given her over the years would compensate her for the inestimable pain you caused her by disappearing into your work for eighteen months—and then by leaving altogether? I'm not saying it was wrong of you to have left, just that the way you reflect on the experience is distorted."

"Hmm."

"Marriages are not banks, Alan. Doing something nice for your wife, being there for her during a difficult period, doesn't 'deposit' money in your relationship savings account that can later be tapped when you've done something mean or hurtful, inadvertently or not. Just because you're maintaining what you believe to be a 'positive balance' in your account doesn't entitle you to immunity from your wife's judgment. Does that resonate with you?"

"Hmm."

Things got very quiet.

"How is the Xanax working?" he said.

"I could use another refill."

"Have you been sleeping? Eating? I have to say, you look thin and pale to me."

"So-so."

Then, as he sat staring at me intently, I started to sob again, all over the poor guy's probably $11,000 vintage sofa.

"I gotta be totally honest with you, Doc," I said. "I'm not doing so hot. At *all*. I just can't . . . I . . . really don't think I'm gonna make it through this."

He handed me a box of Kleenex.

"What do you mean by that?"

"I mean . . . this is all fine and well. You and I can sit here, and you can tell me my thinking is 'self-downing' and warped—about my marriage, my dick, my self-ideal, blah blah blah—and you can teach me methods for replacing my 'hot' thoughts with 'cool' thoughts and repairing the broken fucking image I see in the mirror . . . but as soon as I walk out that door and back into my life I feel *exactly* the same as I did—no, I feel even *more* frustrated and hopeless because *this*—this new thing I've invested so much hope in—see, there I go with the money analogies again!—"

"Alan, Alan, I'm going to stop you. Let me ask you something. When I see you, I see a person who wants to get better— who is *determined* to emerge from this shit and have a normal life. Am I wrong?"

"No . . . Yes . . . I don't know."

He smiled benevolently. "Here's what we're gonna do. I'm going to prescribe you a dose of Lexapro. A *small* dose, five milligrams to start, maybe we'll go to ten. It'll take a few weeks to kick in, but it should lift the floor of your depression and boost your spirits a bit. And I want to start seeing you one more time a week."

"*Three* times a week, you want to see me now?" I exclaimed, sounding very old Jewish man-ish.

"We have a lot of work to do. We'll figure out something on the money. But you *will* be fine, Alan. I promise. I can help you through this. Do you trust me?"

"No . . . Yes . . . I don't know," I said, only half-kidding.

9.4

D R. GOODSON WAS—is—an excellent therapist. He was right—annoyingly *right* about so many things that I stubbornly, repeatedly had all wrong. And the process was working. I could tell that, slowly but surely, therapy was chipping away at the self-lacerating illogic that had taken hold of me; that eventually it would restore my common sense, the sense of *normalcy* I'd so cockily shunned and now wanted back more than anything.

But I was running out of time. I was dying—Couldn't the doctor *tell* that I was *dying,* falling into total extinction where I belonged, a little more each day?

I started taking the Lexapro, another—the last—of the long list of things that failed to afford me a single brief fucking instant of relief from my suffering. I was now totally holed up in my apartment like a shut-in, not leaving my building except for my thrice-weekly shrink appointments or an occasional Trader Joe's or Ralph's run for more booze or American Spirits. I downed bottle after bottle of Bushmills and Powers whiskey (which, admittedly, probably had a lot to do with why the antidepressants were ineffective), vomited my insides out, fought off the urge to exercise my cock, sat in the bathtub and succumbed to it, measured, remeasured with a different ruler, climbed the walls, took the mirror out of the closet, stared into it and put it back again, scrutinized my fingers, yanked at my hair, didn't eat, didn't sleep.

Pretty much the only thing I was still man enough to do was admit—out of desperate need, but also out of deepening grief—that without my wife I had no reason to live and no chance at living. I had reached *that point*—the absolute nadir of despair that a long line of impetuous wife-abandoning schnooks had reached before me, bowed with humiliation and regret.

The point at which—*oh yes*—it was time to come crawling back home.

It was my only recourse: At ten on a Saturday morning, I

showed up at my old apartment—my wife's apartment now—uninvited and unannounced, clutching $200 worth of pineapple lilies and flax blossoms from her favorite exotic flower place. Tail firmly between my legs, I lumbered up the back staircase prepared to grovel, beg, supplicate, self-immolate, do whatever it took to convince her to take me back.

Knock knock.

No answer.

Come on, woman, open the bloody door!

Knock knock knock.

Fuck fuck fuck! She wasn't home. *Where could she be, on a Saturday morning, and with whom other than me? At the gym? Hiking in Runyon Canyon? Having brunch at Urth Caffe with her new hot screenwriter boyfriend, heading back to his downtown loft afterward to spend the entire day in bed with him, watching Italian movies and taking his ten-inch cock up her ass just to spite me?*

I tried my key, the same key that, a few days after moving out, I'd almost thrown into the Pacific Ocean as a way of saying fuck that place, I didn't *need* it anymore and—*Yes!* The door opened! She hadn't changed the locks! She probably should have, but she didn't, God bless her! There was hope yet! *I'll wait for her,* I thought, *I'll wait till she comes home and surprise her with these ridiculously overpriced flowers she's going to love, get on my knees and go from there.*

I waited and waited and waited, going absolutely bonkers. Noon came. One o'clock. Three o'clock. At five I put the wilting flowers in a vase. At six thirty I pounded down half a bottle of wine that I found in the fridge and called her cell phone.

She picked up on the first ring.

"Hello?" she said, like she didn't recognize the number and was talking to a stranger.

"Hon—Sam, it's me."

"Oh—hi—" all surprised "—um, can I call you back? Lia and I are just sitting down to dinner—"

I was relieved: Lia was an old friend from New York and one of Sam's closest confidantes. She also happened to be a fan of mine—or had used to be, anyway—who was more likely to soothe than stoke Sam's animus toward me. *Surely* Sam was raging about how shittily I'd treated her—*the nerve I had, calling her out of the blue, after six months, to tell her how badly I missed her and wanted to come home!*—and *surely* Lia was advising her to give me the benefit of the doubt, and a second chance . . .

"Is Lia in L.A.?" I asked.

"No, Alan. I'm in New York."

"New York? As of when?"

"As of Monday," she said—*a week ago already!*

"On business?"

"Well, yes and no. I'm looking at apartments. I'm moving back to the city at the end of the month."

I could hear behind her the low roar of restaurantgoers clinking cocktails, digging into hearty plates, chatting about stuff other than the Hollywood baloney that invariably dominates dinner conversation in L.A.

"Oh . . . okay. Are you having fun?" I said.

"I am. We're at BLT Steak right now."

She *had* to get that in: She was eating at the then very-in joint where she and I had had a memorable meal together the year before, where we'd pledged to return the next time we weekended in New York, which we never did.

"Well, when are you coming home?" I said.

"Um . . . next week?" Sam said. "Maybe the week after? I

dunno. Lia is leaving town on business Friday for a month and said I could use her place, so I might stick around for a while— But can I talk to you later? We're about to eat."

She's LOVING this, smiting me, tying me to the topmast and making me SUFFER for everything I've done to her.

"Sure. Sorry. Talk to you later."

We—*she*—hung up, and I stood in my old living room, not knowing what the fuck to do with myself.

I looked around the apartment and noticed straight off that something about the place was different: It became suddenly, brutally clear that every trace of me had been erased. Sam had taken down from the dining room wall a triptych of framed canvases I'd painted; three crude holes in the plaster marked the spots where I'd inexpertly hung them myself. The art books of mine that had been mingled among Sam's on the mantle—Raymond Pettibon's *Whatever it is you're looking for you won't find it here,* Robbe-Grillet & Magritte's *La Belle Captive,* Gerhard Richter's *100 Pictures*—had been put away somewhere; the potted orchid cactus that had sat alongside them, given to us by my close friend as an engagement gift, tossed. My CDs had been extracted from the two hundred-disc changer, my vintage cereal toys removed from the kitchen windowsill, the closetful of clothes I'd left behind completely cleared out, my toiletries— *every last sign of me*—disappeared, unremembered.

Tucked away in the closet were three large cardboard boxes she'd clearly stuffed in an angry haste with this pile of things that were mine, now, to remove from her sight forever.

I should perhaps have loaded the boxes into my car and gone on my not-so-merry way. I should have given my wife the space that she deserved and had clearly gained the strength to want and need.

I should have, but I didn't.

Sam was going to be gone for a week at least, so I figured, fuck, I'm still paying the rent: *Why don't I just stay in the apartment for a few days, try my old life on for size, see how it fits?* My hope was that even if Sam were to kick my ass to the curb the moment she returned to L.A., the feel of being in my former home—even if for only a few days—would soothe me somehow; that being in my old kitchen would give me the comfort I needed to eat, my old bed the peace of mind to sleep.

It did not. In my old apartment I felt like the tiniest, most loathsome, most forgettable man in the universe. Within a few hours every obsessive, self-abasing thought returned full force, fastening me down, boxing me in. And yet I *couldn't leave*; I would have sooner died there than leave. I sat in front of the TV all day in a Xanax-and-whiskey haze, surviving on plain noodles, unable to silence my mind, sleeping on the couch in sweaty fits when the drugs and booze overtook me. I gazed and gazed into the mirror: *My hands, my hair, my hands, my hair, not mine, not mine, I'm dying, everyone is dying, I'm so sorry.* My penis was absurdly small again, more miniscule than ever, atomic. I lay in the bathtub late nights, tugging on it, stretching it to its full length, to the left, to the right, back between the cheeks—but now out of raw compulsion, emptied of any hope or goal.

For several interminable days this went on, until a week had passed and Sam still wasn't home and I hit absolute rock fucking bottom.

But then—then, all of a sudden, I had a realization that changed everything.

I was wallowing on the sofa, my former sofa, in the middle of the night, drunker than shit and gazing blankly at a

Jeff Corwin Experience rerun, the one where he's blindfolded, taken to an undisclosed location somewhere on the U.S. mainland, and given forty-eight hours to figure out which state he's in, based only on the snakes he finds. I was cupping my testicles and penis to make sure they hadn't vanished completely, waiting for a massive heart attack, a pulmonary embolism, stray AK fire, some merciful tragedy to come put me out of my misery. And something occurred to me; somehow, an insight crept through my mental morass and brought with it, for the first time in months, a brief but piercing moment of lucidity and peace.

Here I am, I thought, *totally incapacitated, a waste of flesh in a smelly bathrobe, at some nadir of abjection and despair whose cause I haven't even begun to comprehend, with no way out or perceivable terminus, and yet . . . I **still** don't want to commit suicide. If I really wanted to die I would have tried already, many times, weeks ago. I'm not going to kill myself, ever, even if this agony goes on another twenty, thirty, fifty years—no, on the contrary, I will survive this, **need** to survive this, for a reason that will become clear to me eventually, not now, not soon, but in time.*

Grandiose as it may sound, it dawned on me that I *needed* to be going through this crisis, that all my life I lived in a false and fragile peace, sequestered, never experiencing anything *real,* never *feeling* anything real, never doing anything with any real feeling. I'd made myself so busy with the pain of others—the women I'd "saved," the reality TV lab rats I'd punished—in order to dodge the possibility that I had any of my own. I understood, in an incandescent instant, that *my life had not yet really begun,* was about to begin—as a human being, just a man, full of irregularities, deficiencies, failings—as long as I held on; that my suffering was indeed, just as it had said in all those Buddhist self-help books I'd read, a pathway to radical acceptance. In that fleeting moment I was able to view all the pernicious thoughts running through my head as *external to me,* foreign, impositions of a prior self that was dying a slow, miserable death, a death that *it* deserved and I, for all my misdeeds, did not.

My thoughts are not me, I thought, *not mine, no, they can't be.*

Whose thoughts they were, exactly, and how I would make them stop, I had no clue.

My penis is too small, too small, too small.

No it isn't.

Yes it is.

The next morning I called Steve and told him I was leaving town for a few days. *Cover for me,* I said, *I'm going to save my marriage.* It seemed so romantic, a movie moment almost too perfect to write, and he was happy for me, because he had no idea how far away I was from Sam, how far from putting my life back together, so much further than New York City.

I packed a bag and drove to Long Beach airport, bought a ticket to JFK at the JetBlue counter. On the plane it took every iota of willpower—and four Jack Daniels minibottles— not to go into the bathroom and check my hands, inspect my hair, pull on my penis. I landed on a hot September afternoon, cabbed it into the city to Lia's brownstone at Twelfth Street and Sixth Avenue.

I sat on the stoop and, again, waited for my wife, hoping she could find a reason to forgive such a fucking cock.

When Sam showed up around nine and saw me sitting there, blubbering like a baby into a twenty-five-ounce Foster's beer can, she smiled—slightly—and said: "Leave me alone. God, Alan, just *leave me be!*"

I stood up to embrace her, and was surprised and relieved to see that she'd let me take her into my trembling arms.

"Sam," I said, my tears dropping into her hair. "I don't want to lose you. I won't lose you. I'm a . . . tiny, tiny fraction of a man without you, disappearing by the day. Don't—*please* don't let me just . . . go away."

She was crying now, too, burying her face in my chest as if she was trying to look inside and see if I had a heart.

"God, you're an asshole," she said.

Then, pushing past me to the front door, she said, "Come upstairs."

Another shot. My only shot.

Thank fucking God.

10.0

So yes: my wife took me back, after everything I did to her, everything I probably would have done if I hadn't cracked up.

In early October I walked up my back staircase with a couple of sloppily packed duffel bags and hugged and kissed Samantha at the door. We held each other close and traded tearful, breathless promises: to forgive and push past it, to love each other more, to do everything we needed to do to make it work.

A week later Sam asked me to unpack the boxes of my things that she'd shoved in the closet. In another week she made room for the hi-fi stereo and schmancy furniture I'd blown so much of our joint funds on. And in another, I came home from the office to find a yummy *tagine* on the table and my triptych hanging again on the dining room wall.

Why Sam took me back—so sweetly and welcomingly, so

like the woman she'd always been—is a question I've pondered to no end; and that I find myself now as unable to answer as I was three hundred pages ago. In the process of writing this book I believe I have uncovered much about myself—to you and to me both—but not, to this day, any adequate rationale for the love and support that made it possible for me to write it.

Maybe what I did wasn't so bad—yeah, *right*—or at least, when all was said and done, maybe I was not as horrible and undeserving of Sam's love and forgiveness as I've made myself out to be. Maybe she liked the idea of taking me in, sick and helpless for a change, *needing* her overtly rather than subconsciously; or maybe, when push came to shove, we needed each other just the same.

Maybe she knew on some level that 2005 was the Year of the Cock—my time to run, and fight, and fall, and return to life as a man.

Maybe Dr. Goodson was wrong. Maybe I did have some currency left in the marriage bank after all.

Maybe she's just an exceptional woman, the one I loved for ten years for the right reasons before I hated her for all the wrong; before I went blind with lust and obsession and, ultimately, self-hatred.

Maybe she just has a thing for jerks.

Whatever the reason, Sam let me back in—through the door, into the remains of the life I'd nearly destroyed, the bed that I'd forever shamed and polluted.

So yes: I am one of the lucky men who got a second chance—one to which I may or may not have been entitled. I moved back home, and got back on my feet, and worked on my marriage and on myself. I let Sam know in a zillion ways how sorry I was and made what I believed were the necessary amends (including one very costly trip to Cartier). And we got back to our routine: working, watching movies, our morning stroll to the Starbucks on Detroit and Beverly Boulevard, south a few blocks to Third Street and back again.

But lest you believe that returning to my former existence was the immediately sanity-restoring remedy I hoped for, it was anything but. No, the months to come were to be the absolute worst yet, for so many reasons I'm ashamed to confess to you and, now for the first time as I write this, to Sam.

For starters, I was a lying piece of shit. In my first weeks back home, I told Sam repeatedly how grateful I was to her for taking me back, what a colossal mistake I felt I'd made by moving out, unforgivable; I barraged her with sweet, shared memories of us, professed my undying love, pledged to make things right and never leave her again—and she, seeing me so sad and shamefaced, had every reason to believe every last word. But the cold truth was that I wasn't even sure I wanted to be home again, with her, in my old apartment, my old life, at all. I desperately wished it *were* the case that I'd realized my existence was hopelessly empty without her; that my whole personal crisis had stemmed from being suddenly deprived of her and therefore could be as quickly reversed through our reunion. My God, what I would have given to just feel *happy* again with my lovely wife, to have been just some dipshit who'd strayed from his marriage on an idiot impulse, quickly realized the grass wasn't greener, and come ruefully knocking on his wife's door like a bitch!

But in actuality, even *after* moving back in, unpacking my boxes, putting my clothes away in the closet, strolling the aisles of Whole Foods together, figuring out what to do for dinner—I'm not gonna bullshit you—I kinda *still* didn't want to be married to Sam, or married at all, any more than I had when I walked out. I was prudent enough to know that I *needed* my wife, sure, because I was ill. But once she nursed me back to health—three, six months from then, tops—I was 42 percent sure that I was going to want to move right back into my bachelor pad and never speak to her again.

Dr. Goodson summed up my circumstance with his typical devastating precision: "You're trapped," he said, "between a miserable present and the prospect of reliving an equally undesirable past." There was that, yes—and also that I felt like a profound failure, a man too weak and inadequate to be what he'd *wanted* to be, which was alone, unto himself, *free*. I flouted my doctor's orders and fell headlong into my old pattern of comfortless rituals: Many nights, after Sam went to sleep, I sat in the bathtub and yanked on my penis till it was red and raw, hating myself, never saying a word to my wife about any of it. I felt as if I couldn't share any of my obsessive thoughts and urges with Sam, not simply because of the freaky nature of my disorder but because I didn't *deserve* to; I simply hadn't earned the right.

When Sam asked what was wrong—she knew well when I was pretending to be well—I told her only (as I had to so many others) that I was depressed, that I felt deeply saddened and ashamed about everything I'd done to her—not *entirely* untrue—and left it at that. I feared that if she caught any inkling that I wanted anything less than to work on our marriage, restore our trust and our household—that I'd come home for any reason other than that I loved her unqualifiedly—she would boot me to the curb. As she should have—and, on a few occasions, nearly did.

If the journal I kept that year offers any indication—its entries drop off considerably after Labor Day—the final months of '05 were torturously slow and uneventful. A mind falling apart can be an exciting thing to witness and is even thrilling to live through in its own way, but *recovery* is a total snooze both to undergo and to watch. I liken it to all the material on a reality show that you *don't* see, the stuff that gets edited out—the countless hours of "reality coverage" between the show's tentpole events (dates, eliminations, surprise twists, and such), when the participants are just sitting around the mansion yammering about nothing usable and waiting to be told what to do next. It's during those periods that we producers, sitting in Video Village, start to get antsy and question our show format—to say, *Fuck, this is so **boring**, why aren't these knuckleheads **doing** anything?* But we roll cameras anyway, capturing every last paint-drying second of it, because tape is cheap and you never know.

I remember most the sense of treading water for hours and hours on end, feeling like any minute I'd be pulled under. For me, drowning had always seemed the most fearsome way to die, and this was the closest I'd come: a state of suspended submersion, with my legs and arms instinctively fighting for survival but the rest of me prepared to surrender to the reality that no one, especially not Sam, was coming to my rescue.

But, following Tupac's indelible mantra, I kept my head up. I had no choice, I thought, but to fix my marriage—and my mind in tandem. I needed to repair the damage I'd done to Sam, to us, but I also needed to change the way I thought, heal my unleashed shame and guilt, get okay with who I was, fuck, *figure out* who I was. Perhaps when I emerged from the process I'd realize—*we'd* realize—that our relationship, beneath it all, was still as adoring and steadfast as it had been for so long; and perhaps by then I'd be strong enough to go my own way if it was not. Perhaps.

Seriously, Your Band Sucks! did not get picked up for series—

we heard that Brian Graden, the head of MTV, thought it was "too mean"—which left me with plenty of time to get my relationship back on track, surely a blessing. Sam and I began my hitherto worst nightmare, the thing I'd most stubbornly dodged when things between us were headed downhill: *marriage counseling.* Out of fairness we alternated between two therapists—a tetchy female MFT in Beverly Hills with whom Sam ganged up on me; and a pushy male Gestaltian in Santa Monica with whom I ganged up on her. We learned and applied the available techniques: replacing criticisms and complaints with helpful suggestions of what might work better. Taking emotional time-outs before responding out of anger or defensiveness, to rid bottled-up feelings of their power to inflame. Assuming goodwill at all costs, that our primary intent was to love rather than antagonize each other.

From opposite ends of a couch Sam told me how much pain I'd dealt her over the last two years—disappearing into my work, silencing her, abandoning her just like everyone else in her family had. I accepted blame—and told *her,* for the first time without hostility, how hard it had become for me to love her through the barrier she'd put up after her father died, a force field of bitterness and self-pity and grief. She told me how much she loved me, admired me, supported me, but I took advantage, became consumed with myself, egomaniacal; and I told her how much I loved her back but also how much pressure I'd felt, at way too early an age, to fill every sorrowful void in her life, become *everything* to her—father, mother, brother, husband—before I ran out of steam and retreated inward, started looking after *me.* We cried and cried and the whole thing was every bit as agonizing and gay as I'd imagined, but you know what? It kinda worked.

In my own thrice-weekly therapy with Dr. Goodson—between the personal and the relationship appointments, suddenly I was in therapy nearly every fucking day—I started to explore how I fell into my strange obsessive episode, my somatic fixations and deathly pangs of guilt, inadequacy, and mortification. How my penis became a stand-in, a metaphor for everything about my life I couldn't alter, extend, or excise: my essence as a man, my life span, ultimately, my love for my wife. How it was that I could have become so thoroughly undone by a single flaw—*perceived* flaw—in my self-reflection.

After many hours with the doc, and some probing conversations with my family, I discovered that my father—a man who had always seemed steady, strong, manly, despite his needless health worries—had suffered from obsessive thinking his whole adult life. What had seemed to us like so much Woody-ish meshugas—*Dad's back at the doctor's again! Such a hypochondriac!*—was actually a manifestation of an anxiety disorder he'd struggled with for decades. His thoughts, too, began the moment he opened his eyes and would not stop till he drank or drugged himself to sleep: punishing, repetitive ideations about his mortality, about his father's failing health and painful death, about how he'd lived in Grandpa Bernie's shadow and failed in his eyes, how he'd deserved to die in the old man's stead. I recalled all the times my father openly worried—or was it wished?—that his achy shoulder or knee was a certain harbinger of his premature demise. I remembered him talking about being ready for the nursing home at his fiftieth birthday party, not in a funny way but in a sad way that took his guests aback. There were so many other signals that this man's mind was not quite right, things I didn't really see till I looked back upon them.

These were just pieces. There were many, many left to pick

up and find a place for. No one buried memory or moment could suffice to explain everything I had been through. The notion that there was a single isolable incident from which all my mental agony stemmed was as preposterous as the idea that a longer schlong could fix it in one fell swoop. I knew that now; the reality was excruciating to accept, but ultimately the illusion was far more afflicting.

Weeks plodded past. Life started to make a little more sense to me, and to Sam. My racking hatred for my cock turned to nagging dissatisfaction. My fatalistic despair about my marriage gave way to an uncomplicated desire to promote its survival. In late November Sam and I decided to take a trip to Mexico City together. We lived so close and had wanted to go for years, but we'd always made excuses not to: A forthcoming shoot whose exact dates were impossible to predict made booking a vacation impossible. An article in the *New York Times* reported rampant "express kidnappings" across Latin America, and we got cold feet. A guilt-tripping phone call from my folks or her mom— about how *far away* we were in California, how we never came home anymore—compelled us to book a weekend in New York or Florida instead.

Now we just got on Expedia, and on a Wednesday we said fuck it and on Friday touched down at AICM. Things were still very shaky between us, but as soon as we arrived in that underrated city, checked into our hotel in the Polanco district, we set it aside. We stayed up all night for a week drinking *micheladas* at the bar of the Condesa DF Hotel, took a tour of the architect Luis Barragan's home, gobbled down street-corner-stand quesadillas at the Plaza San Jacinto. It was the honeymoon we never had. And we started to have sex again, good sex despite the fact that half my mind was telling me, before every thrust, that my dick was the size of a Tic Tac. But it was getting better, a little better at a time.

When we got back to L.A. we worked on our apartment. We had too much stuff, we decided, too much clutter, in our closets, our garage. We tossed everything we no longer wanted or used. We made more room for my record collection, which had always been stuffed in a corner of the closet, out of reach. We sold our sharp-angled architectural sofa on eBay and bought something a lot comfier to watch Netflix on. We upgraded our Smokey Joe camping grill to a Weber Spirit with a gas tank and everything. We potted succulents, changed fixtures and repainted walls, fought horribly over nothing, laughed afterward, collaborated.

A month or so later, at Steve's wedding, Sam and I showed up as a pair, which many friends were thrilled to see. *We knew you'd work things out,* people said, *you guys were just too good together.* Since I've obnoxiously bragged about so many other things I might as well add that as Steve's best man, I gave an A+ toast—ruthlessly humiliating my best friend before bringing it home with a heart-stirring ode to the love between these two people, Steve and Marita, a rousing *l'chaim*: yup, I knocked that shit right out of the park. And when I told everyone how lucky Steve Sobel, this hapless yutz I loved like a brother, was for finding a woman who'd put up with him—how lucky *any* of us guys were to find a good woman to love and to love us—I looked over at my wife and saw that she believed I actually meant it, because I did.

By year's end Sam and I—good idea or bad—were trying to have a child. In preparation I sold the Porsche and bought a Subaru Outback—literally, the safest car in its class. I got the turbo model and added a performance chip, which took it up to 300 horses and made it actually quicker off the line than the 951—but who was I kidding.

The Rooster surrendered his angry posturing—his bravado and burning pride—and made room for the Dog: playful, loyal, companionable. I was on my way. We were on our way. Two years later now, it still occurs to me, almost daily, that my penis is woefully small, laughably tiny, imperceptible to the human eye, but life goes on. Holy shit, does it go on. Besides, I should count my lucky stars that the thing still works, after the miserable beating it took.

Plus, I got much more important things to think about now. And one of 'em's about to wake up from his eleven o'clock nap.

And lemme tell ya: unlike his old man, the kid's got a helluva cock on him.

Los Angeles
Sept. 5, 2007
Year of the Pig

Epilogue

In full disclosure: I must very regretfully report that in the late summer of 2008, about a year after the completion of this book and a month from our son Roman's second birthday, Samantha and I filed for divorce, ending our thirteen-year relationship.

Though in many ways as ugly and difficult as the first—especially because our young boy's future was at stake—our second parting was mutual and, for the most part, amicable. Sam's story of what spelled the end differs wildly from mine, so it's probably best left between her and me. On my part, what I will say is that, in the long run, the damage I did by walking out in '05 was not as recoverable as I thought it might be in the happy months following our reunion, when we were grateful simply to have a second chance at finding each other. A first child on the way helped further divert our attention from the profound anger and sense of betrayal Sam was harboring—with good reason—from the moment I came home.

I thought about changing the ending of my story. I considered making the final chapter more ambiguous or tense, less happy and hopeful, adding details that might help fill in the blanks between our mostly joyful reunion and the ultimately sad outcome of our discord.

But in truth, the ending of *Year of the Cock* is accurate to the time in which I wrote it, when it really seemed that Sam and I, despite everything we'd put each other through, were on the right path. And to alter the picture of the past to make better sense of the present——for which I really can offer no good explanation——felt too neat and disingenuous.

Samantha and I are both still living in Los Angeles and raising our son, Roman, together. We're good friends and are trying our damnedest to remain so for Roman's sake, which has presented a whole new set of challenges. All in all, though, it's a pretty fucking messy situation and I don't recommend it to any of you who have a little one and are thinking of ending your marriage. If there's even the remotest chance you can work things out, take it from me and do everything possible, because part-timing it with your kid is a real bummer.

And even without a kid, frankly, breaking up is——as I hope I've shown——no picnic.

About the Author

Alan Wieder is a writer and producer in Los Angeles. Along with his film and television partner Steve Sobel, he was the creative producer of several network reality television hits, including *My Big Fat Obnoxious Fiancé*. Alan and Steve are now writing feature films for several major studios. This is Alan's first book.

DEMCO